Medieval Philosophy & Theology
VOLUME 3 (1993)

Medieval Philosophy & Theology

VOLUME 3 (1993)

EDITORIAL BOARD
Norman Kretzmann (chair)
Mark D. Jordan (managing editor)
Stephen F. Brown, David B. Burrell, Kent Emery, Jr., Eleonore Stump

EDITORIAL ADVISORS
Marilyn McCord Adams, Jan A. Aertsen, E. J. Ashworth, Thérèse-Anne Druart, Stephen Dumont, Sten Ebbesen, Alfred J. Freddoso, Charles H. Lohr, Scott MacDonald, Aryeh L. Motzkin, Luca Obertello, Edith Sylla, Avital Wohlman

EDITORIAL ASSISTANT
C. Elizabeth Boyett

Editorial correspondence and manuscripts should be addressed to Mark D. Jordan, Medieval Institute, University of Notre Dame, 715 Hesburgh Library, Notre Dame, IN 46556. Authors should send two copies of their manuscripts, which should conform to the *Chicago Manual of Style*, 13th edition, and which should be suitable for anonymous reviewing. Prepaid orders (for individuals) and standing orders (for libraries) should be addressed to the University of Notre Dame Press, Notre Dame, IN 46556.

Medieval Philosophy & Theology

VOLUME 3 (1993)

University of Notre Dame Press
Notre Dame & London

Copyright © 1994
University of Notre Dame Press
Notre Dame, IN 46556
All rights reserved
Manufactured in the United States of America

ISSN 1057-0608
ISBN 0-268-01404-3

Medieval Philosophy & Theology
VOLUME 3 (1993)

Abbreviations	vii
Rewriting the Narrative of Scripture: 12th-Century Debates over Reason and Theological Form EILEEN SWEENEY	1
The Certainty and Scope of Knowledge: Bonaventure's *Disputed Questions on the Knowledge of Christ* ANDREAS SPEER	35
Good and the Object of Natural Inclinations in St. Thomas Aquinas JOHN I. JENKINS	62
Duns Scotus on Signification DOMINIK PERLER	97
Medieval Supposition Theory in Its Theological Context STEPHEN F. BROWN	121
Nominalism Meets Indivisibilism JACK ZUPKO	158
The Church in the Light of Learned Ignorance THOMAS M. IZBICKI	186

Abbreviations

AHDLMA	*Archives d'histoire doctrinale et littéraire du moyen âge*
AL	Aristoteles Latinus
BFSMA	Bibliotheca Franciscana Scholastica Medii Aevi
BGP(T)M	Beiträge zur Geschichte der Philosophie (und Theologie) des Mittelalters
BT	Bibliothèque Thomiste
CCCM	Corpus Christianorum, Continuatio Mediaevalis
CCSL	Corpus Christianorum, Series Latina
CHLMP	*Cambridge History of Later Medieval Philosophy*, ed. Norman Kretzmann et al.
CIMAGL	Cahiers de l'Institut du moyen âge grec et latin
CPDMA	Corpus Philosophorum Danicorum Medii Aevi
CSB	Collegium Sancti Bonaventurae (Quaracchi, then Grottaferatta)
CSEL	Corpus Scriptorum Ecclesiasticorum Latinorum
CSIC	Consejo Superior de Investigaciones Científicas (Madrid and elsewhere)
DS	*Dictionnaire de spiritualité ascétique et mystique, doctrine et histoire*
DTC	*Dictionnaire de théologie catholique*
LM	*Lexikon des Mittelalters*
LTK	*Lexikon für Theologie und Kirche*
MGH	Monumenta Germaniae Historica
NCE	*New Catholic Encyclopedia*

PG	*Patrologiae cursus completus . . . , Series Graeca*, ed. J.-P. Migne
PIMS	Pontifical Institute of Mediaeval Studies (Toronto)
PL	*Patrologiae cursus completus . . . , Series Latina*, ed. J.-P. Migne
PM	Philosophes Médiévaux
RTAM	*Recherches de théologie ancienne et médiévale*
SCC	*Sacrorum Conciliorum nova et amplissima collectio*, ed. J. D. Mansi
STGM	Studien und Texte zur Geistesgeschichte der Mittelalters
TRE	*Theologische Realenzyklopädie*

Rewriting the Narrative of Scripture: Twelfth-Century Debates over Reason and Theological Form

EILEEN SWEENEY

While the history of Western philosophy as a whole can be seen as the appropriation by philosophers of the discourse of truth from the poets and makers of myth, of the replacement of narrative form by the 'properly philosophical' form of argument, it is an appropriation that also takes place within medieval thought, particularly in the construction of theology as a legitimate academic discipline.[1] Whether that appropriation constitutes progress or loss was as much debated in the Middle Ages as it is in recent thought.

---

1. Though this will receive more substance below, I note here that the standards of 'legitimacy' for the study of Scripture I am interested in here are not institutional but internal, i.e., those sacred study is measured against in order to take its place among the secular arts, in an age of increasing emphasis on these arts and increasing formality and rigor in their study and construction. Viewing twelfth-century debates in terms of the opposition between narrative and dialectical forms in theology was suggested to me by the topic of the 1989 International Association of Philosophy and Literature conference, whose subject was "Dialectic and Narrative," at which an early version of this paper was presented. I am greatly indebted to discussions with Louis Mackey concerning these twelfth-century figures. I am also indebted to Emmet Flood's "The Narrative Structure of Augustine's *Confessions*: Time's Quest for Eternity," *International Philosophical Quarterly* 28 (1988): 141–162.

I offer this medieval chapter not to take a side on the issue, but as an example of some of the presuppositions and dangers awaiting both sides of the polemic. The particular episode I would like to examine is a well-known one, the conflicts over and changes in the nature of theology in the Latin twelfth century, beginning with the even more familiar conflict between Abelard and Bernard of Clairvaux. I offer this essay with full knowledge that characterizations of this conflict are cliché-ridden. It has been seen as the conflict between the first stirrings of the modern critical spirit and the conservative, fideistic opposition, between an emerging 'scholastic' and a revised 'monastic' theology, and/or between 'systematic' and 'mystical' theologies.[2]

Instead of supporting or rejecting any of these clichés, I would like to tell a different version of this familiar story, to argue for another layer of meaning embedded in the events and terms of this debate. I will, then, recast the conflict in two ways: first, by inserting a third party into the debate, Hugh of St. Victor and, second, by focusing on the account of theological form given by these three figures, more specifically on the degree to which they think theology can and should be recast in dialectical form, given the narrative form of its text, Scripture. What I shall show is that it is no accident that differences over narrative and dialectical form accompany the more well-known

---

2. I am thinking here specifically of Marcia Colish's recent caricature of the traditional caricatures in "Systematic Theology and Theological Renewal in the Twelfth Century," *Journal of Medieval and Renaissance Studies* 18 (1988): 135–137. The history of scholarship surrounding the types and tendencies of twelfth-century theology Colish alludes to is complicated. Typical of the early twentieth century, Martin Grabmann's two-volume *Die Geschichte der Scholastischen Methode* (Freiburg i.B.: Herder, 1911) devotes scant attention to Bernard of Clairvaux and refers to all twelfth-century projects simply as 'pre-scholastic'. Charles Homer Haskins, in *The Renaissance of the Twelfth Century* (Cambridge, Mass.: Harvard University Press, 1927), helped originate the distinction between 'monastic' and 'scholastic' theology. Leclercq reassesses Haskins's claim in "The Renewal of Theology," in *Renaissance and Renewal in the Twelfth Century*, eds. Robert L. Benson and Giles Constable (Cambridge, Mass.: Harvard University Press, 1982), pp. 68–87, arguing for not two, but three types of theology: 'monastic', 'speculative', and 'pastoral' (the theology of the cathedral schools). As an advocate of the superiority of monastic writers, Leclercq seems to be the main object of Colish's caricature, while Colish's recent work (e.g., the article cited above) argues for the superiority and vitality of the schools and the sentence collectors. See also Leclercq's response to Colish, "Naming the Theologies of the Early Twelfth Century," forthcoming in *Mediaeval Studies*.

conflict over the roles of faith and reason. Seen in this light, the medieval conflict between faith and reason becomes a version of the current conflict over philosophical form and the nature of inquiry in general, over whether inquiry is most truly represented by narrative or dialectical structures.

I use the notions of 'narrative' as opposed to 'dialectical' form at one level as a way of characterizing the traditionally assumed and articulated (though never perfectly realized) distinction between 'philosophical' and 'literary' texts, between argument and story, truth-telling and fiction, logic and rhetoric or poetry, univocal and figurative language. The indigenous version of these distinctions, articulated and placed in question in these twelfth-century discussions of theological form, is between the study of Scripture conceived as *lectio* as opposed to *disputatio*. The former is described as slow, continuous reading of Scripture, following its narrative order and interpreting 'narratively', giving multiple meanings to the text which imitate its narrative order at higher levels. The latter, however, stops Scripture's own narrative order to ask questions from another order, e.g., about consistency with other parts of the 'story' or with other interpretations and conclusions. It issues not in interpretations paralleling and retelling the stories of Scripture, but in arguments, positions, and conclusions. The goal of the *lectio* is a synthetic grasp of the text that is almost affective and experiential, while *disputatio* is analytic and critical and aimed at understanding.

Now anyone familiar with the twelfth century will recognize these sketches as caricatures, as pure forms never found in practice. Nonetheless these are, as we shall see, the terms in which the conflicts between Bernard and Abelard are cast, terms their own rhetoric pushes toward unrealized and, I will show, unrealizable extremes. What prevents the realization of these caricatured versions of narrative and dialectical theologies is that, like all discourse, theological discourse can only be practiced in time—in a time that breaks down the synthesis of the *lectio* before it is ever achieved, and that configures the moments, questions, objections of the *disputatio* into a sequenced pattern, a kind of whole.

My own 'narrative' of this chapter in the history of philosophy will be broken down into the following parts. I turn first to a variety of texts on the forms of theology, either as articulated by Abelard and Bernard, or from texts reflecting or forming their views. I will discuss, second, their differences over and respective emphases on the roles of faith and reason, and the relationship between this conflict and that over theological form. My 'argument' is that despite their differences over faith and reason, and over Scripture study conceived of as *lectio* vs. *disputatio*, Bernard and Abelard at their most extreme (and, I might add, at their worst) share a desire for certainty that would make theology (and philosophy) either unnecessary or impossible—Bernard because he demands a certainty of faith which makes inquiry unnecessary, Abelard because his doubt is so pervasive and irremediable that it makes inquiry impossible. Hence, they serve as an example of what Louis Mackey has called the "strange but perennial alliance between theological reaction and philosophical rationalism."[3] Third, I turn to Hugh of St. Victor's attempt to construct a theology that is both narrative and dialectical—one which, like Bernard's, is based in the tradition of *lectio* of Scripture, undertaken in faith and oriented toward spiritual growth, and, like Abelard's, is a rationally rigorous, speculative enterprise that begins in the doubt which makes inquiry both necessary and possible. Hugh accomplishes this rapprochement between faith and reason, narrative and dialectic, by recognizing, on the one hand, that faith as well as doubt makes inquiry possible and, on the other, that dialectical inquiry has an intrinsically narrative structure. In other words, Hugh's theology is one whose dialectic of faith seeking understanding imitates the structure of the Christian *narrative* of fall and redemption and reflects the predicament of the Christian as *viator*, as a pilgrim who is always already fallen and who is moving toward, but never quite reaching, redemption. I will end by making a very tentative suggestion about the way in which these dialectical and narrative patterns inform the structure of Peter Lombard's *Sentences*.

A final *caveat* before I begin my story/argument. It is important to note that the material I will consider is somewhat more complex than simply Bernard and Abelard's *ex professo* statements on the nature of theological reflection, though these are the most important *dicta* for my argument. I shall also consider the form of their own theological writing, though not its content on given questions or interpretations of Scripture, and I shall also consider the account of theological reflection implied in some of the texts and practices that formed

---

3. Louis Mackey, "On Terms and Terminations: The Dissolution of the Medieval Metaphor," *Texas Quarterly* (1978): 79.

Bernard and Abelard's thinking, and against which they reacted. This is a complicated but still incomplete consideration of their authorships, and my selectiveness in choosing the material for this narrative (the necessity of selection itself illustrating the way story slides into argument and vice versa) I shall try to make convincing 'narratively' by the coherence of the story itself in the paper as a whole. But I offer here as downpayment a small attempt to justify it 'dialectically'. In this essay, I am not interested in the actual conclusions on given theological questions reached by Bernard, Abelard, or Hugh, nor with assessing their actual and direct influence on their own or succeeding generations of scholars. What I am interested in is their formation in and vision of their own enterprise, their sense of the form, nature, and purpose of theological reflection. No doubt Bernard and Abelard's practices do not reflect the extreme 'theoretical' positions they were prone to articulate, and no doubt Hugh's falls short of the synthesis it promises. In fact, with regard to Bernard and Abelard, my point in one sense is that if they are actually to engage in theological thought they must contradict their meta-theologies. This is exactly what they seem to be blind to and what constitutes the symmetry between their seemingly opposite positions. And, though it prevents them from being 'mainstream' in these articulations of and reactions to each other, it is also exactly what makes them representative of their age and beyond. The extremes to which they are prone map out a center in which, recognized or not, there must be a mixture of narrative and dialectic, faith and reason.[4]

BERNARD'S NARRATIVE AND ABELARD'S DIALECTIC

Since Bernard's theology derives from the life and practices of the monastery and he is the spokesman for the 'tradition' against which Abelard reacts and which Hugh of St. Victor attempts

---

4. Compare Colish, "Systematic Theology," p. 156, who uses the metaphor of a current to characterize the importance of the neglected 'mainstream' of twelfth-century thought, systematic theologians who were neither the 'radical' Abelard is usually depicted to be, nor the 'reactionary' Bernard is thought to be.

to rearticulate, I turn first to Bernard. In a very real sense, of course, Bernard has no 'theology', if by that term one means, as Abelard did, a discipline based on revelation but modeled in some ways on the liberal arts and distinct from its traditional form as the study of *sacra pagina*.[5] The forms Bernard's reflection on Scripture takes, sermons and devotional works, obviate a theoretical consideration of the possibility and nature of theology.[6] Hence, a discussion of Bernard's training and practice must take the place of a theoretical account of sacred study. Or, again to use the terms in which this discussion is couched, explicit reflection on 'method' is characteristic of dialectic's emphasis on universal and timeless perspective. By contrast, one can only tell the 'story' of Bernard's development.

William of St. Thierry's *Golden Epistle* gives an account of the proper steps and method for the reading of Scripture that reflects a model Bernard used and helped shape. It contrasts two forms of *lectio*: one, the careful and slow reading of a single text; another, the quick and scattered reading of many texts at once. The reader is admonished first that "[c]asual and varied reading (*lectio*), making discoveries as if by chance, does not edify but makes the spirit unstable, for that which is lightly taken in easily disappears from memory."[7] Instead,

---

5. The term 'theology' was, of course, used before Abelard even within the monastic and scriptural tradition. See Jean Leclercq, "Etudes sur le vocabulaire monastique du moyen âge," *Studia Anselmiana* 48 (1961): 145. Alf Härdelin even argues for the appropriateness of 'theology' as a description of the monastic enterprise, which he calls "practical theology." But he describes this theology as one always aimed at spiritual experience and expressed in the language and mode of Scripture. See his "Monastiche Theologie: Eine praktische theologie vor der Scholastik," *Zeitschrift für Katholische Theologie* 109 (1987): 400–415. On Abelard's notion of theology as a science separate from scriptural exegesis, see J. Cottiaux, "La conception de la théologie chez Abélard," *Revue d'histoire ecclésiastique* 28 (1932): 269–276.

6. Jean Leclercq argues that it was the concrete and timely literary genres of the letter, history, sermon (rather than the abstract *summa* or uninterrupted commentary) that monastic writers preferred. See *The Love of Learning and the Desire for God: A Study of Monastic Culture* (New York: Fordam University Press, 1961), pp. 153–154. But there are surely counter-examples. Colish, for example, cites the 'systematic' works of two Benedictine writers, Rupert of Deutz and Honorius Augustodunensis (Colish, "Systematic Theology," pp. 138–142). Even Colish admits, however, that these writers had 'monastic' purposes in mind, either mystical contemplation or helping monks minister to the laity.

7. William of St. Thierry *Epistola ad Fratres de Monte Dei* (PL 184:327C).

what is recommended is "from daily reading (*quotidiana lectione*) the commitment of something every day to the belly of memory, to be faithfully digested and recalled again and frequently ruminated upon."⁸ The goal seems to be to conform one's spirit to that of the text, to become inured to its message and tone. This kind of reading, like all reading, is aimed at understanding, but it is the understanding of friendship rather than mere acquaintance, an understanding that results from a relationship with the text that is sympathetic rather than adversarial. The *Epistle* admonishes readers,

> You will never enter into Paul's meaning until by careful attention to reading (*lectione*) him and by giving yourself to assiduous meditation you have imbibed his spirit. You will never understand (*intelliges*) David until by experience (*experientia*) you have put on the very affections of the psalms as your own. And the same with the rest. For all of Scripture, study is as distant from mere reading (*lectione*) as friendship from hospitality, and companionable affection from chance meeting.⁹

In the true kind of 'reading', understanding (*intellectus*) is effected by experiencing the truth of the text rather than its shortcomings. It is an understanding that grows like affection, not for separate and distinct attributes of the beloved, but for the person as a whole. The hermeneutic described here asks the reader to immerse herself in the text as a whole, not to ask questions of it, nor break it down into its parts. The moments of skepticism are repressed as one takes over the perspective and categories of the text in order to understand, or rather experience, it in its own terms.

There is every indication that this is the form Bernard's own reading took. William tells us that Bernard "read willingly and frequently in order (*saepius*) through the canonical Scriptures as a whole (*simpliciter*), for no other reason than to understand (*intelligere*) the very words."¹⁰ Bernard's practice, following this model, is one of assimilation and submission to the narrative order, language, and authority of Scripture. It is an order that preserves the unity of the text as a whole and, hence, produces understanding. The texts of

---

8. William of St. Thierry *Epistola* (PL 184:327C). On rumination, see Leclercq, *The Love of Learning*, p. 73.
9. William of St. Thierry *Epistola* (PL 184:327D).
10. William of St. Thierry *Sancti Bernardi: Vita et res gestae* 1 (PL 185:241A–B). This work is usually referred to as *Vita prima*.

Scripture and the Fathers were to be read, reread, memorized, and rewritten in every sermon. More than once Bernard stated that he did not wish to add anything to what the Fathers taught.[11] His writings at least attempt to follow his remarks in the preface to *De gradibus humilitati et superbiae*. Bernard writes to Brother Godfrey, "if there is anything you approve of in what I have said, you will pray that I do not become proud; if, however—which I think more likely—I have produced nothing worthy of your study, I will have nothing of which to become proud."[12] Bernard, then, denies any originality, but, almost simultaneously in the *retractio* that opens the same work, apologizes for any that might have crept in, noting that he wrote something about the seraphim which he had neither heard nor read elsewhere.[13] Thus, as it was for Augustine, redeemed language and rhetoric for Bernard are the language and rhetoric of Scripture, not the philosophers, the language of God, not the individual.

In Bernard's letters one frequent complaint about his contemporaries (most notably Abelard) is their seeking of 'novelty', of a new language to explain the mysteries contained in Scripture. For example, Bernard writes of Abelard, "He prefers [the philosophers'] innovations and his own novelties to the doctrines and faith of the Catholic Fathers," and he "introduces profane novelties of word and meaning in his discourses."[14] For Bernard, whatever difficulties might arise are not to be resolved by the importation of new categories, especially (and we will see why later) those of logic. Rather, they are resolved in terms of the structure of the discourse of Scripture itself, by becoming more immersed in the text, by opening one's mind and submitting one's will to its 'logic'. Such a hermeneutic views the nature of salvation

---

11. Leclercq cites a number of these passages. See *Love of Learning*, pp. 201–202.

12. Bernard of Clairvaux *De gradibus humilitatis et superbiae* in *Sancti Bernardi Opera* 3, ed. J. Leclercq and H. Rochaix (Rome: Cistercian Editions, 1963), p. 16.

13. Bernard of Clairvaux *De gradibus* (Leclerq-Rochaix 3:15).

14. Bernard of Clairvaux *Epistolae*, in Leclercq-Rochaix *Opera* 8 nos. 189, 332. The fact that, as Edward Little tells us, charges of 'novelty' were frequently made not only by Bernard in many contexts, but also by other writers, only underscores the significance of Bernard's remarks. A standard insult tells us something about an *ethos* and what it fears most. See Edward F. Little, "Relations between St. Bernard and Abelard before 1139," in *St. Bernard of Clairvaux: Studies Commemorating the 8th Centenary of his Canonization*, ed. M. Basil Pennington (Kalamazoo: Cistercian Publications, 1977), pp. 155–168.

and its text as the unfolding of a whole rather than as an analysis of something built up of atomic parts. It demands from the reader that she begin her interpretation from the stance of faith, from a kind of surrendering to the otherness of Scripture's language and structure, rather than from the reader's own perspective and questions.

Bernard was by no means incapable of *disputatio*, of using logical distinctions to construct arguments and resolve verbal contradictions in Scripture. He seems to doubt both the spirit in which it is undertaken and its ultimate usefulness. In *De gradibus*, Bernard constructs a disputation on a line of Scripture which in the *retractatio* to the work he confesses to misquoting. Bernard quotes Mark 13:32 as "Not even the Son *of Man* knows" instead of "Not even the Son knows." He then argues that Christ says, "Not even the Son *of Man* knows the day of judgment," to signify that his ignorance was a function of his human rather than divine nature.[15] What Bernard is relying on here is the logicians' distinction between Christ's divine and human natures. The distinction is used to dissolve contradictions arising from the attribution of predicates to Christ appropriate only to his divine rather than to his human nature, or vice versa. Bernard uses this distinction between the different ways of referring to Christ to explain the passage that Christ as divine is ignorant of nothing, while as human he has human ignorance. So, his ill-fated argument goes, Christ refers to himself as "the Son *of Man*" referring to his human nature in which the ignorance of the day of judgment resides, leaving intact his omniscience as divine. Bernard concludes, "Hence, trying to prove a true conclusion, I constructed the whole following *disputatio* on what was false."[16] Bernard's retraction points out the vanity of his effort. The conclusion he wished to prove, that Christ is God and has all the attributes of divinity, including knowledge, he knew before he began. Out of desire to prove it, to show the logical distinction hidden in the text, he constructs an argument that reveals only his finitude (his less than complete memory) and the inappropriateness of humanly devised distinctions to the text.

---

15. Bernard *De gradibus* (Leclercq-Rochaix 3:15). Bernard explains the mistake as follows, "For while the text has only 'Neither the Son knows,' I, mistaken rather than deliberately erring, misremembered the letter to be sure, but not the sense: 'Not even,' I say, 'the Son of Man knows.'"

16. Bernard *De gradibus* (Leclercq-Rochaix 3:15).

While Evans calls Bernard's excursion into scholastic disputation "unfortunate," I would like to suggest that it might be for Bernard an illustration of the dangers of relying on oneself, on categories invented by us and foreign to Scripture, and of wandering away from the text of Scripture.[17] Following the opening retraction of *De gradibus* in which Bernard lists mistakes and apologizes for innovation, the preface reflects on the perils, the ultimate paradox, of putting oneself forward as an expert on humility. Bernard writes "of fearing, on the one hand, speaking usefully of humility, but being found without it, or, on the other hand, keeping a humble silence, but being found useless."[18] Such an author is too self-conscious not at least to turn his mistakes into part of the lesson to be learned. The lesson is not rooted in his failed memory of the passage, but rather on his expectation that the text of Scripture should conform to our questions and, hence, our answers. The logicians' reduction of the text to propositions, which are true and consistent with others found elsewhere in it, imposes new categories on the text in order to solve contradictions essentially of its own making. It also breaks up its unity and disburses its message. Hence Bernard is not disparaging the search for a kind of 'logic' (in the broad sense) or coherence from the text, but rather the way in which the newness and elaborate cleverness of logical distinctions (like different referents for different names of Christ) result in the destruction of the 'logic' and coherence intrinsic to Scripture.

If Bernard recommends a reading of Scripture that begins in humble submission to mode of expression, in a kind of complete submersion into the whole, he also makes it clear that the end of such study is practical rather than theoretical. What begins with slow, careful *lectio* works toward and ends with prayer and meditation, with the transformation of one's character. Bernard's reading issues not in textbooks, in logically ordered *summae* of theology, but in sermons,

---

17. G. R. Evans, *The Mind of Saint Bernard of Clairvaux* (Oxford: Clarendon Press, 1932), p. 88. John R. Sommerfeldt cites some "happier" example of Bernard's use of disputation in his "Epistemology, Education, and Social Theory in the Thought of Bernard of Clairvaux," in *St. Bernard of Clairvaux: Studies*, pp. 169–179. But these examples are not drawn from discussions of speculative theological questions. They occur in contexts where Bernard is dealing with heresy or with the application of Scripture to contemporary problems.

18. Bernard *De gradibus* (Leclercq-Rochaix 3:16).

in exhortations based in Scripture to the moral and spiritual life. Predictably, Bernard's main concern in his letters about the heresy in the schools such as Abelard's is not theoretical but practical, a concern for the effect of such novelties and subtleties on the faith of common people.[19] Thus, Bernard keeps his eye firmly fixed on what, for him, is the only meaningful context for reading, interpretation, and argument—the enrichment of one's spirituality and commitment to the faith.

Abelard's goal is not different from this, but he certainly chooses different rhetoric and a different path to arrive there. His path lies no longer through submission to the order and language of Scripture, nor to the tradition of commentary on it, nor, perhaps most importantly, to instruction under a master.[20] The master Abelard most explicitly rejected was, of course, Anselm of Laon. Though Anselm was certainly less conservative than Bernard, he is still, at least for Abelard, spokesman for the traditional method of reading and interpreting Scripture in order and from accepted authorities.[21] What was novel at Laon, according to Beryl Smalley, was that this reading was both wider and less deep than elsewhere, and was interrupted for

---

19. See, for example, Bernard *Epistolae*, in Leclercq-Rochaix *Opera* 8, nos. 188, 338, 336.

20. For the argument that the goal of Abelard's theology, like Bernard's, is spiritual enrichment, see the next section below.

21. The School of Laon is the subject of almost as much controversy as the school of Chartres. Colish reports that Grabmann (*Geschichte der Scholastichen Methode*, pp. 157–168) and de Ghellinck (*Le mouvement théologique de XIIe siècle* [Bruges: Editions "De Tempel," 1948], pp. 138–148) originally argued for the roots of a systematic science of theology at Laon. A more careful look at the texts has revealed that their 'systematic' organization is the result of later compilers. Valerie Flint, by raising questions about the filiation of these texts with Laon and Anselm, has argued that there was no 'school' at Laon at all. See her "The School of Laon: A Reconsideration," RTAM 43 (1976): 89–111. For an account of these controversies, see Marcia Colish, "Another Look at the School of Laon," ADHLMA 53 (1986): 7–13. Colish argues that the Laon masters did not make an original methodological contribution to the development of theology, either in giving it a systematic organization or in applying dialectical methods to theology. They were creative in using traditional authorities to solve contemporary problems. I am here much less concerned with assessing the facts about the school of Laon or even the accuracy of Abelard's portrayal than I am with noting the way Abelard understands his own work as a reaction to the shortcomings of Anselm and others like him.

short and, apparently, shallow discussion of questions or problems.²² Such a compromise (like most such hybrids) could not have pleased either those looking for an opportunity to dispute or those hoping to 'taste' (*sapere*) the wisdom (*sapientia*) of Scripture fully. It surely did not please Abelard, who describes Anselm as "admirable in the eyes of an audience, but of no account in the examination of a question." Anselm, Abelard continues, "had a marvelous way of using words, but their meaning (*sensum*) was minimal (*contemptibilem*) and empty of reason (*ratione*)."²³ The contrast Abelard sets up here is between surface ('use') and depth (meaning), between the production of admiration from mere facility with language and understanding, words informed with a discernible meaning.

The contrast between surface and depth is one Abelard's *Historia* returns to repeatedly. At the Council of Soissons condemning Abelard's work on the Trinity, Abelard is both humiliated and frustrated at being forced to recite, but forbidden to explain the Athanasian Creed—after having been criticized for espousing a view for which Athanasius was the authority.²⁴ He also tells of being asked for the authority (namely Augustine) behind the claim that God did not beget Himself, but being cut off from both rational explanation and interpretation of both his own and Augustine's remarks.²⁵ Abelard's criticism of his accusers is the same he leveled at Anselm of Laon, that they are concerned only with surface correctness rather than with inner meaning or understanding, interested in following the received form blindly rather than breaking its order and structure to question and reorder it.

Abelard's rejection of others' authority for his own is, then, simultaneously the rejection of the authority of the text's own narrative categories which Abelard translated into the language and structures of dialectic, unlike Bernard, who has been described as translating the

---

22. Beryl Smalley, "Some Gospel Commentaries of the Early 12th Century," RTAM 45 (1978): 149. Compare Ermenegildo Bertola, "Le critiche di Abelardo ad Anselmo di Laon e ad Guglielmo di Champeaux," *Rivista della filosofia neo-scolastica* 52 (1960): 495–522.

23. Peter Abelard *Historia calamitatum*, ed. Jacques Monfrin, 3rd ed. (Paris: J. Vrin, 1978), p. 68.

24. Abelard *Historia* (Monfrin 88–89).

25. Abelard *Historia* (Monfrin 84–85).

'scholastic' language of correspondents back into biblical language.[26] In the *Historia*, Abelard tells of his rejection both of Anselm's method and authority and of beginning his study of Scripture as an expert, giving a master's lecture without having studied with a master, telling his fellow students, "it was not my custom to progress by practice (*usum*), but by my own intelligence (*ingenium*)."[27] Rejecting the performance of an outward act uninformed by the control, expertise, or understanding which would make it one's own, Abelard seeks to give his words the interiority Anselm and his accusers' words lack. He cannot follow their tracks but must make his own, must rely on his own *ingenium*. And what began as giving a lecture on Ezekiel before having ever been instructed by a master, continued in Abelard's other theological ventures. In them, Abelard thinks of himself as *sui generis* (even if he is not), as following no previously laid down pattern of questioning, form, or interpretation.

What Abelard's *ingenium* produced were several works in systematic theology, the first of which was the *Sic et non*. In a way the *Sic et Non* is Abelard's response to the *Glossa ordinaria*, in which Anselm and his school played a large role.[28] The latter follows the text of Scripture, but appends to that text solutions to textual problems (both grammatical and logical), guides to whether a given passage should be taken historically or allegorically, and clear, if brief, interpretations of passages.[29] The *Glossa*, constructed by many hands over a long period, supplements rather than supplants the tradition and its authority by adding interpretations to those of the Fathers. Thus, in the terms of

---

26. This is Erich Kleineidam's description of Bernard in *Wissen, Wissenschaft und Theologie bei Bernhard von Clairvaux* (Leipzig: St. Benno, 1955), pp. 147, 153, 156. It is repeated by Leclercq, *Love of Learning*, p. 201.

27. Abelard *Historia* (Monfrin 69).

28. On Anselm and the School of Laon's role in the construction of the *Glossa Ordinaria*, see Smalley, "Some Gospel Commentaries," pp. 149ff., and *The Study of the Bible in the Middle Ages* (Oxford: Clarendon Press, 1952), p. 60; Flint, "School of Laon," p. 92. On the construction of the *Glossa* more generally, see Margaret Gibson, *Lanfranc of Bec* (Oxford: Clarendon Press, 1978), and her "The Place of the *Glossa ordinaria* in Medieval Exegesis," in *Ad litteram: Authoritative Texts and their Medieval Readers*, ed. Mark D. Jordan and Kent Emery, Jr. (Notre Dame, Ind.: University of Notre Dame Press, 1992), pp. 5–27.

29. G. R. Evans, *The Language and Logic of the Bible: The Earlier Middle Ages* (Cambridge: Cambridge University Press, 1984), pp. 37–47.

this essay, it tries to combine adherence to the narrative structure of the text with submission to the history and tradition of interpretation and emerging standards of intelligibility and academic rigor. It accomplishes the first by remaining tied to the order of Scripture, the second by starting with earlier traditions of commentary, and the third, by adding comments to address contemporary questions ranging from problems arising from minor discrepancies in the text to larger grammatical, dialectical, and historical difficulties. That the *Glossa* as such has no author except the tradition as a whole, is not even associated with a single or discernible group of compilers, makes it of a piece with the narrative that it reiterates. It does not break the temporal sequence or assert itself as something standing over or outside of that story, to question or reorder it. Nonetheless, its own questions and additions attempt to take into account the demands of reason and understanding, without which one cannot follow the 'story' of Scripture and salvation in any meaningful way.

Abelard seems not to have seen in this tradition and in Anselm's teaching the attempt to combine the dialectical and narrative forms. His *Sic et non*, in contrast to the *Glossa*, is in no way connected to the narrative movement of Scripture and uses authorities not to solve but to raise problems. Its collection of scriptural and patristic passages, organized around questions such as "God is three-fold and contra" and "God is not a substance and contra," breaks down the narrative order of the scriptual text and the tradition of commentary it generated.[30] The *Sic et non*'s lack of connection to Scripture does have precedents in the *florilegia*, collections of sayings of the Fathers. In fact, consistent with his own methods, Abelard seems to have gotten most of his knowledge from such collections, in striking contrast to Bernard, who seems to have read many patristic works entire.[31] The *Sic et non* is

---

30. Peter Abelard *Sic et Non*, ed. Blanche B. Boyer and Richard McKeon (Chicago: University of Chicago Press, 1976–77), "Index quaestionum," p. 709, questions 6 and 9.

31. On Abelard's knowledge of the Fathers from such sources, especially the collection of Ivo of Chartres, see J. G. Sikes, *Peter Abailard* (London: Cambridge University Press, 1932), p. 77. On the *florilegia* in general see, for example, Joseph de Ghellinck, *Le mouvement théologique*, chapter 1. On Bernard's reading of the Fathers, especially Origen, see Evans, *Mind of Saint Bernard*, pp. 81–85. Leclercq reports that while there were monastic *florilegia*, they remained instruments of reading and meditation rather than dispute. See Leclercq, *Love of Learning*, pp. 182–184.

different from the *florilegia*, however, in its two organizing principles, abstract questions of speculative theology and contradictions among authorities in the tradition. Thus, the *Sic et non* represents a departure from earlier projects because it is not tied to the order and language of Scripture. Its rhetorical effect is to displace Scripture in its narrative form from the center of sacred study and turn theology into a set of problems to be resolved dialectically rather than a set of texts to be read narratively. Abelard clearly did not intend to use the collection to undermine faith, either in the authority of Scripture or in its interpreters. Rather, he constructed it as an aid for teaching methods of interpretation and argument by which contradiction might be resolved. Nonetheless, once Scripture and the tradition is removed from the center, a gap is created that can only be filled by the reader of these texts whose task it must be to take them in their newly ordered form, as expressing contradictory views, and give to this order another new and consistent ordering.

This formal difference is reflected and justified in Abelard's long prologue to the work. Smalley's thoughtful look at its prologue connects the *Sic et Non* with the tradition as a broader version of Augustine's project in his *Quaestiones in Heptateuchum*, in which Augustine examines and tries to resolve differences among biblical translations.[32] This seems to have been Abelard's intention, and, to this end, he liberally salts the introduction with quotes from Augustine on the problems and methods of interpretation. As Colish and others have remarked, the examples of and rules for the resolution of contradiction contained in Abelard's long prologue to the *Sic et non* are not unlike those found in Augustine's *De doctrina christiana*. These rules were to a large degree already in use, even by Anselm, whom Abelard criticizes as offering no reasons for his conclusions.[33]

However, the quotations he selects from Augustine and others and the way he weaves them into the prologue underline his text's

---

According to R. W. Southern even the texts selected by 'monastic' and 'scholastic' compilers were different, reflecting their different goals. See Southern, *The Making of the Middle Ages* (New Haven: Yale University Press, 1953), p. 207.

32. Beryl Smalley, "Prima Clavis Sapientiae: Augustine and Abelard," in *Studies in Medieval Thought and Learning From Abelard to Wyclif* (London: Hambleton Press, 1981), pp. 1–8.

33. Colish, "Systematic Theology," pp. 142–143.

preoccupation with the fallenness of language and human understanding, even the supposedly redeemed language of Scripture and the Fathers. The reader is left with a strong impression of the overwhelming odds against arriving at any correct interpretation. This stands in sharp contrast with Augustine, Abelard's putative model. Augustine, while recognizing as many difficulties of interpretation as Abelard, chooses to place them in the context of the multiplicity of possible readings consistent with the faith, revelling in the plenitude rather than, as Abelard does, the poverty of meaning. Abelard's prologue is a litany of the ways in which texts and our interpretations can fail to represent reality and their author's intentions. A text may be miscopied or misattributed to an authority, Abelard explains, may repeat opinions not held by the author, may only lay out problems rather than solutions, or may take a human rather than divine perspective in its use of language.[34] Besides concentrating within these few pages the many possible ways texts and interpretations can go wrong, already noted by Augustine and others, Abelard carries the possibility of error one more step, to Scripture itself.[35] Though Abelard's point is ultimately to underscore the possibility of error in the Fathers, he reaches that conclusion by noting that the human writers of Scripture, the prophets or apostles "did not remain wholly strangers to error," that they may have been mistaken in their prophecies or theology.[36] So much more, Abelard counsels, must lesser authorities be evaluated critically. Although always in light of the larger context of crafting coherent answers to the questions posed, the *Sic et non* structures the achievement of this goal as emerging out of conflict and contradiction in the tradition, and from an attitude of doubt and self-reliance on the part of the student.

Even more radical, perhaps, than the *Sic et non* were Abelard's *Introductio ad theologiam* and *Theologia Christiana*. They are neither commentaries, nor collections of *sententiae*, nor specialized treatises on some particular aspect of Christian teaching, but rather *summae*

---

34. Abelard *Sic et Non* (Boyer-McKeon 91–94).

35. Abelard *Sic et Non* (Boyer-Mckeon 97). Evans notes that Abelard does make a substantive change to the tradition in giving up "the assumption that the divine inspiration of Scripture extends to the minutest detail of the choice of words." See G. R. Evans, *Language and Logic*, p. 138.

36. Abelard *Sic et Non* (Boyer-Mckeon 97).

of theology organized in a way completely unconnected to the order of Scripture.[37] The preface to the *Introductio* describes a theology based upon a logical ordering of topics; it divides theology into faith or dogma (the Trinity, Incarnation, creation, original sin), charity or moral theology (the virtues, vices, and commandments) and the sacraments.[38] This is a division which, as Chenu remarks, disregards the notion that salvation history is, in fact, a history, events taking place in time, and that the text which forms its substance follows the order of this history.[39] If the *Sic et non* disintegrates the temporal ordering of Scripture into isolated problems and questions, the *Introductio* goes further in giving to theology another order not even nominally drawn from its narrative form.

What is the purpose of this new, non-temporal order? It is as if Abelard was thinking of a list of things to be believed (dogma) and to be done, both through our own activity (morality) and through grace (sacraments), rather than the thinking of these as arising out of the story which is salvation history and the tradition of reflection on that history. As we shall see, Hugh also divides theology into that which is to be believed and that which is to be done, but he understands these as the aim of the different levels of meaning of Scripture. Abelard, on the other hand, thinks these matters must be reconstituted in the mind of the theologian, in a different order, in one that distinguishes the content of belief from what is to be done. Mary's pondering of the words of the annunciation in her heart for Abelard signifies that she "carefully (*studiose*) examined each one [i.e., word] separately (*singula*) and compared them with each other, seeing how closely all agreed with one another."[40] Only after the separation of topics and comparison of authorities can the crucial connection between belief and action be made, Abelard implies by following this account of Mary with the question, "who can observe the words or

---

37. See Constant J. Mews, "On Dating the Writings of Peter Abelard," AHDLMA 52 (1985): 73–134.

38. Peter Abelard *Theologia "Scholarium"* 1, ed. E. M. Buytaert and C. J. Mews, CCCM 13 (Turnhout: Brepols, 1987), pp. 317–318.

39. Cf. Marie-Dominique Chenu, *Toward Understanding St. Thomas*, trans. A.-M. Landry and D. Hughes (Chicago: Henry Regnery, 1964), p. 260.

40. Terence P. McLaughlin, "Abelard's Rule for Religious Women," *Medieval Studies* 18 (1956): 292.

precepts of the Lord by obeying them unless he has first understood them?"[41] Just as in the *Historia*, Abelard explains his frustrations with the old and attempts at innovation as motivated by the demands of teaching the faithful. Thus, Abelard's rejection of the traditional *lectio* as the form for reflection on Scripture, like Bernard's rejection of *disputatio*, seems to be based ultimately on pedagogical considerations; they simply place different kinds and degrees of emphasis on different moments in the pedagogical process. And it is here that we arrive at the connection between dialectic and narrative form, on the one hand, and faith and reason, on the other.

FAITH AND REASON, NARRATIVE AND DIALECTIC

It is a truism to say that in the debate between Abelard and Bernard, Abelard represents 'reason' and Bernard 'faith'. However, the debate about faith and reason is, on another level, about the conflict between the narrative and dialectical forms which theology can take. For Bernard, Abelard's attempt to organize theology logically rather than around Scripture's historical structure is an attempt to overcome the need for faith. Equally, Abelard sees his own rewriting of theology in logical terms as satisfying reason's legitimate demand for understanding what it believes. What is surprising and what qualifies the truth of the truism, however, is that both Abelard and Bernard end up denying the narrative structure of reason that should, for Bernard, mirror the narrative structure of Scripture, and which should, for Abelard, be acknowledged in the doubt and desire for understanding which is the impetus for inquiry.

I turn first to Abelard's attempt to satisfy the demand for understanding. In the prologue to the *Sic et non*, Abelard writes that "the first key to wisdom" is "constant questioning."[42] This questioning is valued not just as an instrument of apologetics, Beryl Smalley argues, but for its own sake, as "a mental exercise making young students

---

41. McLaughlin, "Rule for Religious Women," p. 292.
42. Abelard *Sic et Non* prologue (Boyer-Mckeon 103).

more eager and quick-witted in the search for truth."[43] But it is more than a mere exercise. The search for truth through questioning is, for Abelard, oriented to the same goal as the repetition of and meditation on Scripture. This is made especially clear by Eileen Kearney's study of Abelard's rule for monastic life at the Paraclete.[44] In it Abelard argues for the same primacy of inquiry and the search for understanding he does in the *Sic et Non* and other systematic texts, but it is primary, Abelard argues, because it is the necessary condition for spiritual life. Only with understanding can we pray for, teach, and do the right things. Even more, Abelard notes, if we do not seek to understand God, we cannot be united with him. "Disdain for doctrine," Abelard warns Heloise, "is the beginning of withdrawal from God."[45] Kearney argues, with convincing evidence from the text, that Abelard reshapes prophecy and meditation into forms of discursive reasoning, not in order to separate reasoning from religious practice but rather as the only way to inform the outward forms of words and practices with meaning and life.[46] Thus an important theme of Abelard's complaints against Anselm of Laon in the *Historia* returns in this later letter to Heloise—the need to give substance to the external word and deed, to inform them with the logic and clarity that produces understanding.

In response to the emptiness of the words and lack of understanding produced by the masters of *sacra pagina*, Abelard began, he tells us, to examine and discuss (*disserendum*) "the foundation of our faith by likenesses with human reason" and to compose the treatise on the Trinity (later condemned) "for the use of students who were asking for human and philosophical reasons (*rationes*) on this subject, and demanded something which could be understood (*intelligi*) more than merely said."[47] These are mere words because they are spoken without

---

43. Smalley, "*Prima Clavis*," p. 7.

44. Eileen Kearney, "*Scientia* and *Sapientia*: Reading Sacred Scripture at the Paraclete," in *From Cloister to Classroom: Monastic and Scholastic Approaches to Truth*, ed. E. Rozanne Elder (Kalamazoo: Cistercian Publications, 1986), pp. 111–129.

45. McLaughlin, "Rule for Religious Women," p. 288; compare Kearney, "*Scientia* and *Sapientia*," p. 115.

46. Kearney, "*Scientia* and *Sapientia*," pp. 115–119.

47. Abelard *Historia* (Monfrin 82–83). The treatise is printed in CCCM 13 as *Theologia "Scholarium"*.

understanding, and, hence, fail to function as signs so far as they have no reference. The "human and philosophical reasons," with which Abelard proposes to replace this empty rhetoric, are new analogies to explain the nature of the Trinity and the relationship between the Persons.

Taken seriously and rigorously, however, Abelard's impatient demand for "human reasons" is a refusal to enter the world created by Scripture and the commentaries on their own terms. He will not, as William of St. Thierry advises, "imbibe the spirit" of Scripture by working slowly and meditatively toward an intimate understanding, allowing his understanding to unfold over time as its story.[48] In other words, he rejects the hermeneutic which William describes and Bernard practices, eschewing their demand for 'faith' not in Christian doctrine *per se* but in its text's power and clarity of signification. Instead, he demands explanation and argument to defend each and every one of its expressions before he will move on to the next. As a teacher, I can only sympathize with Anselm when I imagine the scenes which led to Abelard's description of his teacher as "of no account in the examination of a question."[49] It signifies an impatience that will not wait for understanding to unfold. What Abelard seems to demand of Anselm is the impossible, that understanding be immediate, that words carry their referents with them, that one need not accept (i.e., have 'faith' in) them as signs and begin a process of seeking out their reference and meaning.[50] Thus, not only does Abelard reject the narrative form of Scripture in attempting to organize synoptically and dialectically what it covers as an unfolding revelation, he also rejects the temporality and partiality of human understanding, i.e., the necessarily narrative structure of reasoning.

What I am arguing here is that this places Abelard in an almost untenable position in regard to the narrative of reasoning and Scripture. On the one hand, Abelard's concern that the intelligence be able to

---

48. Compare William of St. Thierry *Epistola* (PL 184:327D), and the discussion of this passage above.

49. Abelard *Historia* (Monfrin 68).

50. Here and in the following paragraphs I am indebted to Louis Mackey's account of signs and the need for 'faith' in them argued for in Augustine's *De Magistro*. See his, "The Mediator Mediated: Faith and Reason in Augustine's *De Magistro*," *Franciscan Studies* 42 (1982): 135–155.

'follow' the words of a text or teacher is a recognition of the narrativity of the learning progress—a recognition that understanding will not emerge full-blown from nothing at some mysterious point in the future, nor can it in any complete form pre-exist the learning process, but must begin somewhere. For Abelard the 'suspension of disbelief' and, hence, of questioning, required of the listener to the story of Anselm and others produces only uncomprehending repetition of the story by the listener to other listeners in turn. Instead, he opts not for a suspension of but an immersion into questioning, a tactic which breaks down the story into its elements and reformulates it in answer to these questions. In other words, Abelard attempts to restructure the process so that the moments of doubt, inquiry, and understanding are really distinct yet follow from one another, so that the outward form of reflection is once again infused with real growth and progress. On the other hand, his objections to the pedagogy of Anselm center around Anselm's failure to produce complete understanding at each and every moment, his failure, in other words, to produce a narrative whose moments are atomic and self-validating, an obvious contradiction in terms. Thus, though Abelard attempts to replace the lack of real progression, of a workable process for achieving understanding in those like Anselm, he seems to hold them to a standard which would make that progression from doubt to understanding impossible.

Abelard could not, without self-contradiction, wholly refuse to acknowledge that understanding is a temporal or narrative process. Merely to speak or write is to ask listeners and readers to wait, to let the 'story' emerge over time. But, insofar as Abelard failed to recognize this contradiction and approached this extreme, Scripture and the tradition seemed to collapse under the demands for certainty and immediacy Abelard made on it. The corpus of Abelard's own work, one could argue, shows the negative result of such an approach. His works in systematic theology, meant to address the questions raised by the collation of authorities in the *Sic et non*, were never finished, and even though they announce a systematic organization for theology, they never completely fill out that schema.

Abelard's work in theology has certain parallels to his more well-known work on universals. Just as he was better at exposing the difficulties confronting realism than he was at constructing a non-nominalistic alternative, so he was better at exposing the tensions and contradictions among theological authorities than he was at resolving them.⁵¹ Abelard's relentless (and rigorously correct) criticisms of realism's naive 'faith' in natures they could not coherently explain are followed by his attempt to map out a middle ground between realism and nominalism which is sketchy at best. In the same way, the promise of understanding from which Abelard begins in the prologue to his introduction to theology, saying, "by doubting we come to inquire and by inquiry we perceive the truth," does not progress measurably beyond doubt and has as its main by-product the opening up of the possibility of radical skepticism.⁵² The desire for complete understanding at every moment before proceeding and for the complete identity of sign and signified cannot be satisfied, the latter because the space between sign and signified is what allows the sign to signify some reality other than itself, the former because for that understanding to be truly complete one cannot and would not need to proceed; understanding would be transformed into *intellectus*, unified and timeless intuition. Hence, it is always possible to break down the ambiguous unity of sign and signified, to divide the sequential and partial grasp of understanding.

It is, I think, exactly the possibility of ending in skepticism, of opening gaps which cannot be closed, that accounts for the viciousness of Bernard of Clairvaux's attack on Abelard. In the many letters Bernard wrote describing Abelard and his teaching, there are two recurrent and, for Bernard, connected themes, Abelard's pride and the 'novel' language he creates and embraces. The following is a typical passage from Bernard's letters:

> [Abelard] transgresses the boundaries placed by our Fathers in disputing and writing about faith, the sacraments, and the Holy Trinity; he changes each thing according to his wish, adding to it or taking from it. In his books and in his works he shows himself to be a fabricator of falsehood, a cultivator of perverse dogmas, proving himself a heretic not so much in his errors but in his stubborn defense of error. He is a man who oversteps his capacity, by the wisdom of his words evacuating the virtue of the cross. He is ignorant of nothing in heaven or on earth, except himself.⁵³

---

51. Abelard's critique of realism and other views on universals are to be found in *Editio super Porphyrium*, ed. Mario Dal Pra in *Scritti di Logica* (Florence: La Nuova Italia, 1969), pp. 3–42.
52. Abelard *Sic et Non* prologue (Boyer-McKeon 103).
53. Bernard of Clairvaux *Epistolae*, in Leclercq-Rochaix *Opera* 8, no. 193.

The preponderance of reference to reasoning and truth is unmistakable. Bernard uses them to turn Abelard's rationalistic pretentions on their head. Abelard's creations of new analogies to explain the Trinity and new genres for theological reflection are, for Bernard, the creation of new doctrines, of falsehood. Hence, Abelard's disputes 'prove' nothing but Abelard's own error, and Abelard's 'wisdom' breaks down the 'virtue' (both the strength and moral substance) of the Christian message. In Bernard's view, Abelard's pride leads him to revel in novelty, in originality, in what is new, his own and necessarily false, rather than, like Bernard, rejecting originality for the humbler task of reiterating the words of the original, authoritative, and true text.

Further, Bernard's strong reaction to Abelard is grounded in his objection to the starting-point for Abelard's rewriting of Scripture and 'perverse dogmas', to doubt and questioning rather than faith. Abelard, Bernard writes, "sees nothing 'through a glass in a dark manner', but contemplates (*intuetur*) everything face to face."[54] For Bernard, Abelard's standard for understanding is immediacy, which Abelard approximates by subjecting Scripture's divine authorship to the categories of human logic, by "striving to explore with his reason what the devout mind grasps with a vigorous faith."[55] Bernard objects to what he sees as Abelard's skeptical suspension of belief which waits to assent until proof has been provided, and it is to Abelard's attitude that Bernard contrasts the immediate faith of Mary and the Good Thief: "but this one [Abelard], suspecting God, does not want to believe anything except that which has been previously discussed by means of reason."[56] Explorations with human reason of what is, for Bernard, grasped immediately by faith give rise not to a unified grasp but rather to dialectic that analyzes, distinguishes, and argues. It is a dialectical analysis that may not be able to reassemble what it has broken down, and which will not, even in principle, be able to restore it to its original state of unity and integration.

---

54. Bernard *Epistolae*, in Leclercq-Rochaix *Opera* 8, no. 338.
55. Bernard *Epistolae*, in Leclercq-Rochaix *Opera* 8, no. 338.
56. Bernard *Epistolae*, in Leclercq-Rochaix *Opera* 8, no. 338. Recall that for Abelard Mary is the model not of immediate and unquestioning faith, but of action and belief informed by understanding. Mary, after all, "pondered the Word in her heart." See Kearney, "*Scientia* and *Sapientia*," p. 117; McLaughlin, "Rule for Religious Women," p. 292. See the second section above, for another discussion of this passage.

In a peculiarly apt metaphor for my analysis of his objections to Abelard, Bernard accuses Abelard of having divided and shredded the seamless tunic of Christ, a garment which, even if it could be resewn, would nonetheless be irrevocably changed.[57] "But," he continues, "the seamless tunic remains unified (*integra*), having been woven as a whole (*contexta per totum*). . . . What has been thus woven, what the Holy Spirit has joined together, cannot be dissolved by human beings."[58] What this tells us about Bernard is perhaps more revealing than what it tells us about Abelard. Scripture for Bernard is this seamless whole, its text and 'context' indivisible. But the wholeness and unity Bernard attributes to Scripture and to faith in its message is fictional. Its 'text' and faith in it, though woven together (*contextum*) in ways perhaps not reflected by Abelard's *Sic et non*, is nonetheless woven of distinct words, stories, and books. Bernard, no less than Abelard it seems, ultimately rejects the construction of a theology whose structure mirrors the structure of its text. With Abelard, he asks for a timeless and unified grasp of the content of revelation, but he does so as a matter of faith rather than reason.

Bernard's letters excoriating Abelard express his fear that the 'faith of the simple' will be lost through their exposure to Abelardian dialectic. Bernard clearly longs for a return to 'simple faith'. He writes, "the faith of the simple is being ridiculed, the secrets of God are being torn to pieces, questions concerning the highest things are being recklessly discussed in the open."[59] William of St. Thierry describes this simplicity as follows: "Simplicity, in fact, is properly the will fundamentally turned toward God asking of the Lord only one thing . . . with no ambition to multiply itself by becoming dispersed in this world."[60] Bernard and William seem to equate 'the faith of the simple' with 'simple faith' (unanalyzed, unmultiplied, immediate faith). The problem, of course, a problem that Bernard does not seem completely unaware of in his better moments, is that it is by definition impossible to return to simple faith. Faith, even if retrieved after having been doubted or lost, is never simple again but is always sophisticated and fragmented, always infected with doubt. Seams, no matter how

---

57. Bernard *Epistolae*, in Leclercq-Rochaix *Opera* 8, no. 334.
58. Bernard *Epistolae*, in Leclercq-Rochaix *Opera* 8, no. 334.
59. Bernard *Epistolae*, in Leclercq-Rochaix *Opera* 8, no. 188.
60. William of St. Thierry *Epistola* (PL 184:316C).

neatly and closely sewn across rifts of doubt can always be pulled apart again, and they will always be points of weakness and stress in the garment. Further, and more importantly, faith which recognizes itself as faith can never completely deny the possibility of doubt. It has never been completely 'seamless'; it cannot, except through self-deception, be immediate, whole. Bernard should have seen that just as moral reform undertaken to repair a fall from Benedict's original model of the religious life could not be a 'simple' return to this earlier innocent state, but must be a complex, imperfect return which bears the mark of the fall which made it necessary, so the intellectual repair of the fall into doubt cannot pretend to erase the traces of that doubt. Bernard's letters about Abelard seem to have forgotten this bit of wisdom; he seems to want not so much to heal the breach and respond to the doubt Abelard has created, as to have prevented it from having ever occurred, to deny the history that precedes and makes possible understanding. With Abelard, he wants to deny, albeit in a different way, the narrative character of reasoning.

Here lies the source of that 'strange allegiance' between philosophical rationalism and theological reaction I mentioned at the outset. Both demand a certainty untainted by doubt and, hence, cooperate in making reasoning and interpretation impossible. For Bernard it is impossible because any recognition of the need for reasoning is a breakdown of 'simple' faith, which cannot be submitted to the mediation and division of argument and explanation. For Abelard it is impossible because doubt and the need for reasoning, once recognized, show the inadequacy of all starting points for the production of certainty. If Abelard is unwilling to move beyond the starting point until all doubt has been answered, Bernard is unwilling to admit that a faith which is firm has been and can be doubted, and should be examined. To put this dialectical lesson in hermeneutical terms, we can say that just as Abelard denies the moment of faith in all interpretation, in which one comes to the text with a certain faith in its signification and reads on, hoping to return later with a more complete grasp, so Bernard denies the moment of doubt in the meaning of a text that begins the process of reading and interpretation by giving it a question. Using the terms of narrative, we might say that just as Abelard remains unable to move beyond the beginning of the reasoning and interpretive process, so Bernard in a sense wants to skip over beginning and middle to the end, to the certain grasp of a faith which does not and has not ever admitted of doubt. This is beautifully illustrated by Bernard and Abelard themselves. It is Bernard who writes, "if you are a saint, you have already understood, you know; if you are not, become one, and you will learn through your own experience."[61] But it is Abelard, by contrast, who asks, "Who can observe the words or precepts of the Lord by obeying them unless he has first understood them?"[62] Together their views form the two halves of the *Meno* paradox: if you know, you do not need to inquire; if you do not know, you cannot even begin to look for that which you seek.

HUGH OF ST. VICTOR: NARRATIVE FORM AND THE NARRATIVE STRUCTURE OF FAITH SEEKING UNDERSTANDING

Hugh of St. Victor fits into this narrative as the one who, with Socrates as against Bernard and Abelard, solves the paradox and attempts to reunite faith and understanding and assimilate theology's academic form with its narrative text.[63] I will begin with the latter. Unlike Bernard, Hugh deems it necessary to ground the practice of reading and meditation on Scripture in a theoretical account of the nature of such a process. It is in this context that Hugh attempts to formulate a discipline of sacred study which will stand on a par with the *artes*, yet in some sense retain a form and project appropriate

---

61. Bernard, *De consideratione ad Eugenium Papam* nos. 5, 14, 30, as in Leclercq-Rochaix *Opera* 3.

62. McLaughlin, "Rule for Religious Women," p. 292.

63. Though I have chosen to recast traditional ways of categorizing Hugh in terms of dialectic and narrative, my view of Hugh is somewhere between the extremes of some early twentieth-century evaluations of Hugh as, on the one hand, "a mere mystic" with no interest in the project of seeking understanding of the things believed, and as a mere forerunner (and less perfect version) of the great scholastic tradition. The former is Barthélemy Hauréau's view in *Les oeuvres de Hughues de Saint-Victor* (Paris: Hachette, 1886), p. 424; the latter, the view of Martin Grabmann in *Geschichte der Scholastischen Methode*, p. 234, and of Joseph Mariétan in *Le problème de la classification des sciences d'Aristote à Saint Thomas* (Paris: Felix Alcan, 1901), p. 131.

to Scripture, not logic.⁶⁴ This is accomplished in two ways using the model of the *artes*. First, sacred study is given a well-defined subject, on the basis of which its text is divided into the Old and New Testaments (each given a further tripartite division). It is then subdivided into the 'disciplines' of the three levels of meaning: history, allegory, and tropology.⁶⁵ Second, it is given a method of reading that moves from the letter, to the sense, to the deeper or spiritual meaning.⁶⁶ What is significant about these divisions of sacred study is that they are, unlike Abelard's, at once grounded in the narrative structure of Scripture and designed to constitute a logical division of its topics or disciplines.

Let me explain. First, the subject of theology is given by Hugh as "the work of restoration," the restoration of our fallen human nature to its pre-lapsarian state, including how we came to need restoration (the fall) and the world into which we were placed (creation).⁶⁷ The subject matter of Scripture is, then, the works of creation (Old Testament) and restoration (New Testament). Hugh's systematic work on theology, *De sacramentis*, is patterned on this description of the subject of sacred study. Thus, the subject of theology is divided temporally, into creation and restoration, mirroring the temporal structure of Scripture. Within this narrative framework and in an order suggested by its order, Hugh touches on what are normally considered the 'topics' of speculative theology, e.g., faith, doctrine, morality, the Trinity, the Incarnation.⁶⁸ Similarly, the three levels of meaning of

---

64. Compare Marie-Dominique Chenu, *Théologie au 12ème siècle* (Paris: J. Vrin, 1957), p. 202.

65. Hugh of St. Victor *Didascalion* 5.2 and 6.2–5, ed. Charles Henry Buttimer (Washington: Catholic University of America Press, 1939), pp. 95–96 and 113–123.

66. Hugh of St. Victor *Didascalicon* 6.9–11 (Buttimer 126–129).

67. Hugh of St. Victor *De sacramentis christianae fidei* (PL 176:183A, 184A–B).

68. Compare G. R. Evans, *Old Arts and New Theology* (New York: Oxford University Press, 1980), p. 27, for whom Hugh's *De sacramentis* is an attempt to combine two approaches to theology, "the study of the Bible and that of speculative theology where Scriptural passages serve principally to pose problems or to furnish proofs for use in problem solving." See also Roger Baron's general assessment of Hugh's organization and definition of theology in *Science et sagesse chez Hughues de Saint-Victor* (Paris: P. Lethielleux, 1957), p. 84. For a view of some of the ways in which Hugh arguably fails to follow through on the coherent schema he has created, see Colish, "Systematic Theology," pp. 143–145. While many of these observations seem quite correct, some of Colish's criticisms of Hugh seem to measure *De sacramentis* against the yardstick of the Lombard's *Sentences*, which, I will argue below, is conformed to a different

Scripture and the 'method' they generate have a double function: they are both logical categories and narrative structures. On the one hand, they give to theology its disciplines—dogma, things to be believed, and morality, things to be done.[69] Hence, the historical and allegorical levels are the repositories of dogmatic and the tropological of moral theology. But the three levels of meaning of Scripture also ground a method of reading, a method that Hugh constructs to mirror the narrative structure of the text it attempts to interpret.

The method of reading for Hugh consists in the movement from the letter of the text, its orthographic and grammatical construction, to its sense, the literal meaning of the words, to its *sententia*, the inner sense or underlying meaning, the meaning, not of the words but of the things those words name.[70] Hence, the sense corresponds to the historical/literal level and the *sententia* to the two spiritual meanings, allegory and tropology. This rather simple model of reading

---

model of theological reflection. Hence, Colish criticizes Hugh for not opening with an account of the divine nature and proofs for God's existence, for example. She argues that Hugh's account is hopelessly confused by beginning with the six days of creation, a discussion of prime matter, the creation of human beings and why creation occurred at all, and so on. But clearly Hugh is following the order of Scripture, which begins not with a definition of the divine nature, but with creation. Hugh seems to be attempting to take up speculative questions, such as whether there is prime matter, as they would arise in a sequential reading of Scripture. What he found out, and what Colish criticizes him for, is that the explanation of events as they occur in Scripture often requires an account of things that have not yet occurred. The account of the fall provokes Hugh into an account of the need for the Incarnation.

69. "You are given in history what God has done to admire, in allegory his sacraments to believe, in morality his perfection to imitate." Hugh of St. Victor *Didascalicon* 6.3 (Buttimer 113–117); compare 5.6 (104–105).

70. Hugh of St. Victor *Didascalicon* 6.9–11 (Buttimer 126–129). See Beryl Smalley, *The Study of the Bible in the Middle Ages* (Oxford: Basil Blackwell, 1957), pp. 97–106, for the view that Hugh's grounding of the other levels of meaning in the literal level constitutes an important departure from previous and contemporary traditions, for whom the spiritual meanings are more important. Compare Henri de Lubac's response to Smalley for the view that Hugh does not create such an emphasis but rather maintains it, in the tradition of Augustine and Gregory the Great. See De Lubac, *Exégèse médiévale* 1/2 (Lyon: Editions Montaigne, 1961), pp. 357–359. De Lubac argues that the literal and spiritual senses are not opposed for Hugh (as they tend to be in the modern mind). Rather the senses arise from "the movement of faith itself, which from simple narration [the literal level], carries itself all the way to mystery [the allegorical level]" (*Exégèse médiévale*, p. 359).

is complicated by the realization that the text of Scripture, while never wrong, cannot always be taken literally. Hugh writes,

> the Divine Page, according to the literal sense, contains many things which seem both to be opposed to each other and, sometimes, to imply something absurd or impossible. But the spiritual meaning (*intelligentia*) admits no opposition; in it many things can be diverse but none can be opposed.[71]

In this context, Hugh repeats Augustine's guidelines for scriptural interpretation in which the foundation and final arbiter of meaning are "the principles of faith."[72] This hermeneutic, of course, yields a structure of inquiry which is circular, i.e., in Scripture are found the things to be believed, yet they can only be extracted when guided by some previous knowledge of the content of that faith. Hugh explains,

> For in such a great sea of books and in the multiple intricacies of meanings (*sententiarum*) whose number and obscurity often confound the soul of the reader, the person who does not recognize briefly in advance, in every genus so to speak, some definite principle which is supported by firm faith and to which all may be referred, will scarcely be able to bring together (*colligere*) any single thing.[73]

The contrast is between the multiplicity and incoherence of words and meanings, which leaves the reader who confronts the text without a faithful grasp of the truth of Christianity as a whole, without preparation, and without teachers 'at sea', and unified understanding, an understanding 'collected' by a process which begins with some fore-understanding of the text, prepared for by teachers and grasped in faith. Hugh's notion of interpretation and reasoning, then, is grounded on the recognition that it is only through some kind of 'faith', some

---

71. Hugh of St. Victor *Didascalicon* 6.4 (Buttimer 117–122).

72. Hugh of St. Victor *Didascalicon* 6.4 (Buttimer 117–122). Hugh also quotes the following hermeneutic principle from Augustine, "When therefore we read the divine books, [and we meet] such a great number of true meanings (*intellectuum*) that are brought out from few words and built up by the soundness of Catholic faith, let us choose in the first place what it seems certain the one we are reading thought. If however it is unclear, [let us choose] surely that which the circumstances of scripture do not impede, and what conforms to sound faith. If however the circumstances cannot be thoroughly examined, at least [let us choose] what sound faith prescribes." Hugh of St. Victor *Didascalicon* 6.11; compare Augustine, *De Genesi ad litteram* 1.11.

73. Hugh of St. Victor *Didascalicon* 6.4 (Buttimer 117–122).

appeal to prior though incomplete knowledge, that both the moment of doubt about the text's signification and its resolution can take place. Thus, as some recent hermeneutical theories argue, Hugh realizes that only with foreknowledge of the text can we proceed to question it, to open the conversation with it, but equally that that foreknowledge only becomes more than prejudice by being questioned and transformed by the text.

The realization that the text must be interpreted, that its signs do not carry with them their signified is the skeptical moment which, Abelard reminds us, begins inquiry. Equally, however, doubt only emerges in relation to some touchstone for truth, some belief in the meaning of the text as a whole or, at the very least, in the possibility of its signification. Hugh seems to grasp, in other words, that though the unity of belief is necessary to reach the unity that is understanding, that unity is not immediate or original; it is 'collected' by faith that moves to the text with an expectation (rather than certainty) of unity, and 'collected' by the process of understanding which weaves together what doubt has separated and distinguished. Thus, Abelard's doubt and Bernard's faith are not mutually exclusive but exactly the opposite. They make each other possible, and it is this recognition that Hugh makes the guiding principle of the method of sacred study. This principle is, of course, that of "faith seeking understanding," and for Hugh it means that one always already believes something (and so can begin, as one must, from something accepted) and has always already doubted (and so has been moved to inquiry in the first place).

Inquiry and interpretation so understood are, I think, recognized as implicitly narrative. Hugh views the process of understanding as temporally structured, as always already having begun and as working toward completion. More specifically, the dialectic of faith seeking understanding so understood mirrors the narrative of Scripture; it projects backward to the moment of creation (faith) and fall (doubt) and projects forward to redemption (complete understanding). Just as Scripture moves toward an end, a closure, the believer moves toward understanding; however, just as no narrative, including Scripture, crosses the infinite distance between temporality and eternity, no believer can pretend to achieve complete understanding. Thus, the need for faith in that closure remains, and so, then, does the need for the recognition of the still and always incomplete nature of understanding, and, equally, of the always present possibility of doubt.

Hugh's notions of reasoning and interpretation, then, view the reader/inquirer as always temporally located, as always already in medias res. It attempts to reconnect the doubt from which Abelard begins (but hardly progresses) and the perfect certainty to which Bernard leaps by giving the 'story' a 'middle', which consists in the dialectic of doubt and inquiry, faith and understanding. Hence, for Hugh the process of inquiry, indeed of education in the broad sense, is a narrative conforming to the narrative, to salvation history, and its necessarily temporal and incomplete character is seen as another emblem and indication of our status as pilgrims in exile in this life, as in viae. Appropriately, Hugh ends his discussion of secular study with the following characterization of the three stages of education:

> Still tender is the one who finds his native land sweet; already strong is he to whom every place is his homeland; but perfect is the one for whom the entire world is a place of exile.[74]

The process of education and growth is a process of moving from one's native land to the assimilation of new territory, a process that would not begin unless the traveler had some place from which to begin (faith) and some sense of what was beyond 'home' (doubt). Even more, Hugh's metaphor of pilgrimage reminds us, because we do not progress to a homecoming in this life but only toward a more and more profound sense of exile, it is a process that is never finished or closed, only rewritten.

EPILOGUE AND CONCLUSION

And rewritten it was. It is (again) a truism to say that Abelard's dialectic (and not Bernard's nor even Hugh's narrative) structures the theology of the next century as the *Sentences* of Peter Lombard and the *summae* of Thomas Aquinas and others become the models for the 'proper' form of theological discourse. There are many reasons which might explain this; for example, that Hugh did not execute his plan for theology as well as he laid it out, that Hugh's model for inquiry did not seem 'rigorous' enough in light

---

74. Hugh of St. Victor *Didascalicon* 3.19 (Buttimer 69).

of the models of knowledge and inquiry embodied in the complete Aristotelian corpus. However, my interest is not to explore the reasons why Hugh's project or others like it did not succeed, but to insist that even the shift to the dialectic of the *summae* is still a troping, a rewriting, rather than a denial of the narrative form of Scripture and theological inquiry.

Since I can only sketch this briefly, I want to do so by taking the most well-known example for theological form and method from the twelfth century, Peter Lombard's *Sentences*. First, Peter structures the *Sentences*'s consideration of subjects in a way that seems indebted to the spirit of Hugh's project, i.e., following salvation history. It moves from the examination of the Trinity (Book I), creation and the fall (Book II), to the Incarnation (Book III), ending with the sacraments and eschatology (Book IV). Thus, Peter devises a topical arrangement of theology that, like Hugh's, mirrors the biblical narrative of creation, fall, and redemption. But that structure has been reshaped in certain ways to reflect the dialectician's concern with logical and ontological rather than temporal priority. So, for example, Peter opens with an account of the Trinity instead of beginning directly with creation, and discusses the creation of angels before the work of the six days. Moreover, the accounts of the human being and Christ are tied to a series of abstract questions organized around their 'natures' and possibilities, rather than linked to the order of Scripture, which displays these natures by telling their story. The very generalized pattern of salvation history which remains, God—creation—Incarnation—sacraments—eschatology, gives its subject matter logical coherence, but also moves Peter's text away from the specific and complex narrative of Scripture and closer to dialectic.

If the ordering of topics in the *Sentences* retains traces of Scripture's narrative, so too does its way of confronting these various topics in its distinctions and questions. Contradictory authorities and arguments like those collected in Abelard's *Sic et non* are incorporated into the text and so made part of the process of inquiry. The opposing views imply a history and context for reasoning and the response moves forward toward resolution, thus inscribing on the inquiry itself its temporal character. Moreover, the authorities expressing opposing views are not chosen for the sake of their opposition, because not all subjects are turned into a question on which opposing sides are lined up; rather, Peter sometimes seems content to state what he takes as an accepted view and to cite an appropriate authority to back him up. In Colish's view, Peter is not merely selective but is judicious in his use of authorities.[75] Even if this is not always the case, as Colish also remarks, "Peter treats theological debate as a normal mode of theological investigation."[76] I would add, however, that he places that debate carefully within a tradition of past wisdom rather than confusion, and gives a model for a resolution of its conflicts in his own present and provisional solutions. Moreover, Peter's theology is also, like Hugh's, oriented toward a future in which it will be superceded. Though Peter's answers sometimes seem a little too pat and unspeculative, the tradition of commentaries on his *Sentences* certainly tended toward the opposite of both of these, i.e., neither simple nor narrow solutions, and Peter himself must be seen as playing some role in what became of his work, in its continual revision and reinterpretation by masters of theology for many generations. Peter's remark at the end of one question he has solved, "if anyone can do better, I am not envious," is perhaps emblematic of his vision of his own work, as not only at the head of a long, illustrious tradition preceding him but also at the tail of a tradition he knew would and should bypass him.[77] Thus Peter's text, like Hugh's, reenacts the narrative of Scripture, creation, fall, and movement toward salvation. It does so by replacing the kinds of disputed questions Abelard and others were asking, which have a tendency to dissolve the narrative line both of inquiry and of salvation, into the narrative out of which they arise, a tradition that articulates what is to be believed, that raises doubt, and that moves toward full understanding.

Hence, the narrative character of inquiry has been rewritten rather than completely erased insofar as Peter aims at harmonizing various authorities and evidence in light of a past tradition of inquiry and in terms of the larger narrative of creation, incarnation, and last judgment mapped out by the four books. This structure serves as the ruling interpretive principle for the issues and problems which arise dialectically, and these problems are provisionally resolved by

75. Colish, "Systematic Theology," p. 152.
76. Colish, "Systematic Theology," p. 152.
77. Peter Lombard *Sent.* 4.5.3 (CSB 3:76). This remark is noted by Elizabeth Rogers in *Peter Lombard and the Sacramental System* (New York: Richwood, 1976), p. 64.

dissolving division and opposition, so that the *Sentences*'s overall narrative is repeated microcosmically in the structure of each topic, which reintegrate the fragmented tradition into a kind of provisional unity. Thus Abelard's dialectic becomes in the *Sentences* a true dialectic, one with 'narrative' features, with a form which mirrors dialectic's temporal character.

What has changed in moving from Hugh's *De sacramentis* to the *Sentences* is the nature and degree of reflection of the narrative character of understanding. While Hugh explains inquiry as a process of interpreting a text, the Lombard's questions and responses make of inquiry the solution to a problem. Textual interpretation more clearly moves from 'faith', because of its clearer reliance on the interpretive principles and foreknowledge we bring to the text, and more obviously moves toward, but never pretends to reach, complete understanding, since interpretation does not aim at the reaching of a conclusion *tout court* but the seeing of the parts in light of the whole and vice versa, a process which is ongoing. Disputation, even within a tradition, though recognizing the two conditions of the possibility of inquiry (doubt and faith), still tends to emphasize doubt over faith, and can be more easily read as achieving closure rather than only provisional understanding.

There are surely other equally thoroughgoing and persuasive attempts which resolve somewhat differently the tensions between narrative and dialectic, faith and reason in the twelfth and thirteenth centuries. But Peter's 'success' is instructive because it is almost too complete. The *Sentences*'s form and 'method', because so formalized and indirectly related to its textual narrative and the narrative structure of reasoning, make it easy to forget their roots. They make it easy, in other words, to suppress the narrative moments in dialectic, the literary quality of theological and philosophical reflection.

Boston College

The Certainty and Scope of Knowledge: Bonaventure's *Disputed Questions on the Knowledge of Christ*

ANDREAS SPEER

I shall be concerned here with two key questions for any theory of knowledge: (1) Is there such a thing as certainty of knowledge and, if so, what is it? (2) How far does our knowledge extend, and what are its possible limits? In answering these questions I shall make use of Bonaventure's seven disputed questions concerning the knowledge of Christ. This procedure surely calls for some explanation, since both the author and the subject matter of these questions seem to fall outside the sphere of philosophical interest. As far as Bonaventure's philosophical importance is concerned, there still seems to be widespread agreement with Etienne Gilson's judgment that, in contrast to Albert the Great or Thomas Aquinas, Bonaventure has nothing that can properly be called philosophy, if by 'philosophy' one means the discoveries of reason alone, independent of the data of revelation.[1] Is not this caveat borne out in the very subject matter of these disputed questions? What can reason alone tell us about the knowledge of Christ?

---

1. Etienne Gilson, *La philosophie de Saint Bonaventure*, 3d ed. (Paris: Vrin, 1924), p. 387.

If, heedless of such considerations, I persist in using Bonaventure to address one of the great questions of philosophy, it is because I am convinced that one can identify in this text an original philosophical contribution to the two questions I posed at the beginning of this paper. To see this, one must first reconstruct the context of the question; in doing so I intend to proceed historically. I shall then focus on the systematic meaning of Bonaventure's answer. Finally, the historical dimension will come back in view when I relate this answer to Bonaventure's work as a whole.

THE HISTORICAL CONTEXT

The *Quaestiones disputatae de scientia Christi* lead us immediately to Bonvaventure's time in Paris. They mark a temporary peak in a typical academic career of that day, a career that Bonaventure began in 1235 as a student in the Faculty of Arts and that reached a provisional climax with the *licentia docendi* and Bonaventure's appointment in 1254 as ordinary regent master in the Faculty of Theology.[2] When he went to Paris in 1235, Bonaventure encountered a university already thirty-five years old and undergoing a stormy period in its development. The founding of the university at Paris was itself an expression of a development with large consequences. It led, among other things, to a reorganization of teaching, which was now to be done in a thoroughly "scholastic" or school-ish fashion.[3] This process, begun in the twelfth century, led eventually to a progressive dissolution of the classical canon of instruction comprising the seven liberal arts and theology. Moreover the unity of faith and reason, which had, as Christian doctrine, earlier been able to meet the need for a comprehensive and persuasive interpretation of the world, now came apart.[4]

---

2. Jacques-Guy Bougerol, *Introduction à Saint Bonaventure*, rev. ed. (Paris: J. Vrin, 1988), pp. 3–4 and 13–14; Fernand Van Steenberghen, *La philosophie au XIIIe siècle* (Louvain: Publications universitaires, and Paris: Béatrice-Nauwelaerts, 1966), pp. 193ff.

3. See for an overview of this point Joseph Koch, "Scholastik," in *Religion in Geschichte und Gegenwart* 5:1494–1498.

4. Wolfgang Kluxen, "Der Begriff der Wissenschaft," in *Die Renaissance der Wissenschaften im 12. Jahrhundert*, ed. Peter Weimar, Zürcher Hochschulforum 2 (Zurich:

When the young Giovanni Fidanza went to Paris in 1235 as a student, just four years had passed since the papal letter of 13 April 1231. With it, Gregory IX had managed to put an end to the fighting at the University of Paris aroused by his letter of 1228 to the professors of the theological faculty. At issue were both the use of speculative method and the employment of philosophical expressions and concepts in the exposition of the doctrine of the faith. The controversies were ignited principally by the employment of Aristotle's writings, especially of the so-called *libri naturales*, in philosophical and theological instruction.[5] The *libri naturales* had already been condemned in 1210 by the decrees of a regional synod of Sens under Peter of Corbeil, Archbishop of Paris. The synodal prohibition was directed in particular against the alleged heresies of Aumary of Bene and David of Dinant, but in August 1215 it entered the new university statutes of the Faculty of Arts, which permitted instruction in Aristotle's logical and dialectical writings but not in the "libri Aristotelis de methaphisica et de naturali philosophia."[6] The effect of the prohibition was minimal, as the intervention of Gregory IX indicates. The pope himself was finally compelled to open a way to the study of Aristotle's writings on natural philosophy and metaphysics.

One would not do justice to the situation at the beginning of the thirteenth century if one were to see in these conflicts merely a power struggle between the Church's *magisterium* and the university. Gregory IX had himself studied theology in Paris. Like Innocent III, who was involved in the dispute over the statutes in 1215, Gregory had been a student of Peter the Chanter, who was master of theology at Notre Dame from about 1170 until his death in 1197. The conflicts had rather to do with a question of fundamental importance. Theology faced the challenge of determining afresh its position in connection with the new understanding of science. In place of the

---

Artemis, 1981), pp. 273–293; and Georg Wieland, *Ethica—scientia practica: Die Anfänge der philosophischen Ethik im 13. Jahrhundert*, BGPTM NS 21 (Munster: Aschendorff, 1981), pp. 9–18; and Speer, "Wissenschaft und Erkenntnis: Zur Wissenschaftslehre Bonaventuras," *Wissenschaft und Weisheit* 49 (1986): 169ff.

5. For an overview, see Van Steenberghen, *La philosophie au XIIIe siècle*, pp. 100–110.

6. *Chartularium Universitatis Parisiensis*, ed. Heinrich Denifle and Emile Chatelain (Paris: Frères Delalain, 1889), 1:78–79, no. 20; Van Steenberghen, *La philosophie au XIIIe siècle*, pp. 89–99.

"holy relevance" of studies directed towards the better understanding of revelation, there now comes *amor scientiae*, scientific knowledge in accordance with rational principles, pursued for its own sake. Theology became a science among sciences, its status determined under universal notions. With that displacement came the question of the relationship between scientific rationality and the revealed truths of salvation.[7]

THE THEOLOGICAL QUESTION

For his first great disputation after becoming ordinary master, Bonaventure chose the question of Christ's knowledge (November 1253–spring 1254). He had already treated it once before in the context of his lectures on the *Sentences*.[8] But in his lectures he had been bound by the program of the *Sentences*, of the anthologized authorities obligatory for all commentators. In the *Quaestiones disputatae de scientia Christi*, we have Bonaventure's independent and systematic grappling with this topic, one chosen by him as suitable to solemn public disputation.

With his choice of topic, Bonaventure seizes an obviously theological problem, the question of Christ's knowledge. This question may now seem academic, but properly considered it leads to a host of theologically and philosophically important issues. To see the philosophical significance, one must first discuss the theological content, which results from the teaching on the hypostatic union by the Council of Chalcedon (451). The dogmatic exposition of the council, that Jesus Christ was one single person, perfect in Godhead and perfect in humanity, formed the provisional endpoint in a struggle that defined

---

7. Albert Zimmermann, "Die Theologie und die Wissenschaften," in *Die Renaissance der Wissenschaften*, pp. 87–93; Kluxen, "Der Begriff der Wissenschaft," pp. 281–283; Joachim Ehlers, "Monastische Theologie, historischer Sinn und Dialektik: Tradition und Neuerung in der Wissenschaft des 12. Jahrhunderts," in *Antiqui und Moderni*, ed. Albert Zimmermann, Miscellanea Mediaevalia 9 (Berlin and New York: W. de Gruyter, 1974), pp. 58–62.

8. For the dating, see Bougerol, *Introduction*, pp. 4–6. For the earlier treatment, see Bougerol, p. 201, and Bonaventure *Sent.* 3.14 as in *Opera omnia* 3, ed. CSB (Quaracchi: CSB, 1887) 295a–326b.

the first centuries of Christianity—the struggle over the mystery of the hypostatic union, which stands at the center of Christian belief about the redemption.[9] The redemption can be thought of as a perfection immanent in a human being only if Jesus Christ is truly human, but it can have universal efficacy only so far as he is also truly God.

If one refuses to leave this as just a paradox, accepted on faith but ultimately intractable to theological reasoning, a host of problems arises from the teaching that Christ has two natures. These problems determined the rapidly evolving dogmatics of the centuries following Chalcedon. How can this union of the two subsistent natures in one person or hypostasis be conceived, when according to the classic formulation of Lateran IV (1215) the distance between Creator and creation is so great that any similarity grounded in the act of creation is conditioned by a far greater dissimilarity? Again, how can one conceive the participation of the human nature in the divine? This second question has wide implications for the problem of the hypostatic union and leads into the deeper realm of the possibilities for philosophical-theological affirmation. The same is true of the question about how properties and attributes can be predicated of this one person. The unity of the person should not be lost from one side or the other, nor can there be an inadmissible exchange of properties (*idiomata*) between the natures that are bound together, though never confused, in Christ—even though these properties can be common to the person or hypostasis as their underlying subject. Over the course of the history of theology, basic rules covering the so-called "communication of idioms" were laid down. These were supposed to help preserve the hard-won Christological *via media* that had been achieved by the orthodox councils.[10]

The seventh disputed question about the knowledge of Christ provides a clear example of this logically engrossing problem. Does the human soul of Christ understand all divine judgments? Does it

---

9. Herbert Vorgrimler, "Hypostatische Union," LTK 5:579–584; Rowan Williams, "Jesus Christus, II: Alte Kirche," TRE 16:726–745, especially pp. 734–742; Alain Michel, "Hypostatique (Union)," DTC 7:437–568.

10. Karl Forster, "Idiomenkommunikation," LTK 5:607–609; J. F. Rigney, "Communication of Idioms," NCE 4:35–37; A. Michel, "Idiomes (Communications des)," DTC 7:595–602; Arthur M. Landgraf, *Dogmengeschichte der Frühscholastik*, 2: *Die Lehre von Christus* (Regensburg: F. Pustet, 1953) 1:138–146.

possess all the knowledge of the divine Word that is united to it? And does it possess it so far as Christ is a human being? The rules for discourse about the communication of idioms, which Bonaventure invokes when replying to the objections raised, help him to grasp the issue. This issue does not consist in the one hypostasis that can bear diverse attributes, but rather in the ordering of the attributes—in this case, of knowledge—to the two natures, because no simple exchange of attributes is admissible.[11]

But then how are we to think of the psychological unity of Christ? Anselm gave this question prominence in *Cur Deus homo*. After him, under the influence of Abelard and Hugh of St. Victor, among others, the emphasis was all on the perfection of Christ's human knowledge.[12] This emphasis remains important for Bonaventure's posing of the question. He learned it in detail from his teacher, Alexander of Hales. Alexander treated the matter in his *Gloss on the Sentences*, in the *Summa* attributed to him, and in a disputed question of his own. He concluded in all three that Christ had in God a perfect knowledge of God and the world, and had a perfect knowledge of things by means of himself. Thus, Christ's human nature has genuine knowledge of its own.[13] In terms of the psychology of knowledge, Alexander teaches, in harmony with the Augustinian tradition, that God is both the first-known (*primum cognitum*) and the psychologically first source of knowledge about the world.[14]

The question of the relative independence of the human being begins to carry more weight within the context of Aristotelian psychology, since the Aristotelian doctrine of the active and possible intellects seems to preclude every priority of divine illumination. Hence, the need for a new psychological and epistemological grounding for the originally theological thesis that God is first known. He is first in

---

11. *De scientia Christi* 7 ob. 1–3 and ad 1–3 (CSB 5:37a–b, 40b).

12. Jan Th. Ernst, *Die Lehre der hochmittelalterlichen Theologen von der vollkommenen Erkenntnis Christi*, Freiburger theologische Studien 89 (Freiburg: Herder, 1971), pp. 53–96. See also Landgraf, *Dogmengeschichte der Frühscholastik*, 2: *Die Lehre von Christus*, 2:44–68.

13. Alexander of Hales *Glossa in Sent.* 3.13.10–3.14.24 (3:131–149), and Alexander *Quaestiones disputatae "antequam esset frater"* 42 (2:414–730). Compare the *Summa "fratris Alexandri"* 3.3.2 (4:163–171). See also Ernst, *Erkenntnis Christi*, pp. 113–129.

14. Ernst, *Erkenntnis Christi*, pp. 151–153.

regard to his noetic priority and in regard to human knowledge of the world, for which the human being's relation to the world must also be taken into account.

THE SOUL OF CHRIST AS MODEL

Against such a complex background, one can begin to appreciate the interest that moved Bonaventure to take up, again, the question of Christ's knowledge. He could now take it up on his own terms and so use the series of disputed questions to go far beyond the answers permitted by the limits of a commentary on *Sentences* 3.

In the fourteenth *distinctio* of that book, Bonaventure poses the questions in the way laid out for him by the authorities. He traces this way in the *divisio textus* on the problem of Christ's omnipotence and omniscience.[15] He finally reaches the overarching issue of this *distinctio*, the question of the perfection of the knowledge that Christ's soul possessed eminently. He unfolds the issue in three articles of three questions each. Much rests on the distinction in the knowledge that Christ's soul had about the divine Word (*de Verbo*), in the divine Word (*in Verbo*), and from the divine Word (*a Verbo*). Bonaventure discusses all three kinds of knowledge in relation to the divine Word, which the prologue to the Gospel of John describes as the exemplary prototype of all that is (1:3). Thus there is self-knowledge in Christ (*de Verbo*) as well as his knowledge of things in their actual and exemplary being (*in Verbo*), and also the perfection of that knowledge in omnipotence and omniscience (*a Verbo*).[16]

If one can already discern here that Bonaventure is less interested in psychological than in epistemological issues, the structure of the seven disputed questions *de scientia Christi* makes it altogether clear that the question of Christ's knowledge cannot be treated even theologically outside an epistemological horizon. Indeed, one can get the well-founded impression that it is precisely the epistemological implications of the question about Christ's knowledge that enticed

---

15. *Sent.* 3.14.1–2 and *divisio textus* (CSB 3:283a–294b and 295a–b).
16. *Sent.* 3.14.1–3 (CSB 3:294a–325b). Compare Ernst, *Erkenntnis Christi*, pp. 144–160.

Bonaventure to treat the question so thoroughly. This is shown both by the polished and well-developed lines of argument in the epistemologically significant questions, especially the fourth, and by the systematic attack, which differs from that in the commentary on the *Sentences*. Consider the order of questions:[17]

1. Does the knowledge of Christ, so far as he is the divine Word, actually extend to the infinite?
2. Does God know things by means of their Ideas or by means of their essence (*"per essentiam"*)?
3. Does God know things by means of Ideas that really differ from one another?

---

4. Is what is known by us with certainty known in the eternal Ideas themselves?

---

5. Was the soul of Christ wise only through the uncreated wisdom, or wise through both created and uncreated wisdom?
6. Did the soul of Christ grasp uncreated wisdom itself?
7. Did the soul of Christ grasp everything that uncreated wisdom grasps?

I have indicated the obvious division into three parts. Christ's divine knowledge is the point of departure in the first three questions. What does this knowledge include? How does it proceed? In what manner does it concern itself with things, and how are they contained in it? We shall return at greater length to the metaphysical background of these questions.

There follows in the fourth question the hinge of the whole collection. In its very articulation, the epistemological interest becomes unmistakably clear. The same is true of the central point of that epistemology, the problem of the certainty of knowledge. Bonaventure sets up the twofold criterion of infallibility on the part of the subject and of the object.[18] How can one know with certainty what something is?

---

17. I have just published a new edition based on the Quaracchi-text with a German translation, corrective notes, and a detailed introduction (Hamburg: F. Meiner, 1992).

18. *Scientia Christi* 4 (5:23b): "cognitio certitudinalis esse non potest, nisi sit ex parte scibilis immutabilitas et infallibilitas ex parte scientis."

By knowing it completely, that is, under all the conditions that cover both object and subject. As Bonaventure says elsewhere, appealing to Aristotle, "For it is then that we know, namely, when we believe that we know the reason why a thing is, and when we know that it is impossible that the thing be otherwise."[19]

The next three questions pursue this issue. They discuss the possibility that Christ's soul grasped wisdom perfectly. But in the Augustinian tradition 'wisdom' is the usual name for the epitome of perfect knowledge, and thus for a knowledge that has a perfect grasp of the conditions under which it exists.[20]

Thus, Bonaventure can take Christ's soul as the model when he discusses comprehensively the conditions of knowledge and of science, bringing together into systematic form elements that appeared at various points when commenting on the *Sentences*. Among the more significant of these points, in addition to 3.14, are 1.35 (on God's knowledge in itself and in general) and 1.43 (on the divine power with regard to illimitability). Both distinctions from the first Book disclose an eminently epistemological interest.[21] The theological implications of the question of Christ's knowledge are always developed against a philosophical background.

Bonaventure himself hands us this key to interpreting the questions concerning Christ's knowledge in their epilogue. He points out retrospectively that from everything "which has been said and determined about the wisdom of Christ with respect to both the divine and the human nature, there can be seen the manner of knowing both in the knowledge of the Creator and in the knowledge of the creature, not only in the fatherland, but even in the pilgrim state"—not only in the state of perfection, but even under the present conditions of mortal

---

19. *Christus unus omnium est magister* 6 (5:568b–569a): "Tunc enim scimus, cum casum arbitramur cognoscere, propter quam res est, et scimus, quoniam impossibile est aliter se habere."

20. See Tilman Borsche, *Was etwas ist: Fragen nach der Wahrheit der Bedeutung bei Platon, Augustinus, Nikolaus von Kues und Nietzsche* (Munich: Fink, 1990), p. 113. But compare to this Aristotle's remarks on knowledge as *episteme* of causes (*aitias*) and principles (*archas*) in *Metaphysics* 1.2 (982a4–6). On the question of the certainty of knowledge, see further Speer, *Triplex veritas: Warheitsverständnis und philosophische Denkform Bonaventuras*, Franziskanische Forschungen 32 (Werl/Westf.: Dietrich Coelde, 1987), pp. 54–56.

21. *Sent.* 1.35 (CSB 1:599a–616b), 1.39 (1:684a–699b), and 1.43 (1:763–778).

existence.²² This statement is worth unfolding more closely, using as a guide the individual questions.

EXEMPLARISM

The issue of the first question arises on the doctrine, which goes back to Augustine, that God's knowledge is the original principle of everything that is. It includes everything actual and everything possible, since God alone, "by beholding himself as truth, knows the entire truth." God alone can, therefore, simply abstract from every cause, for he is ultimately the cause of all that is.²³ But things must not be considered only in themselves and their own causality, in their own species, but also in their exemplarity, in their essential relatedness to the ultimate creative cause.²⁴ This cause lies in God's knowledge, the creative principle of the existence and intelligibility of all creatures. God's knowledge in the "exemplary forms" (*formae exemplares*) and according to the "eternal ideas" (*sempiternae rationes*) describes at once the ontological distance and the ontological proximity of Creator and creation. It also suggests the gnoseological consequences.²⁵

That is the subject of the second question. The eternal ideas cannot be the true essences (*essentiae*) and quiddities (*quidditates*) of things, since the eternal ideas cannot be separated from the Creator. "Creator and creature necessarily have different essences."²⁶ The principal concepts through which Bonaventure attempts to describe adequately the relationship between Creator and creature are *similitudo, assimilatio, expressio, exemplaritas,* and *repraesentatio*. This group of terms poses many problems for translation, and any particular rendering will depend on the context. But Bonaventure maintains consistency of meaning throughout, as becomes clear in the following example.

In the conceptual field of exemplarism, there stands out one concept that is peculiarly suited to encompass all significant aspects—*similitudo*. *Similitudo* describes a relation, indeed an immediate and

---

22. *Scientia Christi* epilogue (CSB 5:42b).
23. *Scientia Christi* 1 (CSB 5:5a–b).
24. *Sent.* 1.39.1.1 ad 3 (CSB 1:686b).
25. *Scientia Christi* 2 (CSB 5:8b); compare Speer, *Triplex veritas*, p. 102.
26. *Scientia Christi* 2 (CSB 5:8b).

simple relation between two relata that are related to each other. "One is the image of the other" (*unum est similitudo alterius*), without its being the case that a third relatum forms the actual standard for this relation.[27] This relation of likeness can now be read in two directions by applying the ontological relationship of created beings to their creative origin. "[O]n the one hand as imitative likeness (*similitudo imitativa*), as the creature is the likeness of the Creator (*similitudo Creatoris*); on the other hand as likeness of the prototype (*similitudo exemplativa*), as the prototypical standard and likeness (*ratio exemplaris et similitudo*) of the creature is in the Creator."[28]

This ontological distinction has as its epistemological corollary the distinction between knowledge that is caused by things (*notitia causata a rebus*) and knowledge that is itself the cause of things (*notitia causans res*). The creature's capacity for knowledge is actualized by principles exhibited in reality; the relation between knower and known is therefore *similitudo imitativa*. The divine intellect, by contrast, holds the principles of knowledge in itself. It compares them with what exists because, as *similitudo exemplativa*, it is truth able to express itself, the expressive principle of the existence and intelligibility of everything that is ("sua summa veritate omnia aeternaliter exprimens").[29] The exemplarity of God, thus, guarantees the truth of what exists, because what exists is first exemplified in the *summa veritas*. If it is known that this highest truth exists, then the identity of the order of knowledge and the order of being is also known. Bonaventure attempts such a proof in several places by trying to show that the denial of a highest truth, in fact, presupposes the existence of such a performative contradiction, or that the notion of highest truth once understood includes the existence of that truth (the *ratio Anselmi*).[30] Here one sees the systematic place of the thesis that God is the first known.

At this point, however, there also appears the crucial difference between Bonaventure's understanding of exemplarism, as decisively

---

27. *Scientia Christi* 2 (CSB 5:9a).
28. *Scientia Christi* 2 (CSB 5:9a). Compare Speer, *Triplex veritas*, pp. 102f.
29. *Scientia Christi* 2 (CSB 5:9a).
30. *Scientia Christi* 4.12 (CSB 5:18b), 6.5 (5:34a), 4 ad 16 (5:25b), 4 ad 23–26 (5:26b–27b). See also *Coll. in Hexaëmeron* 4.1 (5:349a) and Speer, *Triplex veritas*, pp. 46–48.

shaped by Augustine, and Platonic or neo-Platonic exemplarisms. The divine prototype does not stand on the summit of a pyramid of being that results from a process of emanation. Rather, as the archetypal expression of the divine ground, as the everlasting Word, the divine prototype is equally immediate to each of its creaturely images. Conversely, things not only possess a meaning in themselves, they bring to mind as creaturely copies the divine original "penes modum repraesentandi."[31] The creature is God's trace (*vestigium*), image (*imago*), and likeness (*similitudo*). Thus, as Bonaventure says in the body of the fourth question, "every creature is a trace because it is from God, an image when it knows God, a likeness so far as God dwells in it. From this threefold gradation of relationship there follows a threefold gradation of divine cooperation."[32]

CERTAINTY OF KNOWLEDGE AND THE DOCTRINE OF IDEAS

The intelligibility of things corresponds to their ontological structure. For Bonaventure, as we have seen, all knowledge lies under the postulate of certainty, which is necessarily valid on account of the excellence of knowledge and the worthiness of the knower.[33] But how can this requirement be met? At the beginning of the fourth question, Bonaventure discusses two positions, both of which seem to him inadequate, indeed erroneous. It is not the case that certain knowledge can exist only in the intelligible world of the eternal prototypes, nor can one speak of a mere influence on knowing of the eternal standard (*ratio aeterna*) without its being the case that the eternal standard itself could be reached.[34]

Created truth (*veritas creata*) is not simply unchangeable, it is unchangeable only in consequence of a fundamental condition. So Bonaventure seeks a third way between the two rejected positions. "In order to achieve with necessity a knowledge that lays claim to

---

31. *Sent.* 1.3.1.1.2 ad 4 (CSB 1:73a); Speer, *Triplex veritas*, pp. 105f.
32. *Scientia Christi* 4 (CSB 5:24a).
33. *Scientia Christi* 4 (CSB 5:23b).
34. *Scientia Christi* 4 (CSB 5:23a).

certainty, there is sought an eternal standard to guide and drive—not by itself and in its perfect clarity, but together with a created standard, and in such a way that it is to some degree seen by us even in the state of imperfection."[35] This eternal standard is the *ars aeterna*, the eternal creative art, in which things are considered according to their conceptual and specific mode of existence.

This complex sphere of the *ars aeterna*, which mediates the orders of being and knowledge, usually appears philosophically in connection with the question of Bonaventure's theory of ideas. The idea has the function of a twofold principle of mediation: it betokens on the level of being the relation of creaturely reality to its creative source; and it shows on the level of knowledge the relationship between subject and object.[36]

Following Augustine, Bonaventure places the source of the ideas in God's knowledge. God, knowing himself, turns upon his own being and expresses himself in his eternal Word.[37] The ideas, thus, participate in God's essence and the mode of his own thinking. With reference to our knowledge, the idea is the "standard of knowledge" (*ratio cognoscendi*).[38] As *regula*, *norma*, or *lex*, the highest truth becomes in the idea the norm for the knowing intellect in regard both to immutability and causation; it is the eternal standard that regulates and sets in motion ("ratio aeterna ut regulans et ratio motiva").[39] But while the idea as standard of the divine knowledge is an expression of God's creative knowledge (*similitudo expressiva*), in relation to the human intellect it betokens a relationship of similarity as guarantor of knowledge (*similitudo impressa*). What is known is the truth itself, even if mediated by the idea. The creative act of the rational creature is to follow this standard of knowledge, without in any way constituting it.[40]

---

35. *Scientia Christi* 4 (CSB 5:23b).
36. See *Sent.* 1.35.1.3 (CSB 1:608a).
37. *Scientia Christi* 3 (CSB 5:13b–14a), 4.23–27 (5:19b–20a, "rationes Augustini"). Compare the entry "Idee" in *Historisches Wörterbuch der Philosophie* 4:63–65 and 4:87f. The classical Augustinian source is *De diversis quaestionibus* 83 46.1–2 (CSEL 44A:70.1–73.73).
38. Compare *Sent.* 1.35.1.1 (CSB 1:601a).
39. *Scientia Christi* 4 (CSB 5:23b).
40. *Sent.* 1.35.1.1 (CSB 1:601b).

For the doctrine of ideas thus conceived, there arises now, as a special problem, the multiplicity of ideas. How can this multiplicity, which serves as pattern for classes and individuals alike, be conceived in relation to God's unity? On the one hand, it cannot be that "to produce a human being is to produce an ass." On the other hand, the multiplicity of appearances cannot import any real multiplicity into God's being.[41] Bonaventure tries to solve this problem by referring to two different moments in the idea. As an expression of the divine creative power, the idea stands more to God's side; as constitutive element of our knowledge, it is more strongly present in the being known now. But since God, in reality, does not turn towards anything other than himself, the ideal standards in God cannot be thought of as a real multiplicity (*secundum rem*), but only as a conceptual one (*secundum rationem*). "[T]he concept arises not only from the side of the knower but also from the side of the object known."[42] That is how the ideas, so far as they are standards of knowledge (*secundum rationem intelligendi*), can denote what is really distinct. The unity-in-reality is the expression of the unity of the one divine truth in itself and with itself. It can express and represent the entire multiplicity of actual and possible reality. The plurality for knowledge, on the other hand, is an expression of the kind and manner of our intellectual participation in the one divine truth. "If the many ideas therefore also possess a unity in fact (*re*), so that they can be called the one truth and the one divine Word, they can nevertheless possess no unity according to their meaning (*ratione*) so that one could speak of several ideas or standards (*ideae vel rationes*) as a single idea or standard."[43] For the human intellect, then, the multiplicity and diversity of ideas represents itself as a reality. It denotes *ad modum rei* the concrete way-of-being of things.[44]

The difficult problem of the unity and plurality of ideas is reflected in Bonaventure's terminology, which is by no means completely consistent. Whereas *idea*, *ratio*, and *similitudo* are used in both singular and plural, *exemplar*, *ars*, and *verbum* are spoken of only in the singular. *Ratio* and *idea* apply primarily to things in their distinctness, while

41. *Scientia Christi* 3 (CSB 5:14a).
42. *Scientia Christi* 3 (CSB 5:14a).
43. *Scientia Christi* 3 ad 19 (CSB 5:16b).
44. *Scientia Christi* 3 ad 2 (CSB 5:14b).

the remaining concepts relate the multiplicity of things to their first principle as source and goal.[45]

It is now clear why Bonaventure must reject the extreme positions cited at the beginning. He thinks that they lead to skeptical aporia, to the conclusion "that one can know absolutely nothing."[46] Beyond the a priori moment, an a posteriori or empirical moment is indispensable for the achievement of knowledge, and conversely. In order to know, the intellect must not only turn itself toward the *rationes aeternae*, but also proceed from the essences abstracted from experience.[47] The ideas are not the *obiectum quod* of human knowledge, but only the *obiectum quo*, through whose influence we attain certainty. Consequently, the ideas can only be grasped reflexively by the human intellect. As formal principles of knowing, they first guarantee certainty on the part of both the objects and subjects of knowledge. But the specifying properties and material principles arise out of experience.[48] One sees here the influence of the Aristotelian theory of knowledge. Bonaventure discusses it thoroughly in the *opposita* of the fourth question and rehearses it again in the following answer.[49] He arrives thus at a distinctive solution that thoroughly modifies the Augustinian conception.

CERTAINTY AND ILLUMINATION

The so-called "theory of illumination" both derives from Augustine and is much modified from Augustine. This doctrine allows us to summarize, under the guidance of the fourth question, the answers that were developed by using exemplarism and the theory of ideas, as it allows us to bring them to bear on the following questions. For Bonaventure, too, light is a "metaphysical conjecture" for truth as well as a "model" for the relation between unity and plurality, between

---

45. See on this point *Sent.* 1.35.1.3 ad 2 (CSB 1:608b) and Speer, *Triplex veritas*, pp. 99f.
46. *Scientia Christi* 4 (CSB 5:23a).
47. *Scientia Christi* 4 (CSB 5:24b).
48. *Scientia Christi* 4 (CSB 5:23b–24a); Speer, *Triplex veritas*, p. 101.
49. See especially *Scientia Christi* 4 ob. 7–16 (CSB 5:21b–22a) and the corresponding replies, ad 7–16 (5:25a–b).

the absolute and the conditioned, between source and descendant.[50] In order to illustrate this, he takes over from Augustine the example of the godless person who can think a concept like eternity and judge rightly regarding rules of practical living because in doing so "he turns himself to that light by which he is always touched, even when he turned himself away from it."[51]

Behind this, the problematic of certainty appears once more, for Bonaventure sees, with Augustine, the cause of the pagan's knowledge in rules "that are written down in the book of that light which is called Truth."[52] These rules are obviously in force quite independently of the mistakes of the knower and the always deficient objects known. The metaphor of "illumination" emphasizes the non-empirical origin of the judgments, which do not have their origin in experience and are not the outcome of a process of abstraction. Although Bonaventure requires, for full knowledge, a tracing back "to an altogether unchangeable and fixed truth as well as to an altogether infallible light," the influence of the light cannot be seen only as general, as if both knowledge and wealth were indebted to that influence in the same manner; nor can it be seen only as special, as if all knowledge were infused and no knowledge were acquired or innate.[53] Thus, the epistemological problematic in the theory of illumination becomes noticeably stronger when focused on the individual subject. How are we to conceive concretely of the cooperation of the infallible light of truth, especially since Bonaventure does not fundamentally reject the Aristotelian arguments, but seeks instead to integrate them into his own theory of knowledge?[54] The distinction between a created standard (*ratio creata*) and an eternal standard (*ratio aeterna*), between the light of the creature (*lux creaturae*) and the infallible light (*lux infallibilis*), between a lower reason (*ratio inferior*) and a higher reason

---

50. Hans Blumenberg, "Licht als Metapher der Wahrheit," *Studium Generale* 10 (1957): 432; Klaus Hedwig, *Sphaera lucis: Studien zur Intelligibilität des Seienden im Kontext der mittelalterlichen Lichtspekulation*, BGPTM NS 18 (Munster: Aschendorff, 1980), pp. 161–165.

51. *Scientia Christi* 4 (CSB 5:23b); Augustine *De Trinitate* 14.15.21 (CCSL 50A: 450.35–39).

52. Augustine *De Trinitate* 14.15.21 (CCSL 50A:451.49–50).

53. *Scientia Christi* 4 (CSB 5:23b).

54. See *Scientia Christi* 4 ob. 7–9 and 14 (CSB 5:21b, 22a), together with ad 7–9 and 14 (5:25a, b).

(*ratio superior*), will open a way that makes possible a nuanced reply to this question.

We see it in the following three questions, which treat the human knowledge of Christ. We already have a preparatory hint in Bonaventure's reply to the second *oppositum*. There, in connection with a quotation from Augustine, Bonaventure proposes the claim that if the light of the eternal truth were the standard of knowledge for all true things, no soul would know anything true unless it were pure and holy. Since the consequent is not the case, the antecedent is also denied.[55] Bonaventure solves this objection by distinguishing between knowledge and wisdom. To be sure, a knower knows by means of the eternal ideas, but not with complete firmness. Only the wise man can do that, since he knows them in peace; the knowledge of the *rationes aeternae* cannot be taken away from him again.[56]

FROM KNOWLEDGE TO WISDOM

What is meant by the distinction between knowledge and wisdom? First, we must recall what we said in the overview of the questions with reference to wisdom as the epitome of perfect knowledge. Consider a figure of speech that Bonaventure uses almost universally in this connection: *in via in patria*.[57] It would be a mistake to see in this figure of speech only a Christian-soteriological motif. It serves primarily to get a better grasp on the dilemma in the analysis of human knowledge that is also expressed as a distinction between wisdom and knowledge.

In the present state of imperfection we sometimes arrive, in our search for a foundation guaranteeing certainty to our knowledge, at such principles in which the *ratio aeterna* is recognized only in its generality, as an a priori ground of epistemic certainty, but not in itself.[58] The discursive intellect of the knower thus attains only principles that regulate knowledge, that guarantee no lasting certainty, because they

---

55. *Scientia Christi* 4 ob. 2 (CSB 5:21a), together with Augustine *De Trinitate* 1.2.4 (CCSL 50:31.9–11).
56. *Scientia Christi* 4 ad 2 (CSB 5:24b).
57. *Scientia Christi* 4 (CSB 5:24a–b), 6 (5:35a–b), 7 (5:40a), epilogue (5:42b).
58. *Scientia Christi* 4 ad 16 (CSB 5:25b).

cannot trace back the knowledge to the ultimate principle. Only in that *reductio* would our struggle for certain knowledge come to rest and to fulfillment.[59] Such a knowledge, however, exceeds the domain of discursive reason and reaches an immediate insight into that ultimate principle, which Bonaventure calls interchangeably "eternal standard" (*ratio aeterna*), "highest truth" (*summa veritas*), "infallible light" (*lux infallibilis*), "supreme creative art" (*superna ars*), and "God." But this perfect knowledge, which both exceeds the natural capacity of the rational soul and perfects its immanent struggle, can no longer be reckoned a part of knowledge in the strict sense. Bonaventure, therefore, speaks of an *excessus*, an "overstepping" or "exceeding" of knowledge into wisdom. It happens only to a few, to the perfected intellects, "which is why only a few are wise and many can know."[60]

Following the twelfth-century tradition of so-called speculative mysticism, which is associated with names like Hugh and Richard of St. Victor,[61] Bonaventure displays in the body of the seventh question six steps of a path from mere belief to perfect comprehension. Perfect comprehension is, of course, reserved for the eternal Trinity. The rational soul reaches the outer limit in insight on the level of overstepping (*excedere*): it sees God and so arrives at an immediate unitary view of the supreme principle and the highest truth itself, without becoming one with that truth. This is true not only of the case *in statu viae* where we are moved, enraptured, and lifted up—which signifies each time a special overstepping of the present state—but also of the state of perfection *in patria*.[62]

PERFECT KNOWLEDGE AND CREATED WISDOM

In the last three questions, Bonaventure opens a second perspective on the understanding of wisdom. The point of departure

---

59. *Scientia Christi* 4 ad 19 (CSB 5:26a).
60. *Scientia Christi* 4 ad 19 (5:26a), 6 (CSB 5:35a). Compare *Itinerarium mentis in Deum* 1.6 (CSB 5:297b), *Collationes in Hexaëmeron* 19.3 (CSB 5:420b).
61. See "Kontemplation," LM 5:1414–1416, and "Extase," DS 14:2113–2120.
62. *Scientia Christi* 4 (CSB 5:24b), 6 (5:35a–b). See also *Itinerarium* 1.2–6 (CSB 5:297a–b), 7.1 (5:312a); Speer, *Triplex veritas*, pp. 75–79 and 118–120. Compare "Extase," DS 4:2120–2125.

for this is an obviously theological one. It begins with Christ's human knowledge, not in its full phenomenological breadth, but rather as it extends to the uncreated wisdom and to everything that Christ can see in that uncreated wisdom. Bonaventure distinguishes created wisdom from this. The distinction follows from the manner of the influence and presence of the supreme light of truth in knowledge that lays claim to certainty. A merely general influence, without the immediate presence of that light, is as obviously insufficient as its mere presence without the possibility of an immediate influence.[63] This addresses, once again, the problem of the participation of the created souls in the *ratio aeterna* and their cooperation in the coming-to-be of certain knowledge. Bonaventure's answer follows from the line of thinking up to this point, but it expands during the discussion of the extent of human knowledge in the last three questions.

If we know with certainty only when we comprehend all of the conditions of knowledge and possess wisdom, then it cannot be satisfactory to suppose such knowledge exclusively in the state of perfection, for then this insight would run the risk of having the character merely of a provisional, relative truth. Human knowledge, striving after certainty, must also have the ability to extend to that uncreated wisdom, which itself can be reached only by a deiform and ecstatic intellect. The manner in which the created intellect can participate in the uncreated wisdom *in statu viae*, and at the same time in the "forming, enabling, and uplifting principle," is created wisdom.[64] According to Bonaventure, the soul of Christ was also, so far as he was a human being, bound to this *sapientia creata* as a necessary condition of his having wisdom. But this knowledge was at the same time limited, since Christ's soul did not have actual knowledge of everything that it knew as the divine Word. In this way, Bonaventure manages to conform to the teaching of the Council of Chalcedon and to the requirements of the communication of idioms.[65]

This brings us back to the first question: Is the knowledge of Christ, so far as he is the divine Word, really infinite? The background of this question is the doctrine, going back to Augustine, of the origin of being in God's knowledge, in his eternal, uncreated wisdom. In the

63. *Scientia Christi* 5 (CSB 5:29b).
64. *Scientia Christi* 5 (CSB 5:30a), 6 (5:34b).
65. *Scientia Christi* 6 (CSB 5:35a), 7 ad 1–3 (5:40b). Compare Ernst, *Erkenntnis Christi*, pp. 163–165.

sixth question too, Bonaventure seizes on the infinite, specifically of infinite truth and goodness which alone can fulfill the understanding and appetite of the rational soul and bring it to rest when the soul is lifted up above its own capacity for understanding.[66]

Driven by the goal of knowing the totality of being and of its ultimate ground, the intellectual capacity experiences its limits with all clarity. But the natural limit of creaturely knowledge lies not so much in a limitation on the domain of objects, but rather in the imperfection of that capacity itself, in its limitation to knowing *secundum esse*, to the knowledge of actual being. By contrast, perfect insight into every structure and condition that determines the universe, knowledge "in accordance with that divine art, through which all things come to be," is denied to the created soul.[67] The reason for this lies in the very nature of knowledge *secundum esse*, which is determined by five criteria: dominance of the subject of knowledge in the act of knowing, fulfillment of only one domain of the striving after knowledge, discursiveness, the analytic quality of the judgments, and limitation to a finite horizon. In contrast, the exceeding knowledge *secundum artem* is likewise distinguished by five analogously formulated criteria: dominance of the object of knowledge as the encompassing goal of all knowledge, perfect fulfillment of the entire appetite for knowledge, the abolition of the discursive limitation as well as of the limitation to analytic and synthetic judgments, and finally the directedness to an infinite horizon.[68]

It should be pointed out that Bonaventure here defines the meaning of comprehending knowledge (*cognitio comprehensiva*) and exceeding knowledge (*cognitio excessiva*) in immediate dependence on pseudo-Dionysius and, so, in contrast to the scheme of levels in the sixth question, which relies on Augustinian speculative mysticisms.[69] With pseudo-Dionysius, Bonaventure describes that exceeding not as *transcensus* but as *excessus*. For the subject of knowledge does not outstrip the object of knowledge; rather, the one who has "exceeding" knowledge is brought to the object of knowledge "by going beyond

---

66. *Scientia Christi* 6 (CSB 5:35a).
67. *Scientia Christi* 7 ad 4 (CSB 5:40b–41a).
68. *Scientia Christi* 7 (CSB 5:40a–b); Speer, *Triplex veritas*, pp. 80f.
69. Compare *Scientia Christi* 6 (CSB 5:35a) and the preceding section. See further "Kontemplation," LM 5:1414–1416, and "Extase," DS 4:2125–2126.

himself in a way that exceeds everything, whereby he lifts himself above himself."[70]

It would be a mistake to see in this determination of the extent of knowledge a boundless epistemological optimism. On the contrary, one sees a string of what are unmistakably epistemological critiques. They hold especially for the knowledge that is founded on reason alone, but also for the possibility of a perfect comprehension of the highest truth on the basis of an acquired and, therefore, created wisdom. Even a supernatural illumination that raised the soul to know things in the eternal divine art would allow it to know the contingent with certainty, but would not effect an actual knowledge of the infinite. Thus, it would not make possible a surpassing of the soul's own finitude.[71]

This is the only explanation of the conclusion of the collection of questions, which had its systematic point of departure in the question of the knowledge of the infinite. In the epilogue, Bonaventure summarizes the line-of-thought of the seven questions in order to draw out what might seem at first a surprising conclusion. The insight into the process of knowledge that he has won, which culminates in surpassing, in exceeding (*excessus*), as the utmost and most excellent manner of knowing, leads Bonaventure to the conclusion that negative propositions are more suitable than affirmative, exceeding predications (*superpositiones*) than positive predications (*positivae praedicationes*), in grasping this true wisdom. Quite in the spirit of Dionysian negative theology and with an appeal to the writings of the alleged disciple of the Apostle Paul, Bonaventure points out that "an inner silence can lead to that experience more than an external word."[72]

THE PERSPECTIVE OF METAPHYSICS

Reflection on the conditions of epistemological certainty and on the extent of our knowledge remain, for Bonaventure, determining motifs even in his later works. This is true, for example, in a

---

70. *Scientia Christi* 7 (CSB 5:40a).
71. *Scientia Christi* 7 ad 11 (CSB 5:41b).
72. *Scientia Christi* epilogue (CSB 5:43b).

scientific-theoretical perspective of *De reductione artium ad theologiam*, which also derives from Bonaventure's lecturing activity in 1255–1257. It holds as well for the *Itinerarium mentis in Deum*, which appeared around the end of 1259. The *Itinerarium* further develops the central thoughts of his epistemology and metaphysics very much in the tradition of speculative mysticism.[73]

When these writings appeared, Bonaventure had already left his teaching position in Paris, having been elected Minister-General of the Friars Minor on February 2, 1257. He faced the difficult task of consolidating an order that, given the numbers of its members, still had only a negligible organization. But Bonaventure stopped in Paris on several later occasions. The three sermon series in particular, which he gave in the Franciscan convent there in 1267 (*De decem praeceptis*), 1268 (*De donis Spiritus Sancti*), and 1273 (*Collationes in Hexaëmeron*), confirm his unbroken interest in the intellectual life at Paris, as they show his attempt to tie the Franciscan movement more strongly to the intellectual developments of its time.[74] This important feature of his work often falls completely into oblivion. It is displaced by a spiritual interpretation in the support of a "Franciscan option" or a "théologie du pauvre."[75] For our point of view, it is telling that Bonaventure—like Thomas Aquinas who also returned to Paris, presumably in 1269, on commission by the general chapter of his order—intervenes anew in current doctrinal controversies in what remains the most significant university, controversies again excited by Aristotelianism.[76] The problems, of course, had changed. At the beginning of his studies, the reception of the *libri naturales* of Aristotle, as well as questions about the speculative penetration of the contents of faith, had stood in the center of the dispute. In the meantime,

---

73. See Bougerol, *Introduction*, pp. 7, 215–220; Speer, "Wissenschaft und Erkenntnis," pp. 180–184; and Speer, "*Metaphysica reducens*: Metaphyik als erste Wissenschaft im Verständnis Bonaventuras," RTAM 57 (1990): 161–165.

74. Bougerol, *Introduction*, pp. 227–241.

75. Speer, "*Metaphysica reducens*," pp. 143–145, in contrast with Werner Dettloff, "Die franziskanische Vorentscheidung im theologischen Denken des heiligen Bonaventura," *Münchener Theologische Zeitschrift* 13 (1962): 107–115, and Bougerol, *Introduction*, pp. 12–30 and 283–288.

76. Van Steenberghen, *La philosophie au XIIIe siècle*, pp. 427–430, following the general overview on pp. 411–426.

the works of Aristotle had at last found a secure place in university instruction and had been commented upon thoroughly in all their extent, especially by Albert the Great.

Now the question was how philosophical and theological truth are related to each other. More precisely, it was how the truth of the sciences could stand to the truth of a theology that was, by this time, equally regarded as science. This conflict caught fire particularly on the questions of the individuality of the intellectual soul and the eternity of the world. The questions were answered by Parisian masters like Siger of Brabant and Boethius of Dacia, who appeal to Averroës in support of a radical Aristotelianism. They call into question the synthesis achieved in different ways by Thomas and Bonaventure.[77] With them, metaphysics begins to develop as a science of first principles founded in reason alone: it enters into competition with theology, which takes its first principles from revelation. Consequently, metaphysics stood in need of a justification of its knowledge-of-principles with regard to revelation, and, conversely, the theology of revelation-principles had to be shown to be possible and necessary with regard to the *philosophi*.[78]

Against the background of this controversy, Bonaventure by no means adopts an anti-philosophical attitude, as he is sometimes reproached for doing. The conviction of the necessity of an explanation that rests on reason, which stamps the collection of questions dating from his earlier teaching activities, also determines his last sermon series on the Hexaemeron. With it, Bonaventure joins an old tradition of commentary. Reacting against the model of Aristotelian metaphysics, he formulates his criteria for a metaphysics that can make good on the claim of metaphysics to be a science that proceeds from the knowledge of principles and the ultimate foundation. Metaphysics

---

77. Van Steenberghen speaks both of "Aristotélisme hétérodoxe" and of "Averroisme" in *La philosophie au XIIIe siècle*, pp. 357–412. On the doctrinal controversy, see pp. 413–471.

78. Ludger Honnefelder, "Der zweite Anfang der Metaphysik: Ansätze und Folgen der Wiederbegründung der Metaphysik im 13./14. Jahrhundert," in *Philosophie im Mittelalter: Entwicklungslinien und Paradigmen*, ed. J. P. Beckmann et al. (Hamburg, 1987), pp. 165–168; Albert Zimmermann, *Ontologie oder Metaphysik? Die Diskussion über den Gegenstand der Metaphysik im 13. und 14. Jahrhundert*, STGM 8 (Leiden and Cologne: Brill, 1965), p. 90.

must bear in mind the emanation, exemplarity, and consummation of reality, and bear them in mind according to the degree of illumination and in the manner of a *reductio* to knowledge of principles.[79]

Nevertheless, Bonaventure keeps in view the limits on the scope and certainty of rational knowledge. To be sure, metaphysics is for him the science of being and its principles. Nonetheless, Bonaventure disputes a broader claim of metaphysics on the way toward a critique of metaphysics that he also executes as a critique of reason.[80] Every science based on reason is under the verdict of fallibilism. It is also true of metaphysics, which is distinguished from an ultimate foundation based on revelation.

Although Bonaventure, once again, underscores the finitude of human knowledge, he does not mean to deny the object-related use of reason where this is required. In Bonaventure's eyes, there opens up a wide field of positive autonomy of scientific rationality, which he undoubtedly acknowledges and by which he—true child of his time—feels challenged. Although he clings more tenaciously than many of his contemporaries to the Augustinian ideal of a comprehensive Christian wisdom, and, thus, to the fundamental desire for a single knowledge, he cannot ignore from the outset the confrontation with the claim of the sciences to explain consistently the connections of reality.[81]

CONCLUSION

I should like to close with two observations that relate to the twofold aspect of this essay expressed at the beginning: to treat one of the great themes of philosophy by looking at a medieval author whose contribution to the philosophical discussion of the time is, in general, judged with reserve.

The first observation is intended to hold for the historical evaluation. We were able to see the background against which Bonaventure

---

79. *Coll. in Hexaëmeron* 1.17 (CSB 5:332b).
80. Compare *Coll. in Hexaëmeron* 12.12 (CSB 5:386a).
81. Speer, "Metaphysica reducens," pp. 172–182; Van Steenberghen, *La philosophie au XIIIe siècle*, pp. 197–200.

develops his epistemological inquiries, the background of contemporary controversies as well as of the tradition preceding Bonaventure. Both backgrounds must be considered in discerning what determines Bonaventure's question and his answer. In this sense, the historical procedure is the necessary condition for philosophical understanding; indeed, of any understanding whatever. The same is true of Bonaventure himself, for the specific appropriation of traditions, the engagement with their pre-understanding, is the condition for anything whatever being understood, for there being any questions. Etienne Gilson speaks of an "Aristotelianizing Augustinianism," and Fernand van Steenberghen, on the contrary, of an "eclectic and neo-Platonizing Aristotelianism."[82] But any such schematizings of Bonaventure betray his appropriation of traditions, which proves to be much more nuanced and topical. His appropriation depends on the question at hand, for which a given tradition may or may not offer a model answer.

Among these traditions, the triplet of Augustine, pseudo-Dionysius, and Aristotle stands out. We can show that Bonaventure is most conversant with the Aristotelian writings, not only by the multitude of explicit and implicit references, but also, for example, by his interest in the new and more exact translations of Aristotle, such as the *nova translatio* of the *Nichomachean Ethics* by Robert Grosseteste.[83] Reference has already been made to Bonaventure's thorough engagement with Aristotelian positions, especially in the fourth question. With Augustine and the pseudo-Dionysian corpus, Bonaventure appeals to the two most influential traditions of Christian reception and transformation of Platonic and neo-Platonic intellectual riches. Their diverse character is reflected clearly in the actual systematic context in which Bonaventure makes use of their arguments. Thus, we find in connection with the question of the unity and the outer limit of knowledge—especially in the last three questions, but also in the third question—multiplied references to the Dionysian concept of negative theology. Yet Bonaventure develops his epistemological position and exemplarist ontology on the foundation of Augustine's

---

82. Gilson, *La philosophie de saint Bonaventure*, pp. 390–395; Van Steenberghen, *La philosophie au XIIIe siècle*, pp. 15–18 and 246–267.
83. Compare *Scientia Christi* 4 arg. 16 (5:18b). On the Aristotelian sources, see the survey by Bougerol, "Saint Bonaventure et Aristote," AHDLMA 40 (1973): 135–222.

affirmation of conceivability, modified by the aforementioned influence of Aristotle.

Or does Bonaventure's epistemological problematic result entirely from the answers that he finds ready-made in the traditions? It is not only the working out of particular individual problems in particular tradition-contexts that suggests such a consideration. The question extends further. In the example of the problem of certainty, it becomes clear that Bonaventure's twofold requirement for certainty on the side of both the object and the subject of knowledge, his connecting of a priori and a posteriori elements in the analysis of knowledge, arises out of an intense confrontation with Augustinian and Aristotelian elements. Here lies Bonaventure's unique contribution.

That brings me to my second observation, which has to do with the systematic meaning that I have claimed for Bonaventure's answer. Is there a conceivable aspect under which Bonaventure's reflections can be answers to today's questions? Such a possibility is, as a rule, widely excluded especially for medieval authors, often by means of an appeal to the so-called transcendental turn in philosophy, behind which no road leads back. But can the reproach that has been made against "pre-critical" metaphysics, that it mistakenly seeks to explain the world that exists only in appearance as "real," give itself any other foundation than to be again merely an appearance? If not, then it stands under the same proviso, that it is merely *one* interpretation of reality that can establish itself in the face of other interpretations only by being a plausible answer to recent questions. More precisely, the focus of understanding is that *my* questions find an answer.[84]

This line of argument of recent philosophizing is found, in another form, within Bonaventure. More strongly than many of his contemporaries he reflects on the limits of philosophical knowledge. He sees the finitude of pure reason. In this sense, all rational knowledge is provisional. It stands, to put it theologically, under an eschatalogical reservation.[85] For Bonaventure, this is true quite literally. Here I have come to the decisive point. The fact that our understanding is only an interpretation of reality is represented by Bonaventure in the manner

---

84. Compare Josef Simon, *Philosophie des Zeichens* (Berlin and New York: W. de Gruyter, 1989), pp. 13 and 170–174.

85. Compare *Collationes de septem donis Spiritus sancti*, especially 4 (CSB 5:473–479) and 8 (5:493–498). On this point, see also Speer, *Triplex veritas*, pp. 123–126.

of a theological critique of philosophy.[86] A renewed parallel appears: the eschatological perfection of the striving after knowledge is not thought of in the sense of scientific generality, as if it were possible to win an "objective" standpoint outside history. It is conceived as the individual coming-to-an-end of questioning and striving. But at that point all discourse is over. We understand without questioning.[87]

Universität zu Köln

---

86. Compare *Coll. in Hexaëmeron* 4.1 (CSB 5:349a), 5.2 (5:357b). On the "tenth Science," which philosophy sought in vain, see Speer, "*Metaphysica reducens*," p. 179.

87. Compare *Scientia Christi* epilogue (CSB 5:43b); *Itinerarium* 1.2–6 (5:297a–b), 7.1 (5:312a–b). See also Simon, *Philosophie des Zeichens*, pp. 39f and 152f.

Good and the Object of Natural Inclinations in St. Thomas Aquinas[1]

JOHN I. JENKINS

What is the relationship between what we, in our most reflective and circumspect moments, desire or approve of and what is our good? In this essay I will explore the views of St. Thomas Aquinas on this issue. I will develop my interpretation of Aquinas dialectically by considering and criticizing aspects of the influential interpretations of Germain Grisez[2] and John Finnis,[3] on one hand, and Ralph McInerny,[4] on the other.[5] These interpretations, I will

---

1. Anthony Kenny, Brian Davies, O.P., Robert George, Ralph McInerny, and David Burrell, C.S.C., were all most generous in reading and commenting upon various versions of this paper, and I am most grateful for their help. Of course, the opinions expressed herein are to be ascribed to me alone. This paper was substantially completed in January, 1991 and I have been unable to take notice of studies published since then.

2. Germain Grisez, "The First Principle of Practical Reason: A Commentary on the *Summa theologiae* 1–2, Question 94, Article 2," *Natural Law Forum* 10 (1965): 168–201.

3. John Finnis, *Natural Law and Natural Rights* (Oxford: Oxford University Press, 1980).

4. McInerny's criticisms of Grisez and Finnis are found in *Ethica Thomistica* (Washington, D.C.: Catholic University of America Press, 1982). Grisez and Finnis responded to McInerny in "The Basic Principles of Natural Law: A Reply to Ralph McInerny," *American Journal of Jurisprudence* 26 (1981): 21–31.

5. Grisez and Finnis's writing has set off a long and vigorous debate. Other recent contributions include the following. Robert George gives an admirably clear

argue, founder because of improper analyses and common misunderstandings of key terms in Aquinas. Once we have a proper grasp of Aquinas's position, we can better appreciate it as the interesting and subtle ethical theory that it is.

Although the Grisez-Finnis interpretation differs from McInerny's on several points, two issues are central. Both of these issues have to do with the putative distinction between facts about our natural inclinations and our good, and one difficulty in adjudicating this debate is that the disputants fail to distinguish clearly between these distinct issues. The first concerns the question of whether Thomas thought that a subject could infer judgments about what is normatively good for herself and about what she ought (normatively) to do from some set of descriptive or factual judgments about her nature, capacities, and inclinations. We can call this the epistemological question or issue: it concerns whether Thomas thought that intellectual assent to certain propositions of one sort tends to make epistemically rational assent to certain propositions of another sort. This epistemological question is distinguishable from, though not entirely independent of, what we can call the conceptual question or issue about the nature of the normatively good for Thomas. This concerns whether Thomas thought that being the object of human inclinations is (at least partly) constitutive of the concept of good, or (to put it in more Thomistic language) of the *ratio boni*. We will discuss these questions consecutively. I will argue that though McInerny is nearer the truth on the first question, Grisez and Finnis are nearer the truth on the second.

---

summary and a brief defense of the Grisez-Finnis interpretation in "Recent Criticism of Natural Law Theory" (Book Review), *University of Chicago Law Review* 55 (1988): 1378–85. Douglas Flippen challenged the Grisez-Finnis view in "Natural Law and Natural Inclinations," *New Scholasticism* 60 (1986): 284–316, and Grisez responded with a defense of his interpretation in "Natural Law and Natural Inclinations: Some Comments and Clarifications," *New Scholasticism* 61 (1987): 307–320. Janice Schultz took up the issues in several articles including: "Is-Ought: Prescribing and a Present Controversy," *Thomist* 49 (1985): 1–23; "'Ought'-Judgments: A Descriptivist Analysis from a Thomistic Perspective," *New Scholasticism* 61 (1987): 400–426; "Thomistic Metaethics and a Present Controversy," *Thomist* 52 (1988): 40–62; and "St. Thomas Aquinas on Necessary Moral Principles," *New Scholasticism* 62 (1988): 150–178. Peter Simpson has also contributed in "St. Thomas on the Naturalistic Fallacy," *Thomist* 51 (1987): 51–69; and in "Practical Knowing: Some Comments on Finnis and Aquinas," *Modern Schoolman* 67 (1990): 111–122.

THE EPISTEMOLOGICAL QUESTION

The principles of practical reason, which Aquinas also calls the precepts of natural law, specify goods to be pursued by actions. These Grisez and Finnis call the basic goods. Did Aquinas think that certain principles of practical reason could be inferred from certain factual judgments about human nature and natural inclinations? Grisez and Finnis are brisk and emphatic in their insistence that Aquinas did not think such an inference could be made.[6] Is this correct?

Let us consider first *Summa theologiae* 1–2.94.2. This passage is the only one which Grisez treats extensively, and from which he develops his interpretation. Since it is, as it were, Grisez's chosen field of battle, we should expect to find strong support for his view here. But I believe McInerny provides a more natural reading of the article.

In the corpus of this article, after saying that practical reason is analogous to theoretical reason, and that the first principle of theoretical reason, the principle of non-contradiction, is based on its first *ratio*, the *ratio* of being, Thomas writes:

> And thus the first principle in practical reasoning is the one based upon the *ratio* of the good, which is: good is 'that to which all things are naturally inclined'. Therefore this is the first precept of the law, that good is to be done and pursued, and evil is to be avoided.[7]

In this passage, then, Thomas tells us that the formula which expresses a subject's intellectual grasp of the *ratio* of good is 'that to which all things are naturally inclined'. Since this seems to suggest that the understanding of the good is as the object of natural inclination, it appears that precepts stating basic goods for humans can be inferred from judgments about our natural inclinations. Thus this passage appears, at least *prima facie*, to undermine Grisez's interpretation.

Grisez, of course, offers an alternative reading of this passage. He distinguishes two senses of 'good'. There is, he concedes, a descriptive sense of 'good' according to which the good is simply the end of some

---

6. Grisez, "First Principle," p. 195; Finnis, *Natural Law and Natural Rights*, p. 33.
7. Thomas Aquinas *Summa theologiae* 1.94.2. As with all the citations from Aquinas in this paper, the translation is mine. The edition of the *Summa* used is the collation of the Piana and Leonine editions (Ottawa: Commissio Piana, 1953–). In this passage, the quotation marks and italics are mine.

natural tendency. As he writes, "for each active principle the end on account of which it acts is a good for it. . . ."[8] Hence, we can say that blooming in spring is good for roses, and they ought to do so.[9] But, he insists, "to get moral principles from metaphysics, it is not from the 'is' of nature to the 'ought' of nature that one must go." [10] The good and ought relevant to practical reason and natural law are the normative senses; in this sense 'good' is not meant as the object of a natural tendency. Grisez, then, sharply distinguishes the normatively good from the descriptively good.

About the passage in question, Grisez writes:

> This formula [i.e., 'bonum est quod omnia appetunt'] is a classic expression of what the word 'good' means. Of course, we often mean more than this by 'good', but any other meaning at least includes this notion.[11]

It is not clear, however, just what Grisez thinks the grasp of the *ratio* of good is. He may be suggesting that the sense of 'good' under discussion in *Summa theologiae* 1–2.94.2 is some generic notion which includes both the descriptive and normative notions as species. Alternatively, Grisez might be suggesting that the notion is initially simply the vague notion of someone who has as yet failed to distinguish the descriptive and normative notions. If he is suggesting the former, he must give us some reason to believe that Aquinas recognizes such a generic notion—but he does not do this. If he is suggesting the latter, he must explain how a correct apprehension of the principles of practical reason can be based upon a vague understanding of the intelligibility of the good—but neither does he do this.

It is difficult to extract from Grisez any clear interpretation of this passage in *Summa theologiae* 1–2.94.2 about the *ratio* of good. His failure to produce a clear interpretation of this passage is not, I believe, due simply to careless writing. It is due, rather, to an incompatibility between key tenets of Grisez's reading of Aquinas and what Aquinas actually says about our understanding of the good.

In the corpus of *Summa theologiae* 1–2.94.2 Aquinas is concerned with a certain order among what is apprehended by the intellect. ("Of

8. Thomas Aquinas *Summa theol.* 1.94.2.
9. Thomas Aquinas *Summa theol.* 1.94.2.
10. Thomas Aquinas *Summa theol.* 1.94.2.
11. Grisez, "First Principle," p. 178.

the things which enter into our apprehension of anything, a certain order is found.") Regarding the principles of practical reason, that which falls first in this order is the grasp of the *ratio* of good as 'that to which all things are naturally inclined', which grasp we have been discussing. Based upon this grasp is the first principle of practical reason, 'Good is to be done and pursued and evil avoided'. ("The first principle in practical reasoning is based on the *ratio* of good.") Thirdly, the subordinate principles of practical reason are based upon the first principle. ("On this [first precept of the law] is based all other precepts of the natural law.")

It is not entirely clear just what Aquinas has in mind when he speaks of "a certain order" which is found among "the things which enter into our apprehension." The order may be that by which people ordinarily become aware of the principles. Alternatively, it may be an order of explanation; that is, though what is prior may not be known before what is posterior in the order, nevertheless we explain what is posterior by reference to what is prior.[12] But, however this order is to be understood, it does seem clear that whatever sense good has in the first principle and subordinate principles, it is that which is apprehended in the initial grasp of the *ratio* of good. If this were not so, it is hard to see how the subordinate principles could be "based upon" the grasp of the *ratio* of good.

According to Grisez, however, the sense of 'good' in the subordinate principles of practical reason is of the normatively good. In this sense, Grisez emphasizes, 'good' is not understood as what is the object of some natural inclination, for that is the understanding of the descriptively good. But then it seems clear that the sense 'good' has in these subordinate principles is not "that to which all things are naturally inclined." Therefore it seems that Grisez is forced to accept some change in the sense of 'good' between the initial grasp of the *ratio* of good and the formulation of the subordinate principles of practical reason.

McInerny, on the other hand, does not recognize a distinction between the descriptively good and the normatively good. He holds that the *ratio* of good is the *ratio* under which we desire all we desire. For McInerny, then, the grasp of the *ratio* of good can be a grasp of

---

12. An argument in subsequent pages implies that it is best understood as an order of explanation.

'that to which all things are naturally inclined', if this is taken as the *ratio* of their inclination. This understanding would be what is presupposed by practical reason. And it would lead us, as McInerny suggests, to a consideration of our natural inclinations and of what is perfective of human nature. This consideration would then lead us to the fundamental precepts of the natural law. And this reasoning seems to accord with that outlined in the corpus of *Summa theologiae* 1–2.94.2.

I have argued, then, that Grisez must read into *Summa theologiae* 1–2.94.2c a shift in the sense of 'good' which Aquinas does not acknowledge, and that consequently Grisez's reading of the passage is more forced and unnatural than McInerny's alternative, and perhaps other alternatives as well. But although this conclusion may weaken Grisez's position, it does not wholly undermine it: Grisez can argue that his interpretation is unavoidable in light of other considerations, and thus, all things considered, it is superior to the alternatives. So we are led to ask what other support Grisez and Finnis offer for their reading. And the answer to this is clear: it is that Thomas says that the principles of practical reason are immediate, indemonstrable and *per se nota*. As Grisez writes, these principles "are not derived from statements of fact. They are principles. They are not derived from any statements at all. . . . They are underivable."[13] This also seems to be Finnis's primary argument: "Aquinas asserts as plainly as possible that the first principles of the basic forms of good and evil, which specify the basic form of good and evil and which can be adequately grasped by anyone of the age of reason . . . are *per se nota* (self-evident) and indemonstrable."[14] Let us say that a proposition, p, is epistemically basic for a subject, S, if S believes p, but S does not believe p on the basis of any other proposition S believes. Grisez and Finnis's point here is that if certain propositions are said to be principles which are *per se nota* and indemonstrable, then, in the normal case at least, they are epistemically basic for a normal subject. This seems to be Grisez and Finnis's primary argument in support of their position on the epistemological question.

---

13. Grisez, "First Principle," p. 195. In a more recent defense of his position, Grisez repeats and reaffirms this argument. See Grisez, "Natural Law and Natural Inclinations."

14. Finnis, *Natural Law and Natural Rights*, p. 33.

I will try to show that this argument of Grisez and Finnis is based upon a common misunderstanding of Thomas's view of a science and scientific demonstration.[15] Aquinas's most extensive discussion of the nature of scientific demonstration is found in his commentary on Aristotle's *Posterior Analytics*. When we turn to Aquinas's Aristotelian commentaries, however, we run into the thorny and controversial question of whether and to what extent we can attribute to Aquinas the views he attributes to Aristotle.[16] My own view is close to Chenu's, who says that a medieval commentator such as Aquinas is presumed to take the contents of the text as his own unless he says otherwise.[17] In what follows, however, although I will quote Aquinas's Aristotelian commentaries as indicating his own view, I will add, in footnotes or in the text, a place where Aquinas asserts or implies the doctrine in question in his own work.

The propositions which are principles of a science are, as Thomas frequently notes, "immediata, indemonstrabiles et per se nota." As he writes, "any proposition whose predicate is contained in the *ratio* of the subject is immediate ['immediata'] and self-evident ['per se nota']. . . ."[18] He seems to have several interrelated points in mind here. A proposition of the form 'A is B' is immediate if there is no further middle term, B*, which one can employ in a demonstrative syllogism to demonstrate the inherence of B in A. That is, 'A is

---

15. Even a persistent critic of many features of the Grisez-Finnis position, Janice Schultz, accepts this point that *per se nota* propositions are epistemically basic for the normal subject, though it presents rather serious problems for her. See Schultz, "Necessary Moral Principles."

16. See Jean Isaac, "Saint Thomas interprète des oeuvres d'Aristote," in *Scholastica Ratione Historico-Critica Instauranda: Acta Congressus Scholastici Internationalis Romae anno sancto 1950 celebrati* (Rome: Pontificium Athenaeum Antonianum, 1951), pp. 355–363; Marie-Dominique Chenu, *Toward Understanding Saint Thomas*, trans. A.-M. Landry and D. Hughes (Chicago: Henry Regnery, 1964); Joseph Owens, "Aquinas as Aristotelian Commentator," in *St. Thomas Aquinas 1274–1974: Commemorative Studies*, ed. Armand A. Maurer (Toronto: PIMS, 1974) 1:213–238; Mark Jordan, "Thomas Aquinas's Disclaimers in the Aristotelian Commentaries," in *Philosophy and the God of Abraham: Essays in Memory of James A. Weisheipl, O.P.*, ed. R. James Long (Toronto: PIMS, 1991), pp. 99–112.

17. Chenu, *Toward Understanding Saint Thomas*, pp. 207–208.

18. Thomas Aquinas *Expositio libri Posteriorum* 1.5, Leonine *Opera omnia* 1*/2 (Rome: Commissio Leonina and Paris: J. Vrin, 1989), p. 25, lines 116–118. Compare *Summa theol.* 1.2.1.

B' is immediate if there is no proper demonstrative syllogism of the form:

$$\frac{\begin{array}{c} A \text{ is } B^* \\ B^* \text{ is } B \end{array}}{A \text{ is } B}$$

And since there is no further middle term B*, there is no demonstrative syllogism which proves that A is B, and this proposition is indemonstrable. Finally, since there is no more ultimate middle term, it is thought that the predicate B is "contained in" the *ratio* of A, and so the proposition 'A is B' can be known by anyone who fully understands the *rationes* involved. That is, it can be known *per se*, or, as Grisez and Finnis say, it is self-evident. The three terms—immediate, indemonstrable, and self-evident—are, it is important to note, co-extensive terms for Aquinas.

Grisez and Finnis realize that not all immediate, self-evident propositions are self-evident to us. Although it is true that for any such proposition a full grasp of the *ratio* of the subject is sufficient for seeing that the predicate is contained in it and thus that the proposition is true, such a grasp of the *ratio* of the subject may be beyond us. This may be so even when we in some sense understand the proposition, yet fall short of a complete understanding which enables us to see that the proposition is true. In such cases, the proposition is self-evident *in se* or *secundum naturam*, but not *quoad nos*. The most extreme cases of such a disparity between what is self-evident in itself and to us are found in theology. That God exists is self-evident in itself, but not to us:

> This proposition, 'God exists', is self-evident in itself, because the predicate and subject are identical; for God is his own existence.... But because we do not possess scientific knowledge of God with respect to what he is, he is not self-evident to us. Rather, [the proposition 'God exists'] needs to be demonstrated through things which are better known to us, and less known according to nature, namely, through God's effects.[19]

So Thomas distinguishes between what is self-evident "in itself" ("*in se*") and "with respect to us" ("*quoad nos*"), and these are by

---

19. Thomas Aquinas *Summa theol.* 1.2.1.

no means co-extensive; though all of what is self-evident to us is self-evident in itself, some of what is self-evident in itself is not evident to us. The proposition 'God exists' is an example of an immediate, indemonstrable, self-evident principle which is not evident to us. As the passage just quoted indicates, such a proposition, though it is indemonstrable, nevertheless admits of demonstration by us. The resolution of this paradoxical claim is found, of course, in distinguishing two sorts of demonstration. A self-evident principle does not admit of demonstration *propter quid*, which, as we see below, is required from scientific demonstration. It does admit of, and can come to be known by, demonstration *quia*, which is demonstration from effect to cause. Thomas writes:

> There are two kinds of demonstration. One is through the cause [to the effect], and it is called a *propter quid* demonstration: and this is [a demonstration] which moves from things which are prior *simpliciter*. The other is through the effect [to the cause], and it is called a demonstration *quia*: and this is [a demonstration] which moves from those things which are prior with respect to us; for when an effect is more manifest to us than its cause, we move from the effect to knowledge of the cause.... Hence, due to the fact that God's existence is not something self-evident with respect to us, it is demonstrable from effects better known to us.[20]

The propositions which concern us are not theological, but the principles of practical reason. Finnis says that Aquinas is "regrettably obscure" on, among other things, the question of to whom the principles are self-evident.[21] Yet, as we have seen above, from Thomas's claim that the principles of practical reason are self-evident and indemonstrable, Grisez and Finnis want to infer that he thinks they are epistemically basic for the ordinary subject who is capable of rational moral judgments. Therefore, they must suppose that, unless there is some more or less clear indication to the contrary, then in the nontheological sciences self-evident means self-evident *quoad nos* as well as *in se*. This supposition would be very plausible if Thomas thought the demonstrative structure of these sciences was epistemological. That is, the claim would be plausible if Thomas thought that the order of demonstration in the various sciences reflected the order in

---

20. Thomas Aquinas *Summa theol.* 1.2.2.
21. Finnis, *Natural Law and Natural Rights*, p. 51.

which one[22] comes to know the various propositions of the science. This may seem a very plausible way to think of the demonstrative structure of a science. I want to argue, however, that this is clearly not the way Aquinas thought of the demonstrative structure of a science, and thus that Grisez and Finnis's supposition that self-evident principles can generally be supposed to be self-evident *quoad nos* is quite unfounded.

One possesses demonstrative knowledge when one knows a proposition as the conclusion of a demonstrative syllogism.[23] A demonstrative syllogism is not just any valid, sound syllogism, but one which Aristotle characterizes as follows:

> ... it is necessary for demonstrative understanding in particular to depend on things which are true and primitive and immediate and more familiar than and prior to and explanatory of the conclusion (for in ths way the principles will also be causal to what is being proved).[24]

According to Aristotle, then, a key requirement of a demonstrative syllogism is that the premises refer to the cause and the conclusion refers to the effect. Aquinas in his own work says that "scientia" can be gained by a demonstration *quia*, one which moves from effects to cause.[25] However, it seems clear that this is scientific knowledge in a secondary or deficient sense, for such an apprehension does not proceed from principles which are *per se nota* or known by a higher science.[26] For science *simpliciter*, demonstrations must be *propter quid*; they must proceed from causes which are prior *simpliciter*.[27] This

---

22. The knower in question may either be the one who first discovered truths of the science, the student who learns them, or both the discoverer and the student.

23. "Scientific knowledge (*scire*) seems to be nothing other than 'to understand' the truth of some conclusion 'through demonstration'" (Thomas Aquinas *Expos. Post.* 1.4 [Leonine 1*/2:20.142–144]). Compare, "*Scientia* causes the intellect to assent through vision and understanding of first principles" (*Summa theol.* 1.12.13.ad 3).

24. Aristotle *Posterior Analytics* 1.2 (71b20–23), trans. Jonathan Barnes, in *The Complete Works of Aristotle*, ed. Barnes (Princeton: Princeton University Press, 1984) 1:115, with modifications.

25. Thomas Aquinas *Summa theol.* 2–2.1.5.

26. Thomas Aquinas *Summa theol.* 1.1.2. Aquinas follows Aristotle in distinguishing between scientific knowledge in its full sense or *simpliciter* and various deficient or *secundum quid* forms of it. See Aristotle *Posterior Analytics* 2 and Thomas Aquinas *Sent. Post. Anal.* 1.4.

27. Thomas Aquinas *Summa theol.* 1.2.2.

requirement that scientific demonstrations are demonstrations *propter quid* implies that the demonstrative structure of a science is not epistemological, but reflects the real causal order. Aquinas realized, for example, that the position of the moon caused high and low tide, and thus, on this view of demonstrative science, the fact that the tide is high must be demonstrated from the fact that the moon is in a certain position. But, clearly, we do not come to know that it is high tide by inferring it from our beliefs about the moon's position; knowledge of the moon's causal influence was no doubt subsequent to the awareness of high tide.

This issue is somewhat complicated, however, by the fact that Aristotle and Aquinas held that epistemological considerations were relevant to a demonstrative syllogism, albeit not in that the former determined the structure of the latter. In the passage just quoted, Aristotle says that premises must be "better known" than conclusions, and the point of this stipulation becomes clear later in the text. For a perfect demonstrative syllogism, it seems that not only must the demonstration be from cause to effect, but our knowledge of the cause must itself be the cause of our knowledge of the effect.[28] That is, although we initially come to know causes through effects, the goal of scientific inquiry is, as it were, 'to restructure' our beliefs so that we come to know effects through causes.

However this 'restructuring' is to go, it seems clear that the stipulation that the principles, which describe the causes, are known better than and prior to conclusions, which describe effects, expresses an ideal and not the norm for initial discovery in a science. God knows effects through causes,[29] but for the weaker intellects of human beings, in a very large number of cases, our knowledge of conclusions of a science is prior to, better known than, and the cause of our knowledge of its principles. Thus the principles of a science are always intrinsically self-evident, but not to us:

> And because prior and better known are said in two ways (viz., with respect to us and according to nature) the Philosopher consequently says

---

28. Aristotle *Posterior Analytics* 1.2 (72a25–33). Compare Thomas Aquinas *Summa theol.* 1.12.13 ad 3 and 1–2.51.2.

29. "God [sees] his effects in himself, which is [to see them] in their cause...." (*Summa theol.* 1.14.7).

that those things from which demonstration moves are prior and better known *simpliciter* and according to nature, and not to us.[30]

Consequently, Aquinas writes, in the normal course of much of scientific inquiry, the immediate and intrinsically self-evident principles are demonstrated from non-immediate, intrinsically less evident conclusions of the science:

> In the acquisition of scientific knowledge principles and elements are not always prior, for sometimes from sensible effects we arrive at knowledge of principles and intelligible causes.[31]

Such a demonstration is, of course, a demonstration *quia*. Thomas, following Aristotle, continues to hold that, though the principles may initially be known through effects, one strives for the ideal of knowing effects through causes, and achieving this ideal often requires a certain restructuring, as it were, of one's system of beliefs.[32] But in whatever way this restructuring is to be achieved, it seems clear that the way in which principles are known according to this ideal is certainly not the way they are first known by a subject.

If the preceding is correct, then we cannot straightforwardly infer from the fact that Aquinas says that certain principles are immediate and self-evident that they are self-evident *quoad nos*, and thus epis-

---

30. Thomas Aquinas *Expos. Post.* 1.4 (Leonine 1*/2:21.245–9). Compare, *Summa theol.* 1.2.2.

31. Thomas Aquinas *Summa theol.* 1.85.8 ad 1. See also my "Aquinas on the Veracity of the Intellect," *Journal of Philosophy* 88/11 (1991): 623–632, especially pp. 629–632. I discuss Aquinas's account of how our apprehension of natural essences arises initially from a grasp of merely accidental properties apparent to sense perception.

32. In several passages Aristotle and Aquinas wrestle with the question of how this restructuring might be carried out. As Aquinas writes, "in the completion of scientific knowledge, the scientific knowledge of the effect always depends on knowledge of principles and elements since, as the Philosopher says..., we do not think we know something scientifically until we can make principles manifest in light of their causes" (*Summa theol.* 1.85.8 ad 1). This is perhaps plausible when we can come to have more immediate knowledge of a cause we initially knew by inference from effects. Neil Armstrong would have achieved such knowledge if an eclipse had occurred while he was standing on the moon. Barring lunar travel, it is difficult to see how this cause could ever be better known if someone were, as Thomas and Aristotle certainly were, restricted to hypothetical inference from effects observable from earth. This is precisely the problem Aristotle struggles with in *Posterior Analytics* 1.13, but with dubious results.

temically basic in the normal case for a normal subject. In the case of very obvious and fundamental tautologies, such as the principle of non-contradiction, he certainly does think these are self-evident to all. But in the case of at least many and perhaps most principles of sciences, we must move from what is most knowable to us to what is most knowable in itself, and so the immediate principles are initially known inferentially. But if this is so, the central argument of Grisez and Finnis regarding the epistemological question collapses. In the absence of some further evidence from the texts of Thomas, we cannot suppose that the principles of practical reason—or any other science for that matter—are, at least initially, epistemically basic for a subject.

There seems to be another consideration which, less overtly but perhaps just as powerfully, motivates Grisez and Finnis's view. In a reply to McInerny they discuss the move from descriptive to normative claims. Generally when Grisez and Finnis discuss this, they ask whether there is a "licit inference,"[33] or about whether ought can be derived from is.[34] Here they say, "Our point ... was that there can be no valid deduction of a normative conclusion without a normative principle, and thus the first practical principle cannot be derived from metaphysical speculation."[35] They move without explanation from a question of rational inference to a question of deduction. The question of the inference or derivation of certain propositions from others is a question about epistemically rational inference, one form of which is logical deduction. But Grisez and Finnis's unexplained shift from speaking of inference generally to deduction suggests that they see the former is restricted to the latter in this case. If this is granted, then Grisez and Finnis are perhaps right that normative conclusions cannot be derived from descriptive premises, but why should we suppose that Aquinas would recognize such a restriction? It makes sense within the tight strictures of a Humean epistemology, and thus it is no surprise that Hume was the one to announce that 'is' cannot be derived from 'ought'. But there is no reason to suppose that Aquinas's epistemology was Humean. And thus there is no reason to suppose that the derivation of normative from descriptive claims must be restricted to logical deduction.

33. Finnis, *Natural Law and Natural Rights*, pp. 33–36.
34. Grisez, "First Principle," p. 194.
35. Grisez and Finnis, "Basic Principles," p. 24.

THE GOOD AND NATURAL INCLINATIONS   75

I conclude that Aquinas did think that normative judgments, and indeed some principles of practical reason, can be inferred from certain judgments about human nature and human inclinations. This interpretation gives us a more natural reading of Thomas's discussions on the principles of practical reason, and Grisez and Finnis's arguments against such a reading are not compelling.

THE CONCEPTUAL QUESTION

In addition to the epistemological question, there is a conceptual question about the good. Is being desirable, being the object of natural inclinations, constitutive of the concept of good for Aquinas? McInerny seems to answer this question affirmatively, while Grisez and Finnis respond negatively. Although I sided with McInerny on the epistemological question, I think Grisez and Finnis are nearer the truth on this question.

The question to be addressed must be formulated more precisely. First of all, the above formulation asks whether being desirable is constitutive of being good, but 'desirable' is ambiguous. Let us introduce some distinctions and corresponding labels. Let us call something 'factually desirable' if it is such that it is either what an agent thinks will satisfy his desires, or what will in fact do so. We can divide this genus into two species. Of the factually desirable objects or states of affairs, let us call those 'merely factually desirable' which an agent thinks will satisfy his desires, though they would not, if attained, in fact do so. And let us call those 'genuinely factually desirable' which are such that, if attained, would in fact satisfy the agent's desires, whether or not the agent realizes this.

For both sorts of the factually desirable, desirability is a relational attribute; it is an attribute something has insofar as it bears a relationship to an agent with certain desires and beliefs, or, at least, certain dispositions to desire and believe. These two are the only senses of 'desirable' which McInerny considers or would accept.[36] It will be helpful, though, to introduce another sense of 'desirable'

---

36. In McInerny's terminology, the factually desirable is called the *desirable$_1$*, and the genuinely factually desirable is called the *desirable$_2$*.

to accord with Grisez and Finnis's understanding of Thomas's basic goods. According to them, these goods are goods for humans because human beings, given their natural inclinations, have a certain affinity to them; but their goodness does not consist in the fact that humans have such an affinity. It is rather a feature some things have independently of whether humans in fact desire them. Such goods are, according to Grisez and Finnis, worthy of desire intrinsically, whether or not they are factually desirable, and whether merely or genuinely so. Let us say that an object which is worthy of desire in this non-relational sense is intrinsically desirable. McInerny's view seems to be that being genuinely factually desirable is constitutive of the concept of good, while Grisez and Finnis seem to think that only being intrinsically desirable is.

A second needed refinement of our question regards the terms 'constitutive' and 'concept'. Although these terms are taken for granted by recent philosophers, it is not obvious how they are to be translated into Aquinas's terminology. For Aquinas, the essence or quiddity of a thing is what makes a thing the sort of thing it is.[37] In the primary senses of the terms, only substances have an essence or quiddity, and the essence is primarily the substantial form.[38] The essence is the principle of intelligibility of the thing, and as intelligible structure (which is the substantial form abstracted from the individuating conditions of matter) it is called the intelligible species or *ratio*.[39] This *ratio* is expressed by a definition.[40] In his commentary on Aristotle's *Metaphysics* Aquinas says that although only substances have an essence or quiddity and a definition in the primary senses of these terms, in a secondary and analogous sense things which are not in the category of substance, such as good, have an essence or quiddity and definition.[41] In what follows, then, I will speak of the essence or

37. See, for example, *De Ente et Essentia* 1 and *Sent. lib. Metaphysicorum* 7.3, ed. R. Spiazzi (Rome: Marietti, 1950), no. 1303.
38. Thomas Aquinas *Sent Metaph.* 7.3 (Spiazzi nos. 1324, 1327).
39. Thomas Aquinas *Expositio Super Librum Boethii De Trinitate* 5.2; *Summa theol.* 1.85.1, corpus ad 1, ad 2.
40. Thomas Aquinas *Expositio libri Peryermenias* 1.2 in the Leonine *Opera omnia* 1*/1 (Rome: Commissio Leonina and Paris: J. Vrin, 1989), pp. 10–11, lines 89–112; *Sent. Metaph.* 7.7 (Spiazzi no. 613).
41. Thomas Aquinas *Sent. Metaph.* 7.4 (Spiazzi nos. 1331, 1335, 1337, 1355).

quiddity of good and its *ratio* and definition in this secondary and analogous sense of these terms.

We can now reformulate our question as follows: Is being an object of natural inclination, in the sense of being genuinely factually desirable, part of the quiddity, or essence, or *ratio* of good for Aquinas? Let us label one who answers this question affirmatively an essentialist. As said above, though I believe McInerny seems to hold an essentialist position, his view is not elaborated. One who does explicitly embrace a version of essentialism and elaborates it is Ronald Duska.[42]

Duska emphasizes *De veritate* 21, articles 1 and 2 in his interpretation of Aquinas. He claims that there we find "a definition of the good as well as explanations of this definition."[43] That is, he explains, in this question Aquinas gives us "necessary conditions for calling something good."[44] Duska quotes two passages in this regard. (He actually quotes Aquinas in an English translation which I find problematic and which does not accord with the terminology I have adopted in this paper. Thus I provide my own translation along with Aquinas's Latin.) These are:

> It is to be said that, since the *ratio* of good consists in this, that something is perfective of another as an end, whatever is found to have the *ratio* of an end also has the *ratio* of good. Two things are of the *ratio* of an end: (1) it is naturally inclined to or desired by those who have not yet attained the end, or (2) it is enjoyed, and, as it were, enjoyable, by those who participate in the end.

> Dicendum quod cum boni ratio in hoc consistat quod aliquid sit perfectum alterius per modum finis, omne illud quod invenitur habere rationem finis

---

42. Ronald Duska, "Aquinas's Definition of Good: Ethical-Theoretical Notes on *De veritate*, Q. 21," *Monist* 58 (1974): 151–162. Ironically, John Finnis refers us to Duska's article for clarification about "the relation between the desired, the desirable, and the perfective in Aquinas's notion of good" (*Natural Law and Natural Rights*, p. 79). Others, as well as myself, find this confusing (see also Janice Schultz, "Thomistic Metaethics and a Present Controversy"). For Duska's reading would not support but undermine Finnis's claim that "for one who considers knowledge to be a good, the true expression of his opinion and attitude is not 'it is good because or in so far as I desire it', but 'I desire it because and in so far as it is good'" (*Natural Law and Natural Rights*, p. 70).

43. Duska, *Natural Law and Natural Rights*, p. 152.

44. Duska, *Natural Law and Natural Rights*, p. 152.

habet et rationem boni. Duo autem sunt de ratione finis: ut sit scilicet appetitum vel desideratum ab his quae finem nondum attingunt, et ut sit delectum et quasi delectibile ab his quae finem participant. . . [45]

Primarily and principally, therefore, a being is called good which is perfective of another as an end.

Sic ergo primo et principaliter dicitur bonum ens perfectivum alterius per modum finis.[46]

Duska discusses what he sees as "two elements in this definition . . . (1) the notion of good as something perfective of another and (2) the notion of good as an end."[47] He comments on the second "element," saying:

> According to the text there are two simple criteria for determining whether something is an end: (1) "It must be sought [*appetitum*] or desired by things which have not yet attained the end," and (2) "it must be loved [*dilectum*] by the things which share the end, and be, as it were, enjoyable [*delectible*] to them.[48]

We find in Duska's Aquinas what I will call a dual component view of the essence or *ratio* of good. The essence or *ratio* of good for something of a certain kind consists of both the notion of being perfective for that sort of thing and the notion of being an end, which is just to be desired or enjoyed by individuals of that kind. As he points out, this second component requires actual desiring and, if attained, actual enjoyment.[49] Duska's position, then, is an essentialist one which sees being the object of natural inclinations of certain creatures, being genuinely factually desirable for them, as one component of the essence or *ratio* of good for creatures of that kind; being perfective for creatures of that kind is the other

---

45. Thomas Aquinas *Quaestiones disputatae de veritate* 21.2, in Leonine *Opera omnia* 22 (Rome: Editio di San Tomasso, 1975), p. 596, lines 61–69.
46. Thomas Aquinas *De verit.* 21.1 (Leonine 22: 594.207–209).
47. Duska, *Natural Law and Natural Rights*, p. 153.
48. Duska, *Natural Law and Natural Rights*, p. 153.
49. As Duska writes, "this criterion for an end of being desired, demands actual desiring" (*Natural Law and Natural Rights*, pp. 153–154, n. 10).

component.⁵⁰ There are some immediate and obvious problems with what Duska says. Firstly, it seems unwise to base an interpretation of Aquinas on the *Quaestiones disputatae de veritate*, one of his earliest works.⁵¹ If we find in the *De veritate* claims which are not repeated in, for instance, the *Summa theologiae*, it is probably because Aquinas came to believe the earlier formulations were vague, or misleading, or just plain wrong. But Duska does not cite later works. Secondly, Duska says that Aquinas gives a "definition" of good in the passage he quotes, though Aquinas does not speak of a *definitio* in this passage. Duska, however, does not mention what Aquinas does call a *definitio*, Aristotle's formula 'that to which all things are naturally inclined'. Thirdly, though Duska does say that though this "characterization" is not a proper definition in terms of genus and species, he calls it a definition because "if any characterization gives necessary condition, it seems to be some attempt to define."⁵² But in saying this he conflates the essence of a thing and its proper accidents, which are not part of the essence but which may also be necessary attributes of things with that essence. Fourthly, Duska distinguishes (1) ends for beings which

---

50. The dual component view of the *ratio* of good seems to be the majority position presently, Grisez and Finnis not withstanding. It is found not only in McInerny and Duska, but in others as well. For example, Peter Simpson in a recent article, "St. Thomas on the Naturalistic Fallacy," writes: "[Good] involves reference to desire. . . . It expresses how that being, just as such a being, is a fulfillment and completion of whatever is directed to it as to an object of desire. Good expresses being along with the idea of end, goal or fulfillment" (p. 61). In interesting twists within this confusing area, Douglas Flippen separates the two components into two distinct senses of good, in "On Two Meanings of Good and the Foundation of Ethics in Aristotle and Aquinas," *Proceedings of the American Catholic Philosophical Association* 58 (1984): 57–59. Janice Schultz, on the other hand, sees the desire component as involving a relationship to a possible, rather than an actual, desire, in "Thomistic Metaethics and a Present Controversy." I do not think that either Flippen's or Schultz's view can be sustained, but I will not discuss them in this paper.

51. The *De veritate* consists of questions disputed during Aquinas's first Parisian regency (1256–59), immediately after the completion of the commentary on the *Sentences* of Peter Lombard and his inception in theology. Questions 21 and 22 were probably disputed during the third year of that regency, 1258–59. For a discussion of the dating, see James A. Weisheipl, *Friar Thomas D'Aquino: His Life, Thought, and Work*, rev. ed. (Washington: Catholic University of America Press, 1983), pp. 123–125, with the summary on pp. 362–363.

52. Duska, *Natural Law and Natural Rights*, p. 152, n. 5.

desire and enjoy, such as humans, and (2) ends which may be ends simply in virtue of being the termination of a natural process, such as becoming an oak is the end for an acorn. He then writes that "in the passage cited [*De veritate* 21.2] the primary use of the word 'good' is the use when [sic] it is applied to beings who desire and enjoy"[53]—such as human beings. But Aquinas speaks of what is desired as "appetitum," and he clearly holds that all creatures, living and nonliving, have "appetitus." Indeed, in the very sentence of *De veritate* 21.2 from which Duska takes the passage he quotes Aquinas illustrates the "desire for" and "enjoyment of" an end with the example of a rock which moves toward and ultimately rests at the center.

There are serious problems with Duska's essay, and anyone wishing to defend Duska's view would have to address them. However, I will assume that a more careful expositor of the dual component view can handle them and will ask whether, these problems aside, the dual component interpretation is defensible. I will argue that although Aquinas sees that there is a close connection between being the object of natural inclination and being good, the former cannot be part of the *ratio* of the latter.

If the dual component view of the *ratio* of good is correct, then being good is, at least partly, a relational attribute. The fact that X is good is partially dependent on X's relation to other beings, viz., to beings with a natural inclination to X or the capacity to enjoy X. If some thing, X, is good for humans, then it is part of the *ratio* of good that there must be a human agent, A, who desires X or would enjoy X if X were attained. The problem for the dual component interpretation of Aquinas is that this does not seem to accord with much of what Aquinas wrote.

Let us recall, first of all, the earlier discussion of scientific demonstration and its principles. There I argued that one may come to know some principles of a science by inferring them from other propositions not themselves principles. The fact that they are principles does not mean they must be epistemically basic for a subject. Although this is so, it is nevertheless clearly Aquinas's position that the principles describe what is the ultimate cause in a certain field. They are therefore ultimate in the order of explanation in demonstrative science. If 'A

---

53. Duska, *Natural Law and Natural Rights*, p. 157.

is B' is a principle of science, then there is no further middle term, B*, with which we can demonstrate that B inheres in A. Rather, if 'A is B*' is a claim within that field of science, B*'s inherence in A is demonstrated with the principle 'A is B', or with some other principle, as a premise.

In the *Summa theologiae* the principles of practical reason include propositions such as 'Knowledge is good' and 'Procreation and rearing of children are good'. Consider a principle such as these. If the dual component view is correct, then procreation is good only if it bears a certain relationship to an agent with certain desires or dispositions to enjoy, for part of what it is to be good is to be the object of desire and enjoyment. Being good is, therefore, partially a relational attribute of procreation. For any such relational attribute, its inherence can be explained with reference to the *relata* and the relationship; that Bill Clinton is the choice of the people, for example, can be explained with reference to the people and their choice. Similarly, according to the dual component view, it would seem that the goodness of procreation and rearing can be explained with reference to the desires and dispositions to enjoyment of human agents. Hence, the following demonstrative syllogism seems possible:

> Procreation is perfective and an object of desire.
> What is perfective and an object of desire is good.
> ---
> Procreation is good.

But if this is so, then the proposition 'Procreation is good' would not be, as Thomas clearly claims it is, an immediate and *per se nota* principle of practical reason. The same would be true for all the other principles of practical reason.

There are also problems for the dual component interpretation arising from the *De veritate* itself. In an article of *De veritate* q. 21, Aquinas asks: "Are all things good by the First Goodness?" There Aquinas tells us how a certain sort of Platonic account of good and goodness can be sustained, for the First Goodness, God, is in a certain way the principle of all good things. He writes:

> If the First Goodness is the efficient cause of all goods, it must be that he informs all his effects with his likeness; and so each thing is called good through likeness to the highest good in the way of an inherent form

infused into it, and further through the First Goodness in the way of the exemplar and efficient cause of all created goods.

Thus God, the first and highest good, is the principle of all goods insofar as he infuses in all good things the form which is the likeness of his goodness, and thus God is the exemplar and efficient cause of their goodness. Here Aquinas only speaks of God being the principle of good things insofar as he is the efficient cause and exemplar of their intrinsic forms. However, if the dual component view is correct, God could only be the principle of things being good if he were also the principle of the inclinations of other creatures for the good thing. Aquinas does not mention such inclinations in this article.

Furthermore, in *De veritate* 22.1 Thomas addresses the question: "Utrum omnia bonum appetunt." It is perhaps obvious that he is not asking whether there is some one thing which is good; the question should not be translated: "Do all things desire the thing which is good?" Rather, as he writes in response to an objection in this article, "when one says 'all things are naturally inclined to good,' the good need not be confined to this or that; it is, rather, to be taken in a general sense, because each thing is naturally inclined to the good naturally fitting to it."[54] Thus, he is asking in this article whether all things are naturally inclined to good. He asks, more precisely, whether they are inclined to the good which is fitting to the sort of creature they are; more simply, whether they are naturally inclined to their good.

Thomas begins his *respondeo* by answering in the affirmative, both for creatures having cognitive awareness, and for those lacking it. After mentioning a contrary view of ancient philosophers and offering an Aristotelian response, Aquinas goes on to explain how it is that all things are naturally inclined to what is good. A thing may be ordered to something in one of two kinds of ways: (1) a creature with some cognitive awareness of its end may be ordered of itself to its end, as a human being moves to the place she wishes to be; (2) a creature may be directed to its end by another, and this may be so even if it lacks cognitive awareness of its end, as an arrow which is directed to its target by an archer. Among cases of kind (2), the direction may come about (2a) violently, which occurs when the

---

54. Thomas Aquinas *De verit.* 22.1 ad 4.

creature has no form in virtue of which there is a natural inclination to the end, as when a rock is thrown upwards. Alternatively, it may come about (2b) naturally, which occurs when the one directing the thing instills a form in virtue of which it is naturally inclined to its end, as when a rock is given a natural inclination to downward movement and moves downward. Non-cognitive, natural things have instilled in them forms in virtue of which they are naturally inclined to their proper ends. Although Aquinas does not emphasize it in this article, this is also true for creatures with cognitive awareness of ends, such as human beings, for they also have natural inclinations to their proper ends instilled by God, who is the first mover.[55] What is naturally inclined to something is naturally inclined to that thing because of what the one who guides or directs it by instilling a form wills. So all natural things are naturally inclined to that to which God wills them to be inclined. Thomas then concludes the main argument of the article:

> Since God has no other end of his will but himself, and since he is the essence of goodness, it must be that all other things are naturally inclined to good.[56]

The main argument of the article that all things are naturally inclined to their good seems to be more or less the following:

(1) Whatever are the objects of natural inclination are what God wills them to be.
(2) The end of God's will is God.
(3) God is the essence of goodness.
(4) The end of God's will is the essence of goodness, goodness itself.
(5) God wills for each creature what is good for that creature.[57]

---

55. See, for example, Thomas Aquinas *De verit.* 22.1 ad 6.
56. Thomas Aquinas *De verit.* 22.1.
57. Only premise (5) is not explicitly in *De verit.* 22.1 or does not follow obviously from what is explicitly stated there. Yet it seems that it must be an implicit premise, for otherwise Aquinas could not move from the claim that God wills goodness itself (premise [4]) to the claim that creatures are naturally inclined to their respective goods (premise [6]). Moreover, it is Aquinas's express view elsewhere that in virtue of God's willing his own goodness he wills creaturely goods (see *Summa contra Gentiles* 3.8).

(6) The objects of a creature's natural inclinations are what is good for that creature.

(7) Therefore, all creatures are naturally inclined to their good.

If this summary is roughly right, then Aquinas infers that creatures are naturally inclined to their good from the facts that (1) God determines the objects of creaturely natural inclinations, and (2) God wills that creatures are inclined to their good. Hence, on Aquinas's view, all things are naturally inclined to their good because of the benevolence of God who instills in a creature the natural inclination to its good. The dual component interpretation, however, cannot make sense of this claim. According to it the fact that something is good for a creature is partially constituted by the creature's inclinations, and so a thing's being good for a creature cannot be prior to that creature existing with certain inclinations. On the dual component view, Aquinas's claim in the *De veritate* 22.1 would be similar to the one that God wills that I most favor my favorite color, and so instills in me a disposition to favor my favorite color. But this is nonsense, of course, because nothing is my favorite color until I exist with certain dispositions to favor one color more than others, so God cannot instill in me inclinations to favor a color in light of what my favorite color is. Similarly, if the dual component interpretation is right, then it would be nonsense for Aquinas to say that God instills in creatures of a certain kind natural inclinations to something because God wills that they are naturally inclined to their good, for what is good for that sort of creature cannot be prior to such creatures having certain natural inclinations. But this is precisely what Aquinas claims. Hence, the dual component interpretation—or any interpretation which makes creaturely natural inclinations constitutive of what it is to be good for that creature—cannot be right.

Duska's dual component essentialist interpretation fails even with regard to the *De veritate*, where Duska believes it is strongly supported; it certainly cannot be sustained for Aquinas's later works in which there is less support. Moreover, I contend, the considerations just advanced show that no essentialist interpretation of Aquinas can succeed; that is, no interpretation which understands being the object of natural inclination as part of the essence or *ratio* of good can be sustained. The question then arises: what is the relationship between being good for a certain sort of creature and being the object of such creatures' natural inclinations?

It is clear that Aquinas sees a close connection between being good and being the object of natural inclination, and in the next section I will say more about this connection. For now let us note that in his commentary on Aristotle's *Nicomachean Ethics*, and particularly on Aristotle's definition of good as "that to which all things are naturally inclined," Aquinas says that being the mover of natural *appetitus* is an effect of good, but a proper effect.[58] That is, being the object of natural inclination is a proper or *per se accident* of good, rather than an attribute which inheres merely *per accidens*, which we can call a mere accident.

My claim against Duska's dual component interpretation—and against any essentialist interpretation—is that being the object of natural inclination (i.e., *appetitus*), or being genuinely factually desirable for humans, is not part of the essence or *ratio* of being good, but is a proper effect and accident of the good. One might be tempted to say, then, that although being the object of actual natural inclination is not part of the essence or *ratio* of good, it is a necessary attribute of the good as such. Although Aquinas does sometimes seem to suggest that proper accidents are necessary and some of his commentators have suggested they are,[59] this must be qualified, at least with respect to potencies of the soul, as desires are. For Aquinas holds that the potencies of the soul are proper accidents of a human being,[60] and among these is the power of sight and hearing.[61] Yet he certainly recognized that some people are blind and deaf, and are not actually able to see and hear. He explains this by saying that although one may have a potency, a first actuality, due to the soul, the exercise,

---

58. Thomas Aquinas *Sententia libri Ethicorum* 1.1 in the Leonine *Opera omnia* 47 (Rome: Editori San Tomasso, 1969), p. 5, lines 155–160.

59. Aquinas writes that "what belongs to a thing *per se* is in that thing of necessity, always and inseparably," in the *Summa contra Gentiles* 2.55, ed. C. Pera (Rome: Marietti, 1961), no. 1432. Further, he writes elsewhere, "necessity results from form, because whatever is consequent on form is of necessity in the subject" (*Summa theol.* 1.86.3). These passages are quoted by Petrus Hoenen, who comments, "the necessity of this relationship between [proper accidents] and their substrate is an *absolute* necessity." See his *Reality and Judgement According to St. Thomas Aquinas*, trans. H. F. Tiblier (Chicago: Regnery, 1952), p. 118.

60. "A potency of the soul flows from its essence, not through a transformation, but as a certain natural result, and it is simultaneous with the soul" (*Summa theol.* 1.77.7 ad 1).

61. Thomas Aquinas *Summa theol.* 1.78.3.

or second actuality, of this potency is impeded by some defect in the matter. Hence, although a mere potency due to the form may be necessary for all who possess that form, still this potency may not be able to be exercised if there is a defect in the matter, and thus there may be members of the kind who cannot exercise the potency. Thus, although all creatures of a kind may have a mere potency to desire or be inclined to their good, it is not necessarily the case that they actually desire or are so inclined. It is therefore not necessary that all creatures have an actual natural inclination to their good. It is only necessary that they have a potency to an actual inclination in virtue of their form.

OBJECTIONS AND REPLIES

The reader is probably aware of a serious problem for the view put forward so far. I have claimed that being the object of natural inclination is not part of the essence or *ratio* of good, but is only a proper effect or accident of being good. Yet in *Summa theologiae* 1–2.94.2 Thomas says that the *ratio* of good is 'quod omnia appetunt', 'that to which all things are naturally inclined'. In another place he calls this formula a definition.[62] It seems obvious enough that if this formula expresses the *ratio* of good, and indeed if it is a definition of 'good', then being object of natural inclination is part of the *ratio* or essence of good. Furthermore, I have argued that Aquinas's view was that we infer what is good for us by considering that to which we are inclined (i.e., that which we genuinely factually desire). But how can we make sense of this if being the object of natural inclination is not part of the *ratio* of good?

The first objection is, I believe, the strongest and I will take much longer to respond to it. My response will consist largely of a discussion of Aquinas's views on our ideas ("rationes") in general and the definitions which express them. This area is obviously broad and complex, and my treatment in this paper must be somewhat sketchy. Yet I hope to present and argue for the outline of an interpretation of Aquinas on these issues which will enable me to respond to this

---

62. Thomas Aquinas *Sent. Ethic.* 1.1 (Leonine 47:5.5.149).

objection and which, I believe, will illumine Aquinas's general views on *rationes* and definitions.[63]

First of all, let us recall that although the ideal sort of definition after which Aquinas strives mentions only essential attributes, he does recognize and use definitions which mention accidents of the *definiendum*. For instance, in *Summa theologiae* 1.29.1 ad. 3 Thomas tells us that, having perceived something as common as fire, we can be ignorant of the substantial difference of its proper definition, and must allow 'hot, dry body'—a definition which employs proper accidents—to stand in as the definition of fire. Again, in *Summa theologiae* 1.77.1 ad.7 he writes:

> Nevertheless because substantial forms, unknown to us of themselves, are known through their accidents, there is no difficulty with sometimes using accidents in place of substantial differences.[64]

How is it, though, that accidents can be used to define an essence when the essential attributes are unknown? How can such a formula serve as a definition of that essence at all? Some light can be shed on these questions from Thomas's commentary on chapters 8–10 of Book II of Aristotle's *Posterior Analytics*. Several writers have recently claimed that these passages are important for understanding Aristotle's views on definition,[65] but little has been written on how Aquinas's commentary on these chapters might illumine his views on definition. According to Thomas, in chapter 8 of Book II Aristotle considers two cases of an imperfect apprehension:

> Aristotle says that we can know scientifically that some thing is, and yet not know from this what the thing is; and this can happen in two ways. In the first way, we know some accident of the thing, as, for example, if

---

63. See my "Aquinas on the Veracity of the Intellect" for a somewhat fuller presentation of and argument for this interpretation.

64. Thomas Aquinas *Summa theol.* 1.77.1 ad 7.

65. Some of these are: Robert Bolton, "Essentialism and Semantic Theory in Aristotle," *Philosophical Review* 85 (1976): 514–544; J. A. Ackrill, "Aristotle's Theory of Definition: Some Questions on An. Post. II.8–10," *Aristotle on Science: The 'Posterior Analytics'*, ed. Enrico Berti (Padua: Antenore, 1981), pp. 359–384; and Richard Sorabji, *Necessity, Cause and Blame: Perspectives on Aristotle's Theory* (London: Duckworth, 1980), pp. 195–201.

we think that a hare exists on the basis of quick movement. In a second way, we know something on the basis of its essence.⁶⁶

The first sort of partial knowledge, of accidents only, is quite deficient: (1) it is insufficient for any sort of scientific knowledge of the essence; (2) it does not constitute scientific knowledge that the substance exists; (3) it is not in potency to a full grasp of the essence. In the second case, something of the essence is grasped. The second sort of apprehension is much more adequate: (1) it does qualify as some sort of grasp of the essence; (2) it does constitute scientific knowledge that the substance exists; and (3) it is in potency to full scientific knowledge of the essence. One instance of this is had, as Aquinas writes, "if we grasp that man is on the basis of the fact that man is rational, while not yet knowing the other attributes which complete the essence of man."⁶⁷ Furthermore, this is the sort of case Thomas takes Aristotle to be speaking of when he offers the following accounts:

(1) The definition of 'thunder' is 'a certain noise in the clouds'.
(2) The definition of 'eclipse' is 'a certain privation of light'.
(3) The definition of 'man' is 'a certain animal'.
(4) The definition of 'soul' is 'that which moves itself'.

When one has a grasp of some part of the essence, one grasps the essence partially and is in potency to a full apprehension. It is important for us to appreciate, however, what the imperfect idea is not. It is not, for some essential attribute, the idea of whatever has that attribute. In the case of thunder, for instance, the claim is not:

(5) The definition of 'thunder' is 'any noise in the clouds'.

This would not be an idea of thunder at all, for, as Thomas says, "not every 'noise in the clouds' is thunder."⁶⁸ If the cognitive grasp in question is to be the idea of thunder, then it must be an idea of the property being a noise in the clouds as part of a yet-to-be-discovered essence. This would involve a presupposition that there is some essence yet to be discovered, and some way in which that essence is signified. The idea must be that expressed by:

---

66. Thomas Aquinas *Expos. Post.* 2.7 (Leonine 1*/2:199.126–131).
67. Thomas Aquinas *Expos. Post.* 2.7 (Leonine 1*/2:199.133–135).
68. Thomas Aquinas *Expos. Post.* 2.7 (Leonine 1*/2:199.146–147).

(6) The definition of 'thunder' is 'a certain sort of noise in the clouds' ("quaedam sonam in nubibus").[69]

I am taking the "certain sort of" as a reference to the as-yet-not-fully-known essence. The reference would seem to be in virtue of the instances of the properties which are taken as part of the essence; the phrase in question refers to their underlying cause. As he says in an analogous case, when speaking of using *accidentia propria* in place of unknown essential properties, the *accidentia propria* are used in the definition as "effects of the substantial forms, and as making these forms known ('manifestant eas')."[70] They are used to identify demonstrably the underlying essence which is to be discovered.

In the chapters of the *Posterior Analytics* under consideration, Aristotle and Aquinas discuss only essences the study of which falls to what Aquinas calls natural philosophy or physics. Aquinas follows what he believes is Aristotle's view, that when our grasp of a certain natural essence is deficient, when some essential attributes are unknown to us, we may employ a definition which mentions accidental attributes. The yet-to-be-fully-grasped essence is identified demonstrably as the underlying cause of the instances of the accidental attribute(s) specified in the definition. Such a definition specifies certain accidental attributes of the essence and refers to the essence, which is not itself fully known, as the underlying cause. Henceforth I will call such definitions 'reference-involving' definitions; I will say that terms which are referentially defined in this way possess semantic depth,[71] for the essence signified (in Aquinas's sense of 'significare') may be beyond what the language-users fully apprehend.

The reader will perhaps have realized that this view which I am attributing to Aquinas is very close to so-called recent accounts of natural kind terms which arose out of the work of Hilary Putnam and Saul Kripke, and which has been developed by Colin McGinn and Tyler Burge, among others. Several writers have found such a view in Aristotle.[72] Although I also think Aristotle did hold such a view, the evidence that he did is somewhat ambiguous. Aquinas, I believe,

---

69. Thomas Aquinas *Expos. Post.* 2.7 (Leonine 1*/2:199.144).
70. Thomas Aquinas *Summa theol.* 1.29.1 ad 3.
71. I take this expression from David Charles, who uses it in an unpublished manuscript on Aristotle's understanding of definition.
72. See note 65 above.

embraced and put forward a more sophisticated and clearer version of this sort of account.[73]

Let us return to the *ratio boni* and its definition. I want to argue that Aquinas's use of 'good' and its definition can be understood as analogous to 'thunder' and its definition. I contend that 'good' is a term with a certain sort of semantic depth, and that its definition, 'that to which all things are naturally inclined,' is reference-involving. On this reading, although being the object of natural inclination is a non-essential attribute of being good, it is used in the definition of the term to refer to that attribute of being good which is in fact what is the object of natural inclination.

This reading is strongly recommended by previous results of this paper. In section II I argued that Aquinas held that being the object of natural inclination is not essential to being good; however, as pointed out above, Aquinas defines good in terms of natural inclination. The reading under consideration allows us to reconcile these two apparently incompatible claims of Aquinas. Yet there is also strong support for this reading from what Aquinas actually says about the formula expressing the *ratio* of good.

In *Summa theologiae* 1–2.94.2 Aquinas gives us the definition of 'bonum' as 'quod omnia appetunt', but he does not elaborate there upon this definition. The definition is, of course, taken from the first lines of Aristotle's *Nicomachean Ethics*, and in Aquinas's commentary on the *Ethics* we do find a discussion of it. Aristotle begins with the well-known lines:

> Every art and every inquiry, and similarly every action and choice, is thought to aim at some good; and for this reason the good has rightly been declared to be that at which all things aim.[74]

---

73. One writer who thinks the Kripke-Putnam account of natural kind terms is relevant to Aquinas is Janice Schultz, who discusses it extensively in "Necessary Moral Principles." However, Schultz does not discuss the Kripke-Putnam account with respect to an incomplete grasp of an essence and reference-involving definitions. Her concern is to show that *per se* predications of proper accidents may be necessarily true, and yet informative. Schultz, however, would not be in agreement with my account of the *ratio* of good and its definition, for she offers a different account in her "Thomistic Metaethics and a Present Controversy."

74. Aristotle *Nicomachean Ethics* 1.1 1094a1–3, trans. W. D. Ross, rev. J. O. Urmson, in *The Complete Works of Aristotle*, ed. Jonathan Barnes (Princeton: Princeton University Press, 1984) 2:1729.

In the Latin translation, the second phrase of the quote (which comes after the semicolon in the translation above) is: "Ideo bene enunciaverunt, bonum quod omnia appetunt."[75] Thus in this phrase Aristotle presents what Aquinas takes as the definition of 'good', 'that to which all things are naturally inclined'. Aquinas begins his comment on this second phrase by saying, "[Aristotle] makes his claim manifest through the definition of good."[76] He notes, however, that there is a certain peculiarity about this definitional formula, for "the good is counted among the first things."[77] He goes on to explain:

> The first things cannot be made known through what is prior, but is made known through what is posterior, as causes [are made known] through their proper effects. And since the good is properly the spring of *appetitus*, the good is marked off [*describitur*] with respect to the movement of *appetitus*, as the moving power is customarily made manifest with respect to what is moved. Thus [Aristotle] says that philosophers have rightly declared that the good is 'that to which all things are naturally inclined [*appetunt*]'.[78]

Aquinas says clearly that the definition, 'that to which all things are naturally inclined', employs what is posterior to and an effect of goodness—viz., the ability to move *appetitus*, or natural inclination—to define what is simple and primary, goodness. Being able to move natural inclination, which, in the case of humans, is being genuinely factually desirable, cannot then be part of the essence or *ratio* of good. If it were, being good could not be said to be simple and prior to being able to move *appetitus*, for the latter would be (at least partially) constitutive of the former. We must, therefore, take being able to move *appetitus* (and being genuinely factually desirable) to be a non-essential attribute of goodness, and to be used in the definition to refer to the simple and primary essence of goodness. Thus, the definition of 'good' is reference-involving and the term has semantic depth.

It seems, then, that the definition of 'good' as 'that to which all things are naturally inclined', as Aquinas understands it, does not undermine my contention that being the object of natural inclination is not part of the essence or *ratio* of good. On the contrary, it supports

---

75. Aristotle, as Thomas reads him in *Sent. Ethic.*
76. Thomas Aquinas *Sent. Ethic.* 1.1 (Leonine 47:5.149).
77. Thomas Aquinas *Sent. Ethic.* 1.1 (Leonine 47:5.150–151).
78. Thomas Aquinas *Sent. Ethic.* 1.1 (Leonine 47:5.153–160).

it. For when Aquinas discusses the definition he implies that it is a reference-involving definition which employs an accidental attribute to specify an essence.

There is, however, an important difference between good and its definition and terms from what Aquinas calls natural philosophy, such as thunder and eclipse, and their respective definitions. In the case of thunder and eclipse, it may be argued, although our grasp of these essences is initially imperfect and impartial, there is reason to believe that through prolonged scientific investigation, we can come to a full grasp of these essences. Indeed, Aquinas follows Aristotle's attempts to arrive at a fuller understanding of thunder and eclipses.[79] It does not seem that we can come to a fuller grasp of the essence of goodness in this way, at least given our cognitive state on this earth.[80] We can, of course, sharpen our ability to make practical moral judgments, but this will get us no nearer a full grasp of good and a definition of 'good' which does not employ accidental attributes.

For terms in Aquinas's natural philosophy, there is an expectation that through scientific inquiry reference-involving definitions may be replaced by definitions which are not reference-involving. In the case of 'good' there seem to be no such expectation, given our cognitive state in this life. An objection may be raised, then, that because the definitions of 'thunder' and 'eclipse' are provisional in a way in which that of 'good' is not, this in some way undermines my contention that 'good' has semantic depth and a reference-involving definition, and my claim that the attribute mentioned in the definition is a nonessential attribute of goodness.

This objection is without great force. There is no reason to think that referential definitions must be provisional until scientific progress brings us to a more adequate formulation. Another term which Aquinas seems clearly to recognize as having semantic depth is 'God'. The term 'God' for Aquinas is not the proper name of an individual, but a general term used "to signify the divine nature."[81] As Thomas says, the essence of God is beyond our intellectual grasp in this life,

---

79. See Aquinas's commentary on *Posterior Analytics* 1.13 for a discussion of eclipses, and on 2.10 for a discussion of thunder.

80. The blessed who enjoy the beatific vision have a fuller grasp of goodness, for they see the essence of God, who is goodness. But they enjoy a cognitive state which cannot be enjoyed by anyone in this life on earth. *Summa theol.* 1–2.5.3 and 5.

81. Thomas Aquinas *Summa theol.* 1.13.8.

and any understanding we have of God is from his effects, from the creatures he has created.[82] Any definition of the term, then, must be in terms of his effects in creation. Being creator of the world, however, is an accidental attribute of God,[83] and this accidental attribute is used to define referentially the divine nature; so the term has semantic depth and a referential definition. In the case of God, Aquinas clearly thinks there is no chance that we may progress toward a full grasp of the divine nature in this life through scientific investigation.[84] In this respect, then, 'good' is more like 'God' than like 'thunder', for the referential definition which employs accidental attributes is not provisional until scientific inquiry leads us to a more adequate grasp of the essence. It is, rather, the best definition we can have, given our cognitive state in this life.

I conclude, then, that the definition of good, 'that to which all things are naturally inclined,' is a reference-involving definition which employs an accidental attribute of goodness to specify the simple and prior essence. This conclusion enables us to reconcile the results of the previous section with Aquinas's definition of good. In light of this conclusion, it seems we must make a distinction among *rationes* which is not always clearly made by Aquinas. Given Aquinas's view that we can use a reference-involving definition to specify an essence which may not itself be fully understood, we must distinguish in such cases between an essence and our imperfect intellectual grasp of it. We must distinguish between the full intelligible structure of certain things, which exist *in rebus* in some way, and our apprehension of it. When our understanding of an essence is complete, then there is no difference between them. When our understanding is incomplete, as when we use reference-involving definitions, there is some difference between them. Thomas adopts no consistent terminology to mark this difference between the essence and our imperfect understanding, but it will be helpful for us to do so. I will henceforth cease to use 'idea' to translate 'ratio', the full intelligibility of the thing, and will use 'concept'.[85] When I speak of the intelligibility insofar as it is

---

82. Thomas Aquinas *Summa theol.* 1.13.1.
83. Thomas Aquinas *Summa contra Gentiles* 1.81.
84. Thomas Aquinas *Summa theol.* 1–2.5.3 and 5.
85. This term should not be confused with Aquinas's "conceptus," for he used this term to denote judgments.

understood by us, I will use 'conception'.[86] As was said, when our apprehension is perfect, the intelligible form in our understanding is identical with that in the thing; in this case our conception is identical with the concept. When our apprehension is imperfect, they differ.

A confusing feature of Aquinas's terminology is that he uses 'ratio' to refer to both concepts and our conceptions. Our intellect forms ideas by abstracting the intelligible from individuating, designated matter ("materia signata"), but not from common matter ("materia communis"), and this is the *ratio* expressed by the definition.[87] If our understanding of, say, a human being is perfect, the intelligible form in our intellects is identical with the intelligible structure of the thing, and we can speak of them both as *ratio hominis*. If the intelligible form is not fully grasped, as in the case of our understanding of thunder, we can speak of our definition of thunder and the intellectual form as grasped by our intellects, but this is not identical with the intelligible structure of the thing. So, similarly he can speak of something being good by an intrinsic form which is a similitude of the First Goodness, and also as the *ratio* of good as including being the object of natural inclination. This is understandable because he considers our imperfect conceptions to be inchoate forms which are in potency to be perfect conceptions,[88] which are identical with the concept. Both the imperfect and perfect members of a species are called by the same name. Yet the matter is confusing, and has, I believe, confused many commentators on Aquinas.

My claim, then, is that although being the object of natural inclination is accidental to the concept of good, it is nevertheless central to our conception of good. This leads us to a response to the second objection raised at the start of this section, namely: how are we to

---

86. The terms 'concept' and 'conception' are derived from Frege, but I certainly do not want to suggest that Thomas accepted Fregean concepts. Nevertheless, it is meant to suggest that Thomas's natures as such have a certain existence independent of our understanding them. As Edwards argues (persuasively, to my mind), on a correct understanding of his view "Aquinas turns out to be almost as strong a realist as Duns Scotus." See Sandra Edwards, "The Realism of Aquinas," *New Scholasticism* 59 (1985): 79.

87. Thomas Aquinas *Summa theol.* 1.85.1; *Expositio Super Librum Boethii de Trinitate* 5.2.

88. Thomas Aquinas *Summa theol.* 1.85.3.

account for the fact that Aquinas infers what is good for humans from what their natural inclinations are, if these are accidental to being good? Clearly, we make inferences about things insofar as we understand the sorts of things they are. Hence, we make inferences on the basis of our conceptions of their form, and not necessarily on the basis of concepts. Since, in the case of good, the feature central to our conception is being the object of natural inclination, inferences about what is good for us are understandable based on that to which we think we are naturally inclined, in the sense of genuinely factually desiring. Of course, there may be a further question about why such an inference is rational, or why it produces knowledge ("scientia"), but this would require a lengthy treatment of Aquinas's epistemological views, which I cannot take up here.[89]

CONCLUSION

A deep difficulty for moral philosophers is that in their analysis of the nature of good they seem to be pulled in opposite directions. That something is good for us must provide some motivation for us to bring that thing about. Our good must be something that interests and attracts us. Hence, it is thought, being the object of our inclinations must be (at least) part of what it is to be good for us. This view leads one in the direction of moral subjectivism and moral relativism.

On the other hand, it seems that the fact that something is good or evil cannot depend on whether we are attracted to it or repulsed by it. As W. D. Ross wrote in his classic work *The Right and the Good*, "it is surely a strange reversal of the natural order of thought to say that our admiring an action either is, or is what necessitates, its being good. We think of its goodness as what we admire in it, and as something it would have even if no one admired it, something it has in itself."[90] This view moves us toward moral objectivism.

---

89. For a fuller discussion of Aquinas's epistemological views, see my "Knowledge, Faith and Philosophy in Thomas Aquinas," doctoral dissertation, Oxford University, 1989, especially chapter 1, "The Natural Light of the Intellect."

90. W. D. Ross, *The Right and the Good* (Oxford: Clarendon, 1930), p. 89.

In this essay I have argued for an interpretation of Aquinas which goes some way toward accommodating both of these apparently conflicting intuitions. Our conception, our understanding, of good is as 'that to which all things are naturally inclined'. This definition takes an accidental attribute of goodness, being the object of creaturely natural inclinations (*appetitus*), and marks off the good as that which is the spring of such actual natural inclinations in the creatures on this earth. In this way an accidental attribute is used in the definition of 'good'. But although our own dispositions to desire are intimately involved in our understanding of and reasoning about what is good for us, nevertheless being good does not consist in being the object of such desires: rather, being able to move us to desire is an effect of and posterior to being good. As Aquinas writes, "bonum numeratur inter prima."[91]

University of Notre Dame

---

91. Thomas Aquinas *Sent. Ethic.* 1.1.

Duns Scotus on Signification
DOMINIK PERLER

In both versions of his *Commentary on the Sentences*, Scotus alludes to a great controversy among his contemporaries over the question of whether a spoken word signifies a thing or a concept. He does not give a detailed account of this controversy, but confines himself to saying, "in short, I grant that what is properly signified by a spoken word is a thing."[1] This brief statement may seem trivial at first sight, but it turns out to be innovative when it is assessed against the background of medieval Aristotelian semantic theory. From Boethius onwards, the overwhelming majority of the commentators on *De interpretatione* held that it is a concept and not a thing that is primarily and directly signified by a spoken word.[2]

---

1. John Duns Scotus *Ordinatio* 1.27.1–3 in *Opera Omnia*, ed. Commissio Scotistica (Vatican City: Typis Polyglottis, 1950–   ) 6:97. "Licet magna altercatio fiat de 'voce,' utrum sit signum rei vel conceptus, tamen breviter concedo quod illud quod signatur per vocem proprie, est res." See also John Duns Scotus *Lectura in librum primum Sententiarum* 1.27.1–3 (Commissio Scotistica 17:357).

2. See Boethius *Commentarii in librum Aristotelis Peri hermeneias* 1.1, ed. C. Meiser (Leipzig: Teubner, 1880 and 1877), pp. 38–40; and Boethius *Commentarii in librum Aristotelis* 2.1 (Meiser pp. 25–29). An extensive commentary on these crucial passages is provided by John Magee, *Boethius on Signification and Mind* (Leiden: Brill, 1989), pp. 49–92. On the medieval reception, see Jean Isaac, *Le Peri hermeneias en occident de Boèce à Saint Thomas: Histoire littéraire d'un traité d'Aristote* (Paris: Vrin, 1953), pp. 35–97. On the most important thirteenth-century commentators, see the thorough

In this paper, I intend to examine the reasons that led Scotus to criticize and revise the dominant theory. Such an examination can scarcely be restricted to a logico-semantical analysis.³ An adequate understanding of the relationship between a sign and its significate not only necessitates an examination of the question of *how* this relationship is established, but also a discussion of the question of *what* exactly the sign and the significate are—what kind of entities they are. Therefore, the following analysis aims at investigating not only the semantic aspects of Scotus's theory of signification, but also its ontological commitments.

CLASSIFICATION OF SIGNS

Scotus discusses the semantic function of words within the framework of a general theory of signs. He states that signs can be classified by regarding either (a) their relation to the significate or (b) the significate itself.⁴ (a) If signs are classified as regards their relation to the significate, they can be divided into natural and conventional signs. Natural signs have a significative function by nature; they are linked to their significate by a real relation. Conventional

---

historical introduction in Thomas Aquinas *Expositio libri Peryermenias*, ed. R.-A. Gauthier (Rome/Paris: Commissio Leonina and Vrin, 1989), pp. 64*–84*. Roger Bacon also claims that a spoken word directly signifies a thing; see his *Compendium studii theologiae* 2.2, ed. T. S. Maloney (Leiden: Brill, 1988), p. 68. However, Bacon differs significantly from Scotus in his explanation of what the signified thing is (for which, see below). Because of this different ontological commitment, it would be misleading to introduce Scotus and Bacon as two allies fighting together against the traditional theory.

3. Daniel O. Dahlstrom, in "Signification and Logic: Scotus on Universals from a Logical Point of View," *Vivarium* 18 (1980): 83, chooses a logico-semantical approach, claiming that "Scotus greatly insures the autonomy of logic from metaphysics, psychology, and grammar." Marmo points out the inadequacies of this approach; see his "Ontology and Semantics in the Logic of Duns Scotus," in *On the Medieval Theory of Signs*, ed. Umberto Eco and C. Marmo (Amsterdam and Philadelphia: John Benjamins, 1989), pp. 143–144. Scotus elaborated a theory of signs, including their epistemological and ontological aspects, rather than an autonomous logic.

4. Scotus *Reportatio* 4.1.2 in *Opera Omnia* 23, ed. L. Wadding (rptd. Paris: Vivès, 1891–95), p. 546.

signs receive their significative function *ad placitum*; they are linked to their significate only by a conceptual relation.[5] Nevertheless, the relation beween conventional signs and their significate does exist. Scotus emphasizes that everything that does not include a contradiction exists, whether it has real or conceptual existence,[6] and he claims that a relation (whether real or conceptual) is a peculiar being that cannot be reduced to any other category of being.[7]

Scotus's distinction between natural and conventional signs is traditional. It can be found in many medieval classifications of signs. Natural signs were usually subdivided into non-linguistic natural signs —the groaning of a sick person (natural sign of the sickness) or the barking of a dog (natural sign of its excitement)—and linguistic natural signs.[8] Following Aristotle's *De interpretatione* 1.16a3–8 and Augustine's *De Trinitate* 15.10–11, many medieval commentators identified the linguistic natural signs with the "affections in the soul" (*passiones animae*) or the "words in the heart" (*verba in corde*) that are the same for all human beings, regardless of the language they speak.[9]

Scotus gives examples only for conventional signs, namely, the gestures of monks living under a vow of silence (non-linguistic conventional signs) and spoken words (linguistic conventional signs). These signs are called conventional, "because they can signify other things as well as these things, if it suited the people who impose [the signs]."[10] Thus, conventional signs are distinguished by two features: they can have significates other than those they happen to have, and their signification is arbitrarily fixed by the sign-users.

5. Scotus *Reportatio* 4.1.2 (Wadding 23:546).
6. Scotus *Quodl.* 3 (Wadding 25:114).
7. See Mark G. Henninger, *Relations: Medieval Theories, 1250–1325* (Oxford: Clarendon Press, 1989), pp. 68–97 (with numerous references).
8. See, for instance, Roger Bacon *De signis* in "An Unedited Part of Roger Bacon's *Opus Maius: De signis*," ed. Karin Margareta Fredborg, Lauge Olaf Nielsen, and Jan Pinborg, *Traditio* 34 (1978): 82–84. On the sources of this division, see Alfonso Maierù, "*Signum* dans la culture médiévale," in *Sprache und Erkenntnis im Mittelalter: Akten des VI. Internationalen Kongresses für mittelalterliche Philosophie*, ed. Wolfgang Kluxen et al., Miscellanea Mediaevalia 13 (Berlin and New York: de Gruyter, 1981) 1:51–72.
9. On the distinction between natural and conventional signs, which was a *topos* of medieval philosophy from Boethius onwards, see J. Engels, "Origine, sens et survie du terme boécien '*secundum placitum*'," *Vivarium* 1 (1963): 87–115.
10. Scotus *Reportatio* 4.1.2 (Wadding 23:546).

The relation between a conventional sign and its significate is conceptual, for the sign exists *qua* sign (not *qua* material thing) only if it is linked to a concept. The spoken word 'human being', for instance, has a significative function only if it is associated with the concept *human being*; otherwise, it would simply be a noise. The monk's gestures can be labeled a sign only if the monk intends to make some other monk understand something; otherwise, the gestures would simply be a movement of the body.

To whose concept must a conventional sign be related in order to have a significative function: to the concept of the sign-user, of the sign-receiver, or of both? Scotus distinguishes between a perfect and an imperfect use of a conventional sign, taking the spoken noun as example. If such a noun is used perfectly, both the utterer and the hearer must associate it with a concept. The use is imperfect if the utterer never associates the spoken noun with a concept (as with a well-trained parrot repeating words it has heard) or if the utterer actually cannot associate the spoken noun with a concept (as with a Latin speaker who utters a Hebrew word without knowing Hebrew).[11] Scotus does not mention the case in which only the utterer, but not the hearer, associates the spoken noun with a concept (as with a Latin speaker talking in Latin to a public that understands only Hebrew). Nor does he discuss the case in which utterer and hearer associate two different concepts with one and the same spoken noun (as with a German speaker who utters the word 'gift' and associates the concept *poison* with it, while an English hearer associates the concept *present*). Presumably, Scotus also classifies these cases as imperfect uses of conventional signs.

(b) If signs are classified as regards their significate, they can be divided as follows: some signs have their "significate with them" (*signatum secum*). They are necessarily accompanied by their significate, thus being "true and effective." Some natural signs, Scotus writes, belong to this class. An eclipse, for instance, is such a sign, since it is necessarily accompanied by the interposition of the earth

---

11. Scotus *Reportatio* 1A.22.unica (Commissio Scotistica 5:390). Although both the parrot and the Latin speaker uttering a Hebrew word lack a concept, Scotus clearly distinguishes the two cases. The Latin speaker is able to learn Hebrew and, consequently, to associate a concept with the Hebrew word; the parrot never has this ability.

between sun and moon.¹² Other signs lack the co-presence of the significate. When someone utters a proposition, the proposition is not necessarily accompanied by its significate, since a proposition can express something that is not the case, no longer the case, or not yet the case. That is why a proposition can be a "false sign" as well as a "true sign."¹³

It is clear from these general distinctions that Scotus classifies spoken words among the conventional signs that are not necessarily accompanied by their significate. This claim raises at least two important questions. (1) How is the relationship between a spoken word and its significate established, and what is the significate—the extramental thing itself or its mental representation? (2) How can the utterer of a spoken word judge whether he or she utters a true sign in the absence of the significate?

RELATIONS OF SIGNIFICATION

Scotus's answers to these questions can be found in his commentary on *De interpretatione* (extant in two versions), where he discusses the question of what a spoken word signifies.¹⁴ He opens the discussion with the remark that "the question is not understood regarding nouns that are imposed to signify likenesses (*similitudines*) or species, but regarding every other noun, whatever it might be imposed on, such as 'human being,' 'animal,' etc."¹⁵ Although this remark seems to be made in passing, it should not be overlooked, since it

---

12. Scotus *Reportatio* (Wadding 23:546). Note that not all natural signs are accompanied by their significate. A hoofprint, for example, is a natural sign referring to a horse, but it is not necessarily accompanied by a horse.

13. Scotus *Reportatio* 4.1.2 (Wadding 23:546).

14. See Scotus *In primum librum Perihermeneias quaestiones* 2 (Wadding 1:540–44), hereafter cited as *In Perih.*, and *In duos libros Perihermeneias, operis secundi, quod appellant, quaestiones octo* 1 (Wadding 1:582–85), hereafter cited as *In Perih. II*. There are still some difficulties concerning the authenticity of and the relationship between these two works, which I will not discuss here. (The final word remains to be said by the scholars at the Franciscan Institute in St. Bonaventure, who are preparing the critical edition.) My analysis will mostly be based on the first set of questions.

15. Scotus *In Perih.* 2 (Wadding 1:540).

fixes the scope of the entire investigation. (i) Scotus excludes nouns exclusively signifying mental entities or mental acts (e.g., 'concept', 'thought'), because such nouns never have an extramental significate. (ii) By citing the examples 'human being' and 'animal', which are nouns of first imposition, Scotus seems to leave out of account the nouns of second imposition, i.e., the nouns that signify other nouns (e.g., 'substantive').[16] (iii) The examples suggest that Scotus confines the investigation to common nouns (or general terms), disregarding singular terms such as 'Socrates'. This restriction deserves special attention, since common nouns are exactly the nouns on which the controversial debate over universals focuses. The common noun 'animal', for instance, is the noun signifying the genus *animal*, so that the question "What is the significance of 'animal'?" is closely related to the question "What is the genus *animal*?"

Scotus gives two alternatives for explaining the significate of a spoken common noun: it is either a thing (*res*) or a species in the soul (*species in anima*). He defines the species as an "intelligible likeness of intelligible objects that is in the intellect as in a subject, just as a sensible species is a likeness of a sensible thing that is in a sense as in a subject."[17] The intelligible species is a mental entity—ontologically speaking, a quality of the intellect—which is produced by the intellect on the basis of a sensible species and which functions to represent the understood thing. The relationship between sensible and intelligible species may be explained as follows. When someone sees a table, he or she first receives a kind of visual image of the table in the sensitive part of the soul (the sensible species of the table), and then he or she is able to produce a cognitive image of the table in the intellective part of the soul (the intelligible species). Sensible and intelligible species are distinct, since they are in two distinct parts (or *facultates*) of the soul.[18] In contrast to the sensible species, the intelligible species is

---

16. On this distinction, which has its origin in late ancient grammar, see Mario Dal Pra, "Sulla dottrina della *impositio prima et secunda*," *Rivista critica di storia della filosofia* 9 (1954): 390–399; and Christian Knudsen, "Intentions and Impositions," in CHLMP, pp. 479–495.

17. Scotus *In Perih.* 2 (Wadding 1:540).

18. This is, of course, a simplified account of the production and interrelation of the species. For a detailed introduction to the epistemological species-theory, which is closely related to optical theory, see A. Mark Smith, "Getting the Big

not merely a passing imprint of the thing, but a cognitive image that can exist even when the represented thing is not present.[19] Being a kind of mental counterpart to the thing, the intelligible species is also called a *similitudo*.[20]

Since the intelligible species is necessary for an act of intellective understanding, one might claim that it is also necessary for an act of signifying, assuming that a person uses the word 'table' significantly (and not just as a noise) if he or she signifies the mental likeness of a table. This assumption is at the core of the discussion, for it raises the question: In what sense is the intelligible species necessary for an act of signifying? Is it only a mediating mental entity between a conventional sign and its significate, or is it the significate itself?

Scotus answers this question by distinguishing two aspects of the intelligible species: its ontological status and its function. He claims that a species can be regarded either insofar as it is an accident affecting the soul, or insofar as it represents a thing.[21] The species considered under the first aspect, i.e., under the ontological aspect of its existence as a mental accident, is not the significate of a spoken word. Otherwise one would be led to make some odd inferences. First, one would have to admit that every noun signifies an accident. Even a noun such as 'human being' would signify only an

---

Picture in Perspectivist Optics," *Isis* 72 (1981): 568–589. The division of the soul into a vegetative, a sensitive, and an intellective part is an Aristotelian *topos*. On the medieval reception, see the thorough historical introduction in Thomas Aquinas *Sentencia libri De anima*, ed. R.-A. Gauthier (Rome and Paris: Commissio Leonina and Vrin, 1984), pp. 201*–282*.

19. Scotus expounds his species-theory in *Ordinatio* 1.3.3.1 (Commissio Scotistica 3:209–44), and *Quaestiones super lib. Arist. De anima* 14 and 17 (Wadding 3:549–53 and 575–93). On the sensible species, see John Duns Scotus *Ordinatio* 1.3.3.2 (Commissio Scotistica 3:299). On the epistemological background of this theory, see Richard E. Dumont, "The Role of Phantasm in the Psychology of Duns Scotus," *Monist* 49 (1965): 617–633, and Katherine H. Tachau, *Vision and Certitude in the Age of Ockham: Optics, Epistemology, and the Foundations of Semantics, 1250–1345* (Leiden: Brill, 1988), pp. 62–81.

20. See Scotus *In Perih.* 2 (Wadding 1:540). The synonymous use of these expressions was probably initiated by Roger Bacon; see his *De multiplicatione specierum* 1.1 in *Roger Bacon's Philosophy of Nature*, ed. David C. Lindberg (Oxford: Clarendon Press, 1983), p. 2. On Bacon's influence on late thirteenth-century semantics, see Tachau, *Vision and Certitude*, pp. 11–26.

21. Scotus *In Perih.* 2 (Wadding 1:541).

accident, for the intelligible species of a human being is an accident existing in the intellect. But this claim is evidently false, since 'human being' signifies a substance and not an accident. Second, one would have to grant that every affirmative predicative proposition is false, since by saying 'Human being is an animal' one affirms that the significate of the predicate term inheres in the significate of the subject term. But the intelligible species of animal considered as a mental accident can never inhere in the intelligible species of human being considered as a mental accident; it is impossible to "merge" two mental accidents. Thus, one could never affirm 'Human being is an animal', which is obviously absurd. Third, every existential claim would be true, even such a claim as 'The Antichrist exists', for the intelligible species of Antichrist considered as a mental accident exists independently of the extramental Antichrist.[22] In light of the odd consequences following from the claim that a spoken word signifies the species *qua* mental accident, Scotus insists that a spoken word signifies the species only if the species is considered under its second aspect, namely in its significative function.[23]

But what is the intelligible species *qua* sign? How is its significative function to be understood? This function, Scotus claims, consists in directing the intellect to something which is not identical with the sign itself. If the intelligible species is taken as a sign, it necessarily directs the intellect to something other than itself, and the same applies to the spoken word. Thus, speaking about signification we have to distinguish two levels of signs. There is a *spoken sign* (word) that directs the intellect to a *mental sign* (intelligible species) that itself directs the intellect to a thing. The spoken sign has two significates: (a) the species as its immediate significate; and, (b) the thing as its mediate significate (also called the *ultimatum significatum*).[24] It is important to note that the immediate significate is *necessarily* a sign; it must direct the intellect to the mediate, ultimate significate.

The distinction of two significates enables Scotus to say that by uttering a word we speak about the thing itself and not merely about our intelligible species of the thing, although it is the intelligible

---

22. Scotus adduces these examples among others in In *Perih.* 2 (Wadding 1:541).
23. See Scotus In *Perih.* 2 (Wadding 1:541).
24. Scotus In *Perih.* 2 (Wadding 1:541). See also In *Perih.* II 1 (Wadding p 1:583).

species that is immediately signified. The fact that we signify the thing mediately does not hinder us from signifying it *simpliciter*.[25]

One might object that this is an oversimplified account, for we do not always signify a thing. When a person speaks about his or her cognitive image of human beings, the noun 'human being' signifies his or her intelligible species of human beings and not the human beings as extramental things. Of course, Scotus replies, it is possible to signify a species not only as a sign for a thing, but also as a significate in itself. But such a signification requires a reflexive act, for the first act of understanding and signifying is always directed toward the thing. For instance, in a first, direct act the noun 'human being' signifies human beings, and in a second, reflexive act it signifies the intelligible species of human beings. Scotus stresses, however, that the significative function is always conventionally imposed on a word. So, the users of the word 'human being' could determine that henceforth this word signifies immediately the intelligible species of human beings and no longer extramental human beings. In that case, there would be a primary signification of a species.[26] But this fact does not weaken or refute the general thesis that a spoken word, taken in its ordinary imposition, signifies a species only by means of a reflexive act, because the direct signification of a species can be obtained only on the basis of a new conventional imposition that cancels the ordinary one. And since such an imposition is purely conventional, there is no reason why 'human being' should receive a new imposition and signify the species of a human being; any word would do as well.

However, there seems to be a conflict between Scotus's position developed in the two commentaries on *De interpretatione* (probably written between 1293 and 1297), and his theory presented in the *Ordinatio* and *Lectura* (written between 1297 and 1304).[27] In his *Ordinatio* and *Lectura*, Scotus does not use the distinction between an immediate and a mediate, ultimate significate, but simply says that

---

25. Scotus *In Perih. II* (Wadding 1:542).
26. Scotus *In Perih.* 2 (Wadding 1:543) and *In Perih. II* 1 (Wadding 1:582).
27. On the chronology of Scotus's work, see C. Balić, "The Life and Works of John Duns Scotus," in *John Duns Scotus 1265–1965*, ed. John K. Ryan and Bernardino M. Bonansea (Washington, D.C.: Catholic University of America Press, 1965), pp. 1–27. See also the brief remarks in Allan B. Wolter, *The Philosophical Theology of John Duns Scotus*, ed. Marilyn McCord Adams (Ithaca: Cornell University Press, 1991), p. 103.

a spoken word signifies a thing.[28] Some scholars have tried to explain this discrepancy by distinguishing an "early theory," according to which the intelligible species is the primary significate and the thing the secondary, mediate significate, from a "later theory," according to which the thing is the primary significate.[29]

But is there enough textual support for an explanation of this sort, based on the hypothesis of a change in Scotus's thought? Although Scotus does not use the expressions 'mediate' and 'immediate' significate' in the putatively later works, he clearly distinguishes between the significate strictly speaking (*proprie*) and the significate by priority (*propter prioritatem*). He explains this distinction by comparing the relationship between thing, intelligible species, and spoken word with the relationship between a cause and its effects:[30]

Let us posit a cause x that has two effects, a and b. The effects are hierarchically structured; a is a proximate effect and b a remote effect. Now one might say that a is the cause of b, since a is between x and b. But that would be a fallacy, for a has only a priority in the hierarchical order of the effects. The proper cause of b is always the cause x. Scotus cites the sun that illumines many parts of a medium as an example,[31] but he does not spell out the hierarchical relationship among the effects. We may fill out his argument with the following example: the sun illumines a table in illuminating all the particles of air, i.e., of the medium between the sun and the table.[32] The table can only be illumined if the mediating air is illumined. But that does

---

28. See note 1 above.
29. See E. P. Bos, "The Theory of the Proposition According to John Duns Scotus' Two Commentaries on Aristotle's *Perihermeneias*," in *Logos and Pragma: Essays on the Philosophy of Language in Honour of Professor Gabriel Nuchelmans*, ed. L. M. de Rijk and H. A. G. Braakhuis (Nijmegen: Ingenium Publishers, 1987), p. 127. Marmo, "Ontology and Semantics," p. 164, speaks more cautiously of a "mature position" in the *Ordinatio* and *Lectura*, without sharply distinguishing it from an early theory.
30. See Scotus *Ordinatio* 1.27.1–3 (Commissio Scotistica 6:97).
31. Scotus *Ordinatio* 1.27.1–3 (Commissio Scotistica 6:97).
32. It is likely that Scotus has the air in mind when he speaks about the medium of the sun. In *Reportatio* 2.13.unica (Wadding 23:42–47), he discusses at length the function of light and of the air as transmitting medium. For an extensive discussion (with a new edition of this passage), see Edward R. McCarthy, "Medieval Light Theory and Optics and Duns Scotus' Treatment of Light in D. 13 of Book II of his Commentary on the Sentences," doctoral dissertation, City University of New York, 1976.

not amount to saying that the air illumines the table. The sun is the proper cause for both the illumination of the medium air (the proximate effect) and of the table (the remote effect).[33]

Identifying the thing with the cause and the signs with the effects, Scotus claims that the intelligible species is the proximate effect a, and the spoken word the remote effect b. Since the intelligible species is between the thing and the spoken word, it may seem to be the cause of the spoken word. But the intelligible species has only a hierarchical priority; there cannot be a spoken word without there previously being an intelligible species (just as the table cannot be illumined if the medium air is not illumined). Despite this priority, the proper cause of the spoken word is always the thing itself (just as the sun is always the proper cause of the illumination of the table).[34]

This relationship between a cause and its two effects, one of which is proximate and the other remote, is a specific type of an essential order, as Scotus explains in the first chapter of *De primo principio*.[35] There he distinguishes two types of essential order obtaining between a cause and two effects. (i) Either the first cause x causes the effect a, and a in turn causes the effect b. In that case there is a causal essential order, for the first effect is the direct cause of the second. (ii) Or the first cause x causes the effect a immediately and the effect b mediately. In that case there is a non-causal essential order; the first effect only has a mediating and not a causal function. Nevertheless, this second type is an essential order, Scotus says, "Since each effect is essentially

---

33. A. Vos in "On the Philosophy of the Young Duns Scotus: Some Semantical and Logical Aspects," in *Medieval Semantics and Metaphysics*, ed. E. P. Bos (Nijmegen: Ingenium, 1985), p. 200, tries to explain Scotus's argument by saying: "The sun illumines the whole medium, but the illumination of the nearest parts comes first." This interpretation is correct as regards *Lectura* 1.27.1–3 (Commissio Scotistica 17:357) where Scotus holds, "pars remota immediate illuminatur a sole sicut pars propinqua, et tamen prius natura illuminatur pars propinqua quam remota (ponendo quod una pars adhuc non illuminet aliam)." But Vos's explanation is hardly adequate for the passage in the *Ordinatio* (cited in note 31), because there Scotus does not simply say that the sun reaches one part earlier than the other. His point is rather that the sun reaches the remote effect only insofar as it is mediated by the proximate effect.

34. Scotus *Ordinatio* 1.27.1–3 (Commissio Scotistica 6:97).

35. See Scotus *De primo principio* 1.9–14 in *A Treatise on God as First Principle*, ed. Allan B. Wolter (Chicago: Franciscan Herald Press, 1966), pp. 4–8, or Scotus *De primo principio* 1.4–6 in *Abhandlung über das erste Prinzip*, ed. Wolfgang Kluxen, 2d ed. (Darmstadt: Wissenschaftliche Buchgesellschaft, 1987), pp. 4–8.

ordered to some common third which is their mutual cause, it follows that these effects are also essentially ordered to one another."[36] So, we may conclude that Scotus applies a metaphysical distinction on a semantic problem by explaining the relationship between a thing (cause), an intelligible species (proximate effect), and a word (remote effect) as the non-causal essential order obtaining between a cause and two hierarchically structured effects.

This explanation makes it clear that Scotus does not completely give up the distinction between an immediate and a mediate, ultimate significate in his so-called later works. It would hardly be adequate to draw a sharp distinction between an "early" and a "late" theory. Nevertheless, there is a certain development in Scotus's works. In his commentaries on *De interpretatione*, he speaks about two ways of explaining signification. According to the first, the spoken word signifies the intelligible species; according to the second, it signifies the thing. He favors the second, but seems to be undecided and does not completely reject the first.[37] In his *Ordinatio* and *Lectura*, instead, he makes it clear that he opts for the second way. But his choice includes a subtle addition, a kind of concession to the first way. The spoken word, he says, is only the remote effect of the thing. Between the thing and the spoken word there is still the intelligible species, the proximate effect of the thing. Because of its hierarchical priority (*propter prioritatem*), the species may be called the immediate significate of the spoken word. Yet it is not the significate strictly speaking (*proprie*).

One might object that it is misleading to claim that the ultimate significate of a spoken word (according to the commentaries on *De interpretatione*) or the proper cause of a spoken word (according to the *Ordinatio* and the *Lectura*) is a thing, if by 'thing' one understands an extramentally existing thing, since we can speak about objects that do not exist any more (e.g., by uttering the proposition 'Caesar is a man') or which do not yet exist (e.g., by uttering 'The Antichrist will come') or which never exist (e.g., by uttering 'Chimera is an animal'). Scotus replies to this objection that "the thing is primarily signified, however, not insofar as it exists (since it is not in this way that it is

---

36. Scotus *De primo principio* 1.14 in *Treatise on God* (Wolter p. 8); see also Wolter's commentary, pp. 170–171.
37. Scotus *In Perih.* 2 (Wadding 1:544) and *In Perih. II* 1 (Wadding 1:585).

understood *per se*), but insofar as it is perceived *per se* by the intellect; that is, [insofar as it is] the essence of the thing which is signified by the definition [and] which is the first object of the intellect."[38] This distinction between the thing insofar as it exists (*res ut existit*) and the thing insofar as it is understood (*res ut intelligitur*) plays a crucial role in Scotus's theory of signification and is extensively discussed in both commentaries on *De interpretatione*.[39]

Before considering the details of this distinction, we should counter the objection that the entire argument is self-contradictory. On the one hand, Scotus claims that the thing and not the intelligible species is signified by a spoken word; on the other hand, he says that the "thing as it is understood" is the significate. Is the "thing as it is understood" not the intelligible species, since this species is by definition a cognitive image of the thing, thus representing the thing exactly as it is understood?

This objection overlooks an important point in Scotus's argument. To signify the "thing as it is understood" is not to signify a mental entity representing the thing. Scotus holds that signifying presupposes understanding; a spoken word can be imposed to signify something only if the thing has previously been understood. But this is not tantamount to saying that what the spoken word signifies is the understanding of the thing (i.e., the mental entity representing the thing). Once the spoken word has received its significative function, it always has the capability to signify the thing, even if no one performs an act of understanding.[40] Thus, 'human being' has the capability to signify human beings even if no one actually thinks about human beings and, consequently, even if no one produces an intelligible species of human beings. It is clear, therefore, that since the "thing as it is understood" is independent of the production of an intelligible species, it ought not to be identified with this species.

The "thing as it is understood," then, is identical neither with the thing as it exists nor with a mental species of the thing. What is it?

---

38. Scotus *In Perih.* 2 (Wadding 1:543).

39. The most important passages are Scotus *In Perih.* 3 (Wadding 1:545–46), the "conclusio" and "solutio," and *In Perih II* 1 (Wadding 1:586). There is no discussion in the *Ordinatio* and *Lectura*. Scotus does not seem to have developed or changed his theory as regards this point.

40. Scotus *In Perih.* 3 (Wadding 1:545–46).

Unfortunately, Scotus does not give a detailed answer to this obvious question. In his first commentary on *De interpretatione*, he simply calls it the "essence of the thing, which is signified by the definition," and in his second commentary, he labels it the *quod quid est*, thus referring to Aristotle's *to ti ên einai*.[41] This scant explanation still leaves open the question of what the essence of the thing is. Is it something in the existing thing or distinct from it?

THE ONTOLOGY OF SIGNIFICATES

In order to find an answer to this ontological question, we shall turn from the commentaries on *De interpretatione* to the commentaries on the *Sentences* and on the *Metaphysics*, which treat ontological problems extensively. In his *Reportata Parisiensia* Scotus discusses at length the question of how essence and existence are related to each other—a much contested issue at the University of Paris in the late thirteenth century.[42] Referring to the principle that one should not posit a plurality of entities without necessity, he holds that the essence of a thing is not in reality a distinct entity, preceding the existing thing.[43] Two entities are distinct in reality only if they are separable, that is, only if one of them can be without the other. The essence of a thing, however, is not a thing separable from the existing thing itself.[44] Nevertheless, there is a distinction between essence and existence, since one can understand the two in distinct ways. Scotus cites the following classical example in order to illustrate this distinction.[45] Let us admit that no rose exists, and let us further admit *per impossibile* that the divine intellect does not exist, so that

---

41. See Scotus *In Perih.* 2 (Wadding 1:543), cited in note 38, and *In Perih II* 1 (Wadding 1:583).

42. On the background of this debate, see John F. Wippel, "Essence and Existence," in CHLMP, pp. 385–410.

43. See Scotus *Reportatio* 2.1.2 (Wadding 22:526).

44. The strong realist designation of the essence as a thing (*res*), opposed to the existence as one thing to another, was used by Giles of Rome. See John F. Wippel, *The Metaphysical Thought of Godfrey of Fontaines: A Study in Late Thirteenth-Century Philosophy* (Washington, D.C.: Catholic University of America Press, 1981), pp. 46–53.

45. See Scotus *Reportatio* 2.1.2 (Wadding 22:527).

there is not even a rose in the divine intellect. If then a created intellect exists, it can still have an understanding of a rose, since it can grasp the essence of a rose. Thus, the essence of a rose can be understood distinct from its existence, though in reality it is not separable from the existing rose.

Now one could suppose that the distinction between essence and existence is purely conceptual; it is a distinction which the intellect produces by conceiving a thing in different ways. But Scotus rejects the conceptual distinction as well as the real distinction. He claims that, in being grasped by the intellect, the essence is not produced by the intellect. It is rather "in potency before the act of existing."[46] Since the essence *is* (though only potentially) before the existence, and since being-in-potency does not depend on being grasped or being conceived, the distinction between essence and existence is preconceptual.

So, how is this distinction to be explained? Some modern commentators[47] have argued that here Scotus applies his famous "formal distinction." This intermediary distinction between the real and the conceptual distinction obtains between two *rationes*[48] of a thing which differ in their definition and can be conceived one without the other, but in reality constitute one thing.[49] For example, God's attributes (omnipotence, omniscience, infinitude, etc.) are formally distinct, since they can be distinctly conceived, but in reality constitute one thing.[50] In the same way, one may argue, essence and existence in creatures are formally distinct, since they are distinctly conceivable, though in reality they constitute one individual thing.

Wolter has challenged this interpretation by referring to a passage in the *Quodlibeta*, where Scotus holds, "One can say that essence

---

46. Scotus *Reportatio* 2.1.2 (Wadding 22:528).

47. See Andrew J. O'Brien, "Duns Scotus' Teaching on the Distinction Between Essence and Existence," *New Scholasticism* 38 (1964): 65–77, with the references there.

48. Besides 'ratio' Scotus also uses the expressions 'formalitas' and 'intentio'. See Scotus *Ordinatio* 1.2.2.1–4 (Commissio Scotistica 2:355–58), and *Reportatio* 2.1.6 (Wadding 12:556).

49. On the formal distinction, see Wolter, *Philosophical Theology*, pp. 27–41.

50. On Scotus's theory of God's nature, see Wolter, *Philosophical Theology*, pp. 254–277. Note that for Scotus there is a *formal distinction only between God's attributes*, not between God's essence and God's existence.

and its existence in creatures are related to each other as quiddity and mode; therefore they are distinct."[51] According to this statement (the authenticity of which is questionable, however, since it occurs in an *additio* rather than in the text itself), there is a modal distinction between essence and existence. Existence adds the proper mode of being to every essence (with the exception of God's). To the essence of a present, living person, for instance, it adds the mode of actual existence, while to the essence of an imaginary person it adds the mode of fictive existence. Since this mode is only added, it is extrinsic to the essence and "quasi-accidental."[52] Yet existence is not a real accident, because accidents, in a strict sense, are descriptive; they increase the conceivability of the substance in which they inhere. The more accidents we can describe, the better we can conceive the substance. When we examine a table (substance) that is brown, square, hard, etc. (accidents), we can say that the more accidents we are able to describe, the better we understand how the table is. Existence, however, does not increase the conceivability of the essence to which it is added; by grasping the existence of a table we do not gain a better knowledge of *how* the table is, we just know *that* it is.

Scotus's ontological discussion of the relationship between essence and existence has a strong impact on his theory of signification. In emphasizing that a spoken word signifies the "thing as it is understood" and not the "thing as it exists," Scotus makes clear that essence and existence are distinctly signified. And what is signified in a distinct way is also understood in a distinct way, since signifying presupposes understanding.[53]

So, we may conclude, Scotus resolves the problem of how a spoken word directly signifies the thing by introducing a crucial metaphysical distinction, namely that between essence and existence. Claiming that a spoken word signifies a thing does not amount to saying that it signifies the thing as it exists, as one may spontaneously suggest. This claim only implies that a spoken word directly signifies the essence of the thing, the essence that is distinguishable from the thing's existence. It is important to note that it is by means of a

---

51. See Wolter, *Philosophical Theology*, p. 281; Scotus *Quodl.* 1 (Wadding 15:9–10).
52. See Wolter, *Philosophical Theology*, p. 283.
53. Scotus *In Perih.* 2 (Wadding 1:540). It is assumed, of course, that what is signified is first understood in the same way.

metaphysical distinction that Scotus answers the *semantical* question of what a spoken word signifies. He needs such a metaphysical distinction because he tries to escape from the following dilemma: either he sticks to the traditional Boethian answer, claiming that a spoken word directly signifies the intelligible species. But then he has to admit that a spoken word merely signifies a mental entity so that we can never establish an immediate relationship between language and reality. Or he preserves this immediate relationship and claims that a spoken word signifies the existing thing. But then he can hardly explain how we are able to signify something although the significate does not actually exist (e.g., the dead Caesar) or not really exist (e.g., a chimera). Scotus clearly sees that both ways are unsatisfying and chooses a third one that is based on a metaphysical assumption: we can preserve an immediate relationship between language and reality *and* the possibility to signify non-existing things if we recognize that a spoken word signifies the essence of a thing, distinct from its existence.

But what is the signified essence? Is it something common, or something individual, or something neither common nor individual? This is obviously a complex metaphysical question that needs to be examined in a separate study. I just want to give some hints.

Scotus has confined himself in this discussion to common nouns such as 'human being' and 'animal'. These nouns signify a common essence or common nature (*natura communis*).[54] 'Human being' signifies the nature of every human being, regardless of its existence or nonexistence. However, this human nature is not something additional to or in reality separable from every individual human being. It is always individuated by the "this-ness" (*haecceitas*) of this or that human being and is therefore signified insofar as it is individuated.[55] When we say 'Caesar is a man', we signify the common nature *man* insofar as it is individuated by Caesar's *haecceitas*. The fact that Caesar no longer

---

54. See, for instance, Scotus *Ordinatio* 2.3 (Commissio Scotistica 7:403). For a thorough discussion of the common nature, see Tamar M. Rudavsky, "The Doctrine of Individuation in Duns Scotus," *Franziskanische Studien* 62 (1980): 62–79.

55. On Scotus's theory of individuation, see Wolter, *Philosophical Theology*, pp. 68–97 (especially 68–69, n. 1, where the most relevant passages are cited); Kenneth C. Clatterbaugh, "Individuation in the Ontology of Duns Scotus," *Franciscan Studies* 32 (1972): 65–73; Tamar M. Rudavsky, "The Doctrine of Individuation in Duns Scotus," *Franziskanische Studien* 59 (1977): 320–377.

exists does not hinder us from signifying his individuated common nature which is distinguishable from his existence. In uttering the true proposition 'Caesar is a man' we predicate of Caesar only the essence *man*, not the essence together with the existence. Such a predication is always true, because the essence is predicated *per se* of a subject.[56] And there must be a *per se* predication (also called 'essential predication'[57]), for according to the ontological order Caesar necessarily belongs to the species *man*. Thus, Caesar necessarily has the essence *man*.

But what about essential predications such as 'Human being is an animal' where the terms do not signify an individuated common nature? And what about tautologies such as 'Human being is human being' where no essence is predicated? Are these propositions always true, even when no human being exists?[58] Yes, Scotus says. The first proposition simply expresses that the genus *animal* (the superior) is predicated of the species[59] *human being* (the inferior). And such a predication is always true, whether genus and species are individuated or not, whether a member of the species *human being* exists or not, because the genus is always predicable of one of its species. Of course, the genus is only predicable of a species belonging to it; 'Gold is an animal', for example, is false because the species *gold* does not belong to the genus *animal*. Thus, true predicability of a genus depends on the ontological classification of genus and species.[60] As for the second proposition, a tautology is merely a particular case of an essential predication. In 'Human being is human being' one predicates the essence human being of the essence human being, and such a self-predication of an essence is always true, whether a human being exists

---

56. Scotus *In Perih.* 7 (Wadding 1:550). See also *In Perih II* 2 (Wadding 1:585–87).

57. On essential predication (*praedicatio in quid*), see Scotus *Super Universalia Porphyrii* 12 (Wadding 1:158).

58. The question *Utrum haec sit vera 'homo est animal' nullo homine existente* was one of the most favored subjects of the sophism-literature in the late thirteenth century. Alain de Libera, "Roger Bacon et la référence vide," in *Lectionum Varietates: Hommage à Paul Vignaux (1904–1987)*, ed. Jean Jolivet and de Libera (Paris: Vrin, 1991), pp. 91–93, lists 36 texts devoted to this question.

59. The word 'species' is equivocal in the philosophical medieval terminology. In epistemological contexts it refers to the cognitive image, in ontological contexts to a kind subordinate to a genus. Here 'species' obviously stands for a kind.

60. On the predicability of a genus, see Scotus *Super Universalia Porphyrii* 12 (Wadding 1:166).

or not. Even 'A chimera is a chimera' (a tautology about a fictive entity) is always true, for in this proposition one predicates the essence of a chimera of the essence of a chimera, regardless of the impossible existence of a chimera.[61]

THE SIGNIFICATION OF ACCIDENTAL TERMS

Since in his commentaries on *De interpretatione* Scotus limits the discussion to substantival terms, I have been confining my analysis to these terms. However, his claim that spoken words signify immediately the essence of things also applies to accidental terms, in particular to denominative (or paronymous) accidental terms, as his remarks in the commentary on the *Categories* make clear. In accordance with Aristotle,[62] he defines the *denominativa* as those (mostly adjectival) terms that receive their *denominatio* from abstract terms.[63] Thus, 'white'—the standard example in the Middle Ages—has its denomination from 'whiteness'. Derived from the abstract substantive, 'white' differs from 'whiteness' only in grammatical form. But does this mean that the denominative term has the same signification as the term from which it has its denomination? This assumption hardly seems convincing, since 'whiteness' is an *abstract* accidental term which signifies the quality white in an abstract form, i.e., without being in a subject.[64] The denominative term 'white,' on the other hand, is a *concrete* accidental term which signifies the quality white insofar as it is in a subject. Used in the proposition 'Socrates is white,' for instance, 'white' signifies exactly Socrates' quality of being white and not whiteness in general. This distinction of abstract and concrete accidental terms raises the question: how can the difference between the significates of 'whiteness' and 'white' be explained ontologically?[65]

61. See Scotus *In Perih.* 8 (Wadding 1:550–57, especially p. 551).
62. See *Categories* 1 (1a12–15) and 8 (10a27–29).
63. See Scotus *Super Universalia Porphyrii* 16 (Wadding 1:207 and 209) and *Super Praedicam.* 8 (Wadding 1:456).
64. In this context, 'subject' is not used for the subject term, but for the *subiectum* (in Greek, *hypokeimenon*), which is the "support" or "bearer" of the accidents.
65. An excellent introduction to this question, which was extensively discussed in the late thirteenth century, is provided by Sten Ebbesen, "Concrete Accidental

Scotus holds that every accidental term, whether abstract or concrete, signifies an essence that is distinct from the essence of the subject. Admittedly, the two essences are not equally perfect, since there can be a subject without accidents but no accident without a subject.[66] Nevertheless, there is an essence of the accident as well as an essence of the subject. One can understand and signify the essence of an accident in two different ways, namely in its own nature (*sub ratione propria*) or insofar as it is in a subject (*inquantum informat subjectum*). The first is the abstract mode of signifying which applies to abstract accidental terms; 'whiteness' signifies the essence of whiteness in its own nature, regardless of the inherence or non-inherence of this quality in a subject. The second is the concrete mode of signifying which applies to concrete accidental terms; 'white' signifies the essence of whiteness insofar as it inheres in a subject, for example, in Socrates. Therefore, abstract and concrete accidental terms do not differ in their significate—both signify the quality white—but in their mode of signifying.[67]

However, 'whiteness' is only a kind of first-level abstract term, for it does not signify the quality white as being completely abstract. Rather, it signifies this quality as being attributable (although not actually attributed) to different kinds of subjects. For instance, it signifies the quality white as it can be in a wall, and as it can be in milk, and as it can be in the face of a human being, etc. Abstracting from these different possible subjects, we can form a second-level abstract term, e.g. 'quiddity of whiteness' (*'quiditas albedinis'* or *'albedineitas'*), that signifes the pure quality white without any inclination toward a specific subject.[68]

Summarizing these subtle distinctions, we can list three kinds of quality terms and, correspondingly, three ways of signifying a quality: (a) concrete accidental terms (e.g., *'album'*) signify the essence of

---

Terms: Late Thirteenth-Century Debates about Problems Relating to Such Terms as 'album'," in *Meaning and Inference in Medieval Philosophy: Studies in Memory of Jan Pinborg*, ed. Norman Kretzmann (Dordrecht: Kluwer, 1988), pp. 107–161. On the competing theories, see p. 118; on Scotus's approach, see especially pp. 120–129. See also Marmo, "Ontology and Semantics," pp. 165–168.

66. Scotus *Super Praedicam.* 8 (Wadding 1:457).
67. Scotus *Super Praedicam.* 8 (Wadding 1:457). See also *Reportatio* 4.12.1 ad 4 (Wadding 24:140).
68. See Scotus *Ordinatio* 1.5.1.unica (Commissio Scotistica 4:20–21).

a quality and indicate by their mode of signifying that the quality inheres in a subject; (b) first-level abstract terms (e.g., '*albedo*') signify the essence of a quality and indicate by their mode of signifying that the quality tends to inhere in different kinds of subjects without, however, indicating an actual inherence; and, (c) second-level abstract terms (e.g., '*albedineitas*') signify the essence of a quality and indicate by their mode of signifying that the quality is taken in its absoluteness.

The appeal to different modes of signifying is obviously due to the so-called "modistic approach" to semantic theory which Scotus shares with other late thirteenth-century authors such as Boethius of Dacia and Radulphus Brito. Scotus's modistic background has already been the subject of some thorough studies and will not be further investigated here.[69] The important point in this context, however, is Scotus's appeal to the *essence* of the accidents. Not only in explaining the signification of substantival terms such as 'human being' and 'animal' but also in delineating the signification of accidental terms he clearly distinguishes between essence and existence. All accidental terms, he claims—whether they are concrete, abstract, or purely abstract—signify the essence of accidents, but by means of their mode of signifying concrete accidental terms make one understand that the accident inheres in an existing subject. So Scotus is consistent in claiming that a spoken word—whether it is a substantival or an accidental term—never signifies the existent thing, but only the essence of a thing.

CONCLUSIONS

After this overview, we can give a more precise answer to the two questions which resulted from Scotus's classification of signs. The first question, namely how the sign-user relates a spoken

---

69. See Jan Pinborg, "Bezeichnung in der Logik des XIII. Jahrhunderts," in *Methoden in Wissenschaften und Kunst des Mittelalters*, ed. Albert Zimmermann, Miscellanea Mediaevalia 7 (Berlin: de Gruyter, 1970), pp. 238–281; and Pinborg, "Die Logik der Modistae," *Studia Mediewistyczne* 16 (1975): 39–97. A concise evaluation of recent interpretations of the theories of *modi significandi* is provided by Robert Lambertini, "*Sicut tabernarius vinum significat per circulum*: Directions in Contemporary Interpretations of the Modistae," in *On the Medieval Theory of Signs*, ed. Eco and Marmo, pp. 107–142.

word to its significate, and what exactly the significate is, can be answered as follows: the relationship between a spoken word and its significate is established by conventional imposition and not by a mental representation of the significate. Even if no person performs an act of understanding and representing, the spoken word does not lose its signification.[70] However, in perfectly using a spoken word the utterer and the hearer of the word need an intelligible species that represents a thing. But this species has only a mediating function; it is not the significate itself. The proper, ultimate significate of a spoken word is always the "thing as it is understood," the essence of a thing, whether the thing is a subject or an accident.

The second question ran as follows: what criteria enable the sign-user to judge whether a sign not accompanied by its significate is a true sign? Since in a strict sense only a proposition and not an isolated noun can be called a true sign,[71] this question is tantamount to the following: what criteria enable the utterer of a proposition to judge whether the proposition is true in the absence of the significate?

An exhaustive answer to this question would require an examination of Scotus's theory of supposition; for in medieval logic, the truth-conditions of a proposition were largely involved with the supposition-conditions of its terms.[72] For the present, I will limit my answer to the truth-conditions that deal with the signification of the terms. These conditions have to be formulated separately for two classes of truth: (a) necessary truth; and (b) contingent truth.

If a proposition is an essential predication such as 'Caesar is a man' and 'Human being is an animal' or a tautology such as 'Human being is human being' it is necessarily *always* true, regardless of the presence or existence of the significate, since the significate of both subject term and predicate term is the "thing as it is understood" (the essence of Caesar, the essence of human being, etc.) and not the "thing as it exists."

If a proposition is a contingent predication such as 'This table is brown' or 'Caesar is white' it is true only if the predicate term

---

70. See note 40.

71. See Scotus *Quaest. subtilissimae super libr. Met. Arist.* 6.3 (Wadding 7:337–48). On Scotus's theory of the proposition, see Bos, "Theory of the Proposition."

72. On Scotus's theory of supposition, see Marmo, "Ontology and Semantics," pp. 168–180.

(a denominative term) signifies a quality with the concrete mode of signifying; that is, if it signifies the quality insofar as it inheres in an *existing* subject. Thus, 'Caesar is white' is false, not because of the significate of 'white' (every accidental term signifies the essence of an accident, not its existence), but because of its mode of signifying. It is false to signify the whiteness as inhering in an existing subject, for Caesar is not an existing subject.[73]

But in what respect is Scotus's theory of signification innovative, as I claimed at the beginning of this paper? The distinction between a mediate and an immediate significate is not unusual among late thirteenth-century authors, and the claim that a spoken word signifies primarily and in a proper sense the thing, not the intelligible species, can also be found in Roger Bacon. Bacon seems, in fact, to be much more radical than Scotus, for he holds that a spoken word signifies the thing as it exists; consequently, he denies that words such as 'Caesar' or 'chimera' have a signification.[74]

The innovative character of Scotus's theory is less apparent in his semantical explanation of the relationship between a spoken word and a thing than in his attempt to give a metaphysical (in modern terminology, an ontological) foundation to this relationship. By establishing the "thing as it is understood"—the essence of a thing (of an accident as well as of a subject)—as the significate of a spoken word, he sets himself apart from theorists such as Boethius and his followers, who, in establishing the intelligible species as the primary significate, give up the direct signification of things. But he also separates himself from logicians such as Roger Bacon, who, in positing the existing thing as significate, can hardly explain the signification of past, future, or fictive things. Admittedly, Scotus is not the only late thirteenth-century author who rejects the Baconian approach as well as the Boethian; Radulphus Brito also calls the "thing as it is understood" the

---

73. See Scotus *In Perih*. 8 (Wadding 1:553–54). See also Bos, "Theory of the Proposition," p. 129.

74. See Roger Bacon *Compendium studii theologiae* 2.2 (Maloney p. 68). On Bacon's semantics, see Thomas S. Maloney, "Roger Bacon on the *Significatum* of Words," in *Archéologie du signe*, ed. Lucie Brind'Amour and Eugene Vance, Papers in Medieval Studies 3 (Toronto: PIMS, 1982), pp. 187–211; and Maloney, "The Semiotics of Roger Bacon," *Medieval Studies* 45 (1983): 120–154. On his theory of terms which signify non-existing things, see de Libera, "Roger Bacon et la référence vide."

immediate significate.⁷⁵ But so far as I can see, Scotus gives the most comprehensive answer, based on an elaborate metaphysical doctrine.

So, is Scotus's appeal to the essence of a thing the perfect solution? Only if one is willing to accept the essence-existence distinction, a distinction that is not unproblematic, as Ockham's harsh critique and the attacks of other fourteenth-century philosophers make plain.⁷⁶ In trying to ensure the direct signification of things and the possibility of signifying non-existing things, Scotus invokes a specific kind of entity as significate. Therefore, who accepts his answer to the *semantical* question of what a spoken word signifies will also have to accept a good deal of his controversial *metaphysical* doctrine.⁷⁷

University of California, Los Angeles

---

75. See Pinborg, "Die Logik der Modistae," p. 46, who quotes the *Quaestiones super Isagogen Porphyrii.*

76. On Ockham's objections, see Marilyn McCord Adams, *William Ockham* (Notre Dame, Ind.: University of Notre Dame Press, 1987), pp. 46–52. The critique was mainly directed against Scotus's modal distinction (or formal distinction, according to other interpretations) between essence and existence. Armand Maurer, "William of Ockham on Language and Reality," *Sprache und Erkenntnis* 2:800, shows clearly that Ockham disagreed with Scotus above all over the ontological commitments of his theory of signification, not over the semantic aspects in a narrow sense.

77. I am grateful to Sten Ebbesen, Gyula Klima, Norman Kretzmann, Robert Pasnau, Fiona Somerset, and Paul Vincent Spade for helpful comments on earlier drafts of this paper.

Medieval Supposition Theory in Its Theological Context

STEPHEN F. BROWN

In his *Historia calamitatum* Abelard recalls a dramatic confrontation between Alberic of Rheims and himself. During the Council of Soissons (1121) Abelard's *Theologia 'Summi boni'*, at Alberic's insistence, was being examined for doctrinal errors. Alberic, carrying a copy of the work, approached the combative Abelard and declared how startled he was by something he found in the book: since God begot God and there was only one God, how could Abelard deny that God had begotten Himself? Alberic didn't want any rational justification the suspected Abelard might want to provide for such a denial. Nor did he even want to know what the wandering teacher from Palais meant. He sought solely the words of the authority on which Abelard based himself. The undaunted Abelard told Alberic to turn over the folio of the work he was carrying. He would find there what he wanted. There indeed, to the consternation of Alberic and the disciples who accompanied him, the words from the opening chapter of Augustine's *De Trinitate* both justified Abelard's denial and undermined the thesis Alberic had taught for years.[1] For Augustine said:

---

1. Peter Abelard *Historia calamitatum*, ed. Jacques Monfrin (Paris: Vrin. 1959), p. 84, line 751 to p. 85, line 781. Compare *Theologia 'Summi boni'* 2.2, ed. Heinrich Östlender, BGPTM 35/2–3 (Munster i. W.: Aschendorff, 1939), pp. 46–47.

He who thinks God to be of such power that He begot His very self errs all the more because not only does God not exist in this way, but neither do spiritual or corporeal creatures: for there exists nothing at all which begets itself.[2]

Abelard's refutation of Alberic's understanding of "Deus genuit Deum" (God begot God) is further recorded in Books 3 and 4 of *Theologia Christiana*.[3] Through the *Summa sententiarum*[4] this Alberic-Abelard debate found its way into the fourth distinction of Peter Lombard's first book of the *Sentences*: "Hic quaeritur utrum concedendum sit quod Deus se genuerit."[5]

Gilbert de la Porrée's denial of the truth of the logically linked proposition "Deus est Trinitas"[6] not only provoked discussion at the

---

2. Peter Abelard *Historia calamitatum* (Monfrin 84.765–85.769). See also Augustine *De Trinitate* 1.1.1 (PL 42:820; CCSL 50:28).

3. Peter Abelard *Theologia Christiana* 3, ed. Eligius M. Buytaert, CCCM 12 (Turnhout: Brepols, 1969), p. 235, line 1287 to p. 236, line 1334, together with 4.70–136, especially no. 78, and 4.138–158 (Buytaert 297.1024–334.2184 and 335.2193–344.2532).

4. *Summa sententiarum* 1.8 (PL 171:1087 and PL 176:60–61).

5. Peter Lombard *Sententiae* 1.4.1, ed. Ignatius Brady (Grottaferrata: CSB, 1971), p. 77, line 21.

6. Gilbert Porretanus *Commentarium in Boethii De praedicatione trium personarum* (PL 64:1309): "Unde et auctor recte infert dicens: Quo fit ut nec Trinitas quidem de Deo substantialiter praedicetur." Compare Nicholas M. Häring, "Notes on the Council and Consistory of Rheims (1148)," *Mediaeval Studies* 28 (1966): 39–59. Damien Van den Eynde contends that Lombard's critique of Gilbert de la Porrée and his followers in *Sent.* 1.4.2 lacks an inner connection with 1.4.1. See his "Essai chronologique sur l'oeuvre littéraire de Pierre Lombard," in *Miscellanea Lombardiana* (Novarra: Istituto geografico De Agostini, 1957), p. 56. While not denying that the attack on the *Porretani* may have been added to an earlier redaction of the *Sentences*, I would suggest that Praepositinus and other theologians show a closer interior link between the contents of the two chapters through their common dependence on an adequate theory regarding the supposition of terms, especially the *suppositio* of the term 'Deus'. For a fuller study of the connection between Peter Lombard and the school of Gilbert in the area of language, see Nicholaus M. Häring, "Petrus Lombardus und die Sprachlogik in der Trinitätslehre der Porretanerschule," in *Miscellanea Lombardiana*, pp. 113–127. For a broad historical perspective on Gilbert and his contemporaries, see H. C. Van Elswijk, *Gilbert Porreta, sa vie, son oeuvre, sa pensée*, Spicilegium Sacrum Lovaniense 33 (Leuven: Spicilegium Sacrum Lovaniense, 1966), pp. 321–364 and Lauge Olaf Nielsen, *Theology and Philosophy in the Twelfth Century* (Leiden: Brill, 1982).

consistories of Paris (1147) and Rheims (1148), it also fostered logical and linguistic precisions regarding the supposition of terms by late twelfth-century theologians, such as Praepositinus.[7]

When Joachim of Flora attacked Peter Lombard's claim in *Sentences* 1.5 that "Pater non genuit divinam essentiam" and "Divina essentia non genuit Filium," not only did Joachim draw to his own teaching the condemnation of the Fourth Lateran Council (1215), he also stimulated early thirteenth-century theologians, such as William of Auxerre, to make further distinctions concerning the *suppositio terminorum*.[8]

In brief, although modern students of medieval supposition theory have, for the most part, based themselves on medieval logic treatises, there is a rich parallel source for studying the development of the theory of the supposition of terms to be found in theological writings. For, especially in dealing with the Trinity and the Incarnation, theologians had to clarify their statements, explaining in each case whether they were speaking about the divine essence or about all or one of the divine persons, or whether they were speaking about Christ as God or Christ as man. Did they develop a certain consistency in their theory of reference or supposition? Did they find some logical principles that governed their use of language and could be applied to each proposition dealing with the Trinity? If they did, would such a theory also be applicable in statements concerning the Incarnate Son, where one is dealing with only one person, but a person with a divine and a human nature?

If we wanted to examine the success of such an endeavor, even in one medieval author, it would require a complete search of all the propositions dealing with the Trinity or the Incarnation in that author's writings. We would have to see if there were explicit or implicit rules governing the referents in each of his statements. Then we would have to see if these rules could be applied in all the other areas of his theological or philosophical discourse in a consistent way.

---

7. Praepositinus *Summa* 1, as in Paris, B. N. lat. 14,526, fol. 4$^{ra\text{-}va}$.

8. Compare *Enchiridion Symbolorum*, ed. Denzinger-Bannwart-Schönmetzer, 32d ed. (Barcelona: Herder, 1963), nos. 431–432 [803–807], and William of Auvergne *Summa aurea* 1.4.4/6, ed. Jean Ribaillier (Paris and Grottaferrata: Editions du CNRS, 1980), pp. 44–49, 56–57.

Our present task is a much more modest one. We are writing this essay as an introduction to a particular text of Walter Chatton. We will be looking at one particular theological case and showing how a small number of Chatton's predecessors dealt with that case and how they tried to develop a theory of supposition to handle it. The particular theological case is found in Lombard's *Sentences* 1.4 where, picking up the Alberic-Abelard debate of 1121, the *Magister Sententiarum* examines the truth of the proposition "Deus genuit Deum." Since the *Sententiae* of Lombard became the official theology textbook at Paris and Oxford before the middle of the thirteenth century, and every medieval *baccalareus* had as one option to present a commentary on Lombard's work as a partial requirement for becoming a Master of Theology, the commentaries *baccalarii* wrote on distinction 4 contain an alternate source for their theories of supposition.[9]

In order to understand better the text of Walter Chatton's *Lectura* 1.4.1.1–2, which we have edited here, we will examine the *Sentences* of Bonaventure (who verbally resembles William of Ockham, Chatton's chief opponent in this text), Praepositinus's *Summa* (he is attacked by both Thomas Aquinas and Henry of Ghent, Ockham's chief opponents), the *Sentences* and *Summa theologiae* of Aquinas, the *Summa quaestionum ordinariarum* of Henry of Ghent, and William of Ockham's *Scriptum in I Sententiarum*.

BONAVENTURE

Bonaventure, in 1.4.1.1 of his *Sentences*, asks the question: Should we concede the statement "Deus genuit Deum"?[10] What does 'Deus' stand for in such a proposition: (1) the divine essence, (2) all three persons of the Trinity, or (3) one of the persons? Such a statement ("Deus genuit Deum") has been granted as true, according to Bonaventure, by the *magistri* and the *sancti*. But we have to get

---

9. For an introduction to the development of the theory of the supposition of terms in the medieval period according to logical works, see Brown, "Walter Burleigh's Treatise *De suppositionibus* and its Influence on William of Ockham," *Franciscan Studies* 32 (1972): 15–64.

10. Bonaventure *Sent.* 1.4.[1].1, ed. CSB, *Opera Omnia* 1 (Quaracchi: CSB, 1882), pp. 97–99.

some things clear if we wish to appreciate exactly what they granted when they admitted the statement as true. Or did they mean that the divine essence begot God? Did they mean the Trinity begot God? In other words, what is the supposition of 'Deus' and 'Deum' in the proposition "Deus genuit Deum"? What do 'Deus' and 'Deum' refer to in this statement?

Bonaventure tells us as a first rule that a concrete term ('Deus' or 'albus') and an abstract term ('deitas' or 'albedo') have different references. The abstract term stands for the form or essence: 'deitas' refers to the divine essence, 'albedo' refers to the form of whiteness. The concrete term stands for the subject in whom or in which the essence or form exists: 'album' refers to a white man or a white swan, a subject in whom or in which whiteness is present, 'deitas' to a divine person in whom the divine essence is present. The need for such a distinction is clear: we could say rightly "albus currit," but not "albedo currit."

Secondly, if we further examine the concrete term ('Deus', 'albus') and find that such a term has many referents ('Deus': 'Pater', 'Filius', 'Spiritus Sanctus'; 'albus': 'homo', 'cygnus'), then if no specific reference is indicated, we should give the benefit of the doubt to whichever one would make the statement true. For example, when someone says "homo currit," the statement is true if any man at all is running. So, we should not focus on the men who are not running. As long as someone is running, the statement "homo currit" is true.

From these two rules Bonaventure arrives at this conclusion concerning the proposition "Deus genuit Deum." According to the first rule: 'Deus' is concrete, and so although the divine essence is present in each person of the Trinity, still the term 'Deus' (as well as 'Deum') refers not to the divine essence, but to a person. Then, according to the second rule: If one person, say the Father, begot another person, say the Son, then if 'Deus' stands for the Father and 'Deum' for the Son, the proposition is true. Unless 'Deus' is limited in its referents to stand only for the Son or the Holy Spirit, or 'Deum' is limited to suppost only for the Father or the Holy Spirit, then the statement "Deus genuit Deum" does not have concrete terms that are limited to specific referents for whom it would be false to say "Deus genuit Deum." As long as there is a referent ('Pater') for whom 'Deus' truly stands, and as long as there is a referent ('Filium') for whom 'Deum' truly stands, then the proposition "Deus genuit Deum" is true. This is the ground of meaning on which Bonaventure agrees with the *magistri* and *sancti* who accept the statement as true.

Notice that Bonaventure, in this *quaestio*,[11] does not elaborate a theory. He simply borrows a few rules[12] which help him solve a concrete problem. He says that the concrete term 'Deus' stands for a person, but he does not say why it stands for a person. Does the term 'Deus' by itself always stand for a person? Or does it stand for a person in this particular proposition because of the verb 'genuit'? As long as he does not further specify the grounds supporting his rules, he will appear, as we shall see later, to be saying the same thing as William of Ockham. In fact, however, Bonaventure does not provide us with the precise ground for his decision that "Deus" stands for a person. When Ockham does, it brings out their differences.

THOMAS AQUINAS

Thomas's discussion of the same proposition "Deus genuit Deum" provides a more theoretical discussion of supposition.[13] He focuses on the opinion of Praepositinus,[14] who follows Gilbert of la Porrée.[15] For Praepositinus 'Deus' by its natural supposition,[16] i.e., taken simply as a term without considering the role it plays in

---

11. Bonaventure, in 1.4.[1].4, does ask explicitly "utrum hoc nomen 'Deus' pro persona supponat, vel pro natura?" In response, Bonaventure does not develop a theory of supposition, but rather notes that 'Deus' is a unique term, "quia habet naturam termini communis et termini discreti: termini communis propter pluralitatem suppositorum, termini discreti ratione formae immultiplicabilis—quod proprie supponit tam naturam quam personam" (CSB 1:102–103).

12. Bonaventure *Sent.* 1.4.[1].1 (CSB 1:98).

13. Thomas Aquinas *Summa theol.* 1.38.4.

14. Thomas Aquinas *Summa theol.* 1.38.4.

15. Thomas Aquinas *Summa theol.* 1.38.4.

16. 'Natural supposition' in the era of Praepositinus is the supposition a term has just on its own. In the latter part of the thirteenth century, supposition will become defined as the property of a term in a proposition, and then natural supposition will be set aside. It does reappear, however, with a different meaning in some later authors. See *Logica 'Ad rudium'*, ed. Lambertus M. de Rijk (Nijmegen: Ingenium, 1981), p. 51, no. 110.

a proposition, stands for the divine essence. In a certain statement it might be limited by the predicate or the context to stand for a particular person. In the statement "Deus genuit Deum," for example, 'Deus' has its natural supposition restricted to stand for the *persona Patris*. For Praepositinus, then, 'Deus' naturally stands for the divine essence, but can in a particular proposition, like "Deus genuit Deum," stand not for the divine essence but for the Father.

Aquinas is critical of this position of Praepositinus.[17] It is true, Aquinas argues, that "Deus" and "deitas" both signify the divine essence. Still when we speak of what some term stands for, what its supposit is, we must consider not only its significate ('Deus' and 'deitas' both signify the divine essence), but also consider the *modus significandi*, the manner in which each word signifies what it signifies. Now 'Deus' and 'deitas' both signify the divine essence, but they do so in different ways. 'Deus' signifies that essence "ut in habente ipsam" (as found in a subject or supposit), whereas 'deitas' signifies that essence as an absolute form. 'Deus' by its concrete mode of signifying signifies the divine essence in a different way than 'deitas', and therefore properly supposits or stands for the divine essence not in its absolute form but as it is present in a supposit.

Aquinas adds to this, in second place, 'Deus' can sometimes properly stand for a supposit, as in the proposition "Deus genuit Deum." In other words, the concrete term 'Deus' can properly at times supposit for the *essentia, ut in habente ipsam* and it can also at times properly stand for the *habens essentiam* or supposit itself.[18]

Finally, if 'Deus' can stand for the *essentia in habente ipsam* in some cases and for the *habens essentiam* or supposit in other instances, then when and why does it properly stand for the former or the latter? Aquinas explains that 'Deus' properly stands for the *essentia in habente ipsam* when it is used in a proposition in which the predicate is affirmed of the subject 'Deus' by reason of the form of divinity that is signified by 'Deus' or 'deitas'. This is, for instance, the case in the proposition "Deus creat." The triune God creates not because He is God the Father, or God the Son, or God the Holy Spirit, but because

17. Compare Thomas Aquinas *Summa theol.* 1.39.4.
18. Thomas Aquinas *Summa theol.* 1.39.4.

of His divine form, nature, or essence. This, however, is not the case in the proposition "Deus generat." In this instance, God generates not because of His divinity but because of His paternity. In formal terms, Aquinas declares:

"Per se [Deus] supponit pro natura communi [in habente ipsam], sed ex adiuncto determinatur eius suppositio ad personam."[19]

HENRY OF GHENT

Henry of Ghent deals with "Deus generat Deum" in his *Summa* 54.3.[20] For him, 'Deus' signifies the deity, which is also what 'deitas' signifies, just as 'album' signifies whiteness, as 'albedo' does. So 'Deus', as far as what it signifies is concerned, signifies the same thing as 'deitas'. Their mode of signification, however, is different, since 'Deus' signifies *per modum suppositi*—or, in John Damascene's terminology,[21] 'Deus' signifies the *natura ut in habente ipsam*—whereas 'deitas' signifies the *natura per modum formae absolutae*.[22]

Henry continues. Although 'Deus' signifies *per modum suppositi*, it does not signify any supposit—not one, not many—because even though 'Deus' is concrete, still it signifies something absolute in an absolute way and after the manner of something absolute, whereas all the divine supposits are *relativa*. For sure, 'Deus' has a different *modus significandi* from 'deitas', but 'Deus' also has a different *modus significandi* from 'persona' or 'Pater'. 'Deus' signifies the divine essence *in habente ipsam per modum absoluti*. 'Deus' does not signify *per modum relativi*, and therefore it primarily and principally stands for the essence (*in habente ipsam*) rather than for a person. Only when a qualifying adjunct is added can 'Deus' stand for a person, and such an adjunct (*genuit*) is added in the statement "Deus genuit Deum." In this case, therefore, 'Deus' supposits for the *persona Patris*, and thus understood, the proposition can be admitted.[23]

---

19. Thomas Aquinas *Summa theol.* 1.39.4.
20. Henry of Ghent *Summa quaestionum ordinariarum* 54.3 (Paris, 1520), 2:82r.
21. Compare Henry of Ghent *Summa* 54.3 (2:81v).
22. Henry of Ghent *Summa* 54.3 (2:81v).
23. Henry of Ghent *Summa* 54.3 (2:81v).

WILLIAM OF OCKHAM

In his *Commentary on the Sentences*,[24] William of Ockham faces off with Thomas Aquinas and Henry of Ghent. He argues that every concrete term has to stand for that in which its form is found, as is clear from 'albus' in the proposition "Homo est albus." Here 'albus' does not stand for the form of whiteness, but for the subject of that form. In the same way, when someone says "Homo est filius Dei," 'homo' does not stand for human nature, but for the person sustaining human nature. This is also the case in regard to 'Deus' in the proposition "Deus genuit Deum": 'Deus' does not stand for the Deity itself, neither *in forma absoluta*, nor *in habente ipsam*, but stands rather for a divine *suppositum* or person. Furthermore, this is not due to any qualifying adjunct in the proposition "Deus genuit Deum" which restricts 'Deus' to stand for a person. 'Deus', as a concrete term, in a proposition where it stands for its significate, stands by that very fact for a divine person.

What explains this difference between Ockham, on the one hand, and Thomas and Henry, on the other? There are a number of issues involved. First, Ockham's theory of signification is different from that of Thomas and Henry. Thomas and Henry follow the traditional view flowing from Boethius's explanation of what Aristotle declares in *Perihermenias*, that "words are signs of passions in the soul."[25] Boethius, following Porphyry, states that: "[a]lthough verbal expressions signify things and concepts, principally they signify concepts and signify by a secondary signification the things which the intellect itself grasps by means of the concepts."[26] Aquinas, walking in Boethius's footsteps, explains:

> 'Passions in the soul' must be understood here as concepts in the intellect, and names, verbs, and speech, signify these conceptions of the intellect immediately according to the teaching of Aristotle. They cannot immediately signify things, as is clear from the mode of signifying, for the name 'man' signifies human nature in abstraction from singulars; hence it is impossible that it immediately signify a singular man. The Platonists for

---

24. William Ockham *Scriptum in I Sententiarum* 4.1, ed. Girard I. Etzkorn, *Opera theologica* 3 (St. Bonaventure: Franciscan Institute, 1977), pp. 3–17.
25. Aristotle *On Interpretation* 1 (16a3–4).
26. Boethius *In librum De interpretatione, editio altera* 1 "De signis" (PL 64:407C).

this reason held that it signified the separated idea of man. But because in Aristotle's teaching man in the abstract does not really subsist, but is only in the mind, it was necessary for Aristotle to say that vocal sounds signify the conceptions of the intellect immediately and things by means of them.[27]

Now Ockham's theory of signification is clearly different from the more traditional Boethian one. He writes,

> Names of this type 'Man', 'animal', 'lion' and universally all first-intention names primarily and principally signify the things themselves outside the mind. The word 'man' primarily signifies all men and the word 'animal' primarily signifies all animals. And the same holds for other words of this type.[28]

Since all concrete first-intention words primarily and principally signify things outside the mind, and there are, for Ockham, no universal things, such words must primarily and principally signify not essences distinct in any way from the individuals, but the individuals themselves. In short, Ockham's theory of signification concerning concrete terms, namely that they primarily and principally signify things, is linked to his theory of universals. For him, there are no universal things, nor any universal natures in things that in some real way are distinct from individuals. When you couple his theory of signification with his theory of universals, the result is that, since a concrete term primarily and principally signifies a thing and the only things are individuals, then concrete terms must primarily and principally signify individuals.

If we swing back to the theological context of *Sentences* 1.4, we can see Ockham's consistency.[29] As 'man', 'animal', and 'lion' primarily and principally signify men, animals, and lions, that is individuals, so 'Deus' signifies primarily and principally the divine persons. And just as 'man' does not specify Socrates, Plato, or Cicero, so 'Deus' does not specify Father, Son, or Holy Spirit. Still, 'Deus' primarily and

---

27. Thomas Aquinas *Super Perihermenias* 2.5, in *Aristotle: On Interpretation*, trans. Jean Osterle (Milwaukee: Marquette Univ. Pr., 1962), p. 25.
28. William Ockham *Expositio in librum Perihermenias* 2.8.12, ed. Angelus Gambatese and Brown, *Opera philosophica* 2 (St. Bonaventure: Franciscan Institute, 1978), p. 502.
29. William Ockham *Scriptum in I Sent.* 4.1 (Etzkorn 12).

principally signifies a person, not the divine essence, whether that essence be considered absolutely or as present in a supposit.

Although first-intention names primarily and principally signify individuals outside the mind and stand for or supposit for such individuals, they can in certain propositions have their supposition restricted by a qualifying adjunct.[30] For instance, in the propositions "Man is a species" or "'Man' is a one-syllable word," the term 'man' is not used significatively or according to what it primarily and principally signifies. In brief, the primary form of supposition for Ockham is personal supposition, the type of supposition a term has in a proposition when it stands for its significate. In the case of concrete names, the principal and primary significate is the individual or supposit; it is for this supposit that a concrete term stands when it is a case of personal supposition. In this he differs from Thomas, Henry, and many others for whom simple supposition is primary. For them simple supposition takes place when a term in a proposition stands for its significate, by which they mean the essence—either taken absolutely or as present in an individual or supposit. Personal supposition is, for them, secondary: it takes place when a term stands for one of the inferiors contained under the essence or significate.

The primacy of personal supposition within Ockham's framework flows from his theory of signification and his theory of universals. Once you accept his position that concrete words signify things and join to it the thesis that the only things are individuals, Ockham's supposition theory, with the primacy of personal supposition, follows of necessity. It is from this viewpoint and from these assumptions that Ockham criticizes Thomas and Henry. Looking at Thomas's *Summa* 1.39.4, Ockham states: "In eadem quaestione non tantum realiter sed vocaliter idem condedit et negat."[31] Why?

Thomas said "ex modo significandi" 'Deus' can stand for a person, then later added that 'Deus' stands *per se* for the divine essence and *per adiunctum* for a person. In Ockham's eyes that is a contradiction. When a terms stands for something precisely by reason of an adjunct, then it does not supposit for it by reason of its *modus significandi*. For Ockham the concrete term has a way of signifying that points

---

30. William Ockham *Scriptum in I Sent.* 4.1 (Etzkorn 8–11).
31. William Ockham *Scriptum in I Sent.* 4.1 (Etzkorn 5–6).

primarily to the supposit; it does not need an adjunct, therefore, to stand for the supposit. For Ockham, it needs an adjunct not to stand for the supposit.

From Ockham's viewpoint, Henry of Ghent's position is likewise faulty. A concrete term has to supposit for that in which its form is found: 'album' doesn't supposit for whiteness but for the subject in which whiteness is found. The abstract term 'albedo' signifies whiteness. The concrete term 'album' is more complex: it is not an absolute term, but a connotative one. 'Album' signifies one thing directly and another indirectly. Directly it signifies a subject; indirectly it signifies the whiteness present in the subject. The same holds for 'Deus'. It is a concrete term that directly signifies a supposit, indirectly the divine nature or essence that exists in the subject. Its primary significate, however, is the subject or supposit; only secondarily and indirectly does it signify the divine essence.

Henry's theory of signification and his theory of universals support the opposite position. The primary significate for him is the essence. He even refuses to speak of a secondary or indirect significate or consignificate. "Unde hoc nomen 'Deus' non significat nisi deitatem quam significat hoc nomen 'deitas', quemadmodum 'album' significat solam albedinem sicut et hoc nomen 'albedo', ita quod hoc nomen 'Deus', quantum est ex parte rei significatae, non significat aliud quam significetur hoc nomine 'deitas'."[32]

WALTER CHATTON

Walter Chatton and William of Ockham spent the early 1320s teaching together.[33] Chatton knew Ockham's works well and criticized them frequently. Ockham's theory of supposition was no exception: Chatton criticized it in the fourth distinction of his *Lectura in I Sententiarum*, which we have edited below.

32. Henry of Ghent *Summa* 54.3 (2:81ᵛ–82ʳ).
33. Compare Stephen F. Brown, "Walter Chatton's *Lectura* and William of Ockham's *Quaestiones in libros Physicorum Aristotelis*," in *Essays Honoring Allan B. Wolter* (St. Bonaventure: Franciscan Institute, 1986), pp. 81–115.

The chief difficulty Chatton found with Ockham in this *quaestio* centers on the general theory of supposition held by the Venerable Inceptor. For Ockham, personal supposition, as we have seen, takes place when a term supposits for its significate, the individual it stands for. In the proposition "Homo currit," 'homo' signifies and stands for a real individual man. Since universals are, for Ockham, words or concepts, never things distinct in some real or formal manner from the individuals, simple supposition takes place when a term stands for a concept. The term 'man' in the statement "Man is a species" does not stand for a universal reality or a common nature in reality but for a universal or common concept. In brief, Ockham's account of supposition follows his theory of universals.

Chatton's theory of universals is different from Ockham's, and this is manifest in his definitions of the different types of supposition. Simple supposition, for Chatton, is manifold. Sometimes a term stands, as it does for Ockham, for a concept or a written or spoken word. At other times, however, we have cases of simple supposition where a term stands for a thing; here Chatton differs from Ockham.[34]

For Chatton, terms both in simple and in personal supposition can stand for things. Yet, he is careful not to make his distinction between simple and personal supposition follow a form of realism where he would claim that a term taken simply, or in simple supposition, stands for a universal thing, whereas a term taken personally, or in personal supposition, stands for a singular thing. He therefore frames his definitions in the following words:

> Personal supposition takes place when a term so stands for a singular individual that the predicate of that proposition can be verified of a proper concept of that thing.[35]
>
> The type of simple supposition that stands for a thing is that by which the subject of a proposition so stands for a thing that is really singular that the predicate of that proposition is not capable of being verified of a proper concept of that thing.[36]

---

34. See the edition below, nos. 8 and 6–6.1.
35. See no. 6, below.
36. See no. 6, below.

Chatton takes great pains to explain the theory of universals which supports[37] this theory of supposition,[38] perhaps because it comes so close to the position of Henry of Harclay, which Ockham attacked in his *Scriptum in I Sententiarum* 2.7.[39] Furthermore, Chatton seems aware that if for him a common term sometimes signifies a reality, and not just a common concept or a common spoken or written word, he might be vulnerable to Ockham's struggle against any claim that a thing can be the subject or predicate of a proposition. Chatton phrases Ockham's doubt in the following words:

> I prove that the subject of this proposition "Man is a species" does not supposit for a thing outside the mind, since 'to be a species' is a second intention just as 'to be predicated of many' is a second intention, and a second intention does not belong to a thing that is signified.[40]

Chatton answers this objection by distinguishing between the admissible and inadmissible meanings that can be given to the phrase 'predicable of many'. If one intends to imply that some thing outside the mind really through its proper entity can be the predicate of a proposition, then certainly such an outside thing cannot be the predicate of a proposition. If, however, you mean by a thing being predicated that a thing outside the mind that is predicated of many is signified *per se* and *primo* by the predicate, then Chatton claims that this is admissible. For it is true, Chatton argues, that human nature, for instance, is signified *per se* and *primo* by the concept of man or by the definition 'rational animal', and that such a concept or definition can be predicated of many.[41]

The traditional question of *Sentences* 1.4 "utrum Deus generet Deum?" allows Chatton to make these clarifications concerning his definitions of supposition and his theory of universals. On the traditional question, nonetheless, there is no serious objection to Ockham's own answer. Chatton's disagreements are minor; they seem strained.

---

37. See no. 6, below.
38. See no. 6, below.
39. William Ockham *Scriptum in I Sententiarum* 2.7, ed. Brown and Gedeon Gàl, *Opera theologica* 2 (St. Bonaventure: Franciscan Institute, 1970), pp. 227–248.
40. See no. 7.1, below.
41. See no. 8.2, below.

Both he and Ockham hold that 'Deus' and 'Deum' have personal supposition in the proposition "Deus generet Deum." Since there is no essential difference in the two men's views of personal supposition itself, there is no serious disagreement on the question inherited from Abelard.[42]

Chatton's text that is edited below provides one example of the theological context within which he and other medieval thinkers developed their theories of supposition. Any careful reader of Ockham's *Summa logicae* would see how often this same example and many other theological examples served as major challenges to the logical theory of supposition. Logic rules and theory to a very great extent were developed to solve such theological challenges. Much broader studies of Chatton, of Ockham, and of most medieval thinkers would be well worth the effort.

Boston College

APPENDIX
[WALTER CHATTON/*LECTURA IN I SENT.* 4.1.1–2]

[1.0] Circa distinctionem quartam quaero utrum Deus generet[1] Deum:

[1.1] Quod non, quia si sic, aut igitur haec esset vera per se aut per accidens. Non primum, quia sic omnis Deus generaret Deum. Non per accidens, quia tunc sibi non repugnaret non generare Deum, et per consequens sibi non repugnaret esse sine Filio Deo.[2]

[1.2] Secundo, quia omnis Deus est necesse esse. Si[3] igitur Deus generaret Deum, tunc necesse esse generaret necesse esse. Quod falsum, quia tunc necesse esse[4] necessario exigeret aliud a se ad hoc

---

42. See nos. 9.1–15.4, below.
1. generet/generat F (= Florence, Bibl. Naz. Cent. MS Conv. soppr C.5.357)
2. Deo/idem P (= Paris, Bibl. Nat. MS lat. 15, 886)
3. Si/quia F
4. esse/est P

quod esset, et per consequens illo alio circumscripto ipsum non esset, igitur ipsum non est necesse esse.

[1.3] Contra: Pater generat Filium et uterque est Deus, igitur Deus generat Deum.

[1.4] [DIVISIO QUAESTIONIS]

In ista quaestione unum supponitur et aliud quaeritur. Supponitur enim quod in divinis una persona generet aliam personam. Et hoc supposito, quaeritur utrum ista propositio debeat concedi 'Deus generat Deum'. Admisso supposito tamquam certissimo ex fide, eo quod Filius a Patre solo est non factus nec creatus sed genitus, in ista tamen[5] quaestione sunt duo facienda: primo enim aliqua sunt tangenda de suppositione per quae quaestio solvetur; secundo est per illa respondendum ad quaestionem.

[2.0] [ARTICULUS PRIMUS]
[OPINIO GUILLELMI DE OCKHAM]

[2.1] Primus igitur articulus est tangere aliqua de suppositione per quae solvetur quaestio. Et hic est opinio Ockham in *Primo*, distinctionis 4 quaestione 1.[6] Distinguit[7] suppositiones in generali, dicens quod suppositio variatur dupliciter: quia aliquando variatur ex hoc quod supponit pro alio et alio et aliquando variatur ex hoc quod supponit aliter et aliter pro eodem.

[2.2] Suppositio isto secundo modo dividitur in suppositionem confusam tantum et in suppositionem confusam et distributivam; suppositio primo modo dividitur in[8] suppositionem simplicem, materialem et personalem. Terminus enim in propositione vocali supponit simpliciter

---

5. tamen *om.* F
6. William Ockham *Scriptum in librum primum Sententiarum* 4.1, ed. Girard I. Etzkorn, *Opera theologica* 3 (St. Bonaventure: Franciscan Institute, 1977), pp. 7–13.
7. Distinguit/quae distinguit F
8. in suppositionem confusam et distributivam... in *om.*(*hom.*) P

quando illa vox supponit pro conceptu. Licet enim vox non significet conceptum illum, tamen quia ista vox et iste conceptus sunt signa subordinata respectu eiusdem significati,[9] ideo respectu praedicati quod convenit conceptui potest vox supponere pro conceptu, ut cum dicitur 'Homo est species'. Sed in propositione in mente terminus supponit simpliciter quando supponit pro se ipso et non pro re extra, ut patet de ista 'Homo est species'—ut patet distinctionis 2 quaestionibus 4 et 5 et alibi frequenter.[10] Terminus[11] autem supponit materialiter quando supponit pro ipsa voce, ut in ista 'Homo est nomen'. Sed terminus supponit personaliter quando supponit pro ipso individuo reali significato.[12]

[3.0] [CONTRA OPINIONEM GUILLELMI DE OCKHAM]

Contra ista: primo, non videtur verum quod vox supponat pro conceptu quem non significat, quia supponere pro aliquo est stare loco sui sicut signum pro significato.[13]

[3.1] Item, si in ista propositione in voce 'Homo est species' subiectum supponat pro conceptu, igitur idem est dicere quod 'Iste conceptus est species'. Sed istae voces quas formavi cum dixi "Iste conceptus" vere significant illum conceptum.

[3.2] Item, sicut conceptus dicitur species seu illud quod est praedicabile de pluribus in propositione in conceptu, eadem ratione haec vox "homo" dicetur species seu id[14] quod praedicatur de pluribus in propositione in voce. Qua ratione igitur in propositione in voce vox, si supponat simpliciter, supponit pro conceptu communi, eadem ratione in propositione in mente si conceptus supponat simpliciter supponit

---

9. significati/signati P
10. William Ockham *Scriptum in librum primum Sententiarum* 2.4–5, ed. Brown and Gedeon Gàl, *Opera theologica* 2 (St. Bonaventure: Franciscan Institute, 1970), pp. 135, 157. Compare Ockham *Summa logicae* 1.64, ed. Philotheus Boehner et al., *Opera philosophica* 1 (St. Bonaventure: Franciscan Institute, 1974), p. 195.
11. Terminus/Tres P
12. significato/signato P
13. significato/signato P
14. id/idem P

pro[15] voce communi vel alio signo corporali, [ut] cum intellectus format hanc[16] propositionem 'Haec vox "homo" praedicatur de pluribus'. Et si ponas quod hoc non sit necesse, eadem ratione dicam quod ibi non sit necesse.

[3.3] Secundo, non apparet verum quod in propositione in mente quando conceptus supponit simpliciter supponit pro se ipso, quia tunc significaret[17] se ipsum; sed significari[18] per intentionem est intelligi; igitur iste conceptus est intentio sui ipsius, et per consequens omnis cognitio intellectiva esset cognitio sui ipsius, quod falsum est, sicut patet in prima quaestione *Prologi*, articulo primo[19]—reducendo primum argumentum contra opinionem, et etiam de prima.[20]

[3.4] Item, eadem ratione in propositione in voce: si vox supponat simpliciter, supponit pro se ipsa.

[3.5] Item, in propositione in mente conceptus potest supponere materialiter ita bene sicut vox in propositione in voce; et hoc non possent ipsi salvare nisi ponendo quod tunc conceptus supponat pro se multo magis quam[21] quando supponit simpliciter.

[3.6] Item, in ista propositione 'Homo est species' vel in ista 'Homo praedicatur de pluribus' "praedicari de pluribus" non convenit illi subiecto pro se sed pro re, nam cum "homo" praedicatur in istis 'Sortes est homo', 'Plato est homo', praedicatur de eis pro rebus extra secundum eos.[22] Igitur subiectum istius propositionis, si supponit pro conceptu, hoc erit in ordine ad rem significatam; igitur licet immediate supponat pro conceptu, tamen[23] mediate supponit pro re significata per conceptum illum. Aut igitur pro re communi, et istam negant;[24]

---

15. conceptu [lin. 5] . . . pro *om.(hom.)* P
16. hanc/habeat P
17. significaret/signaret P
18. significari/signari P
19. Maria Elena Reina, "La prima questione del prologo del 'Commento alle Sentenze' di Walter Catton," *Rivista critica di storia della filosofia* 25 (1970): 53.90–59.281; also Chatton, *Reportatio et Lectura super Sententias: Collatio ad librum primum et prologus*, ed. Joseph C. Wey (Toronto: PIMS, 1989) 24.213–27.279.
20. Namely of the first opinion reported and refuted there, that is, of the first opinion of William Ockham.
21. quam *om.* P
22. Namely according to William Ockham, *Summa logicae* 1.64 (Boehner et al. 195).
23. tamen *om.* P
24. William Ockham *Summa logicae* 1.64 (Boehner et al. 195).

aut pro re singulari. Tunc mediate saltem supponit personaliter, quia secundum eos[25] hoc est supponere personaliter: supponere pro supposito reali significato.[26] Igitur si supponat mediate pro illo individo vel supposito, tunc supponit personaliter mediate.

[3.7] Confirmo, quia cum dicitur quod Sortes praedicatur de uno solo, quaero utrum subiectum supponat simpliciter vel materialiter vel personaliter. Non simpliciter, quia subiectum non est commune; nec materialiter, quia stat significative. Si personaliter, igitur cum suppositione personali stat quod immediate supponat pro conceptu et mediate pro re significata per illum.

[4.0] [OPINIO REDUCENS OMNEM SUPPOSITIONEM AD SUPPOSITIONEM PERSONALEM]

Quantum igitur ad istud diceret forte aliquis[27] quod omnis suppositio est personalis, tam suppositio simplex quam materialis, quam etiam quaelibet alia, quia quilibet terminus supponens supponit pro aliquo singulari quod significatur[28] per ipsum. Aut enim supponit pro re extra singulari quod significat;[29] tunc habetur intentum. Aut significat[30] conceptum aliquem et supponit pro illo: adhuc tunc supponit pro una singulari qualitate sive illa qualitas sit eadem cum ipsomet conceptu supponente sive non sit eadem sibi, ut verius credo.[31]

Aut significat[32] vocem unam et supponit pro ea sive illa sit eadem cum subiecto supponente sive non, adhuc supponit pro quadam qualitate significata per ipsum. Et eodem modo de scripto arguendum est, et etiam de quocumque alio signo.

---

25. William Ockham *Summa logicae* 1.64 (Boehner et al. 195).
26. significato/signato P
27. This opinion, here presented as possible, will later be held by Peter of Mantua. Compare Paul of Venice *Logica magna: Tractatus de suppositionibus*, ed. Alan R. Perreiah (St. Bonaventure: Franciscan Institute, 1971), pp. xi, 53–73.
28. significatur/signatur P
29. significat/signat P
30. significat/signat P
31. See Gedeon Gàl, "Gualteri de Chatton et Guillelmi de Ockham controversia de natura conceptus universalis," *Franciscan Studies* 27 (1967): 191–212.
32. significat/signat P

[4.1] Diceretur igitur quod suppositio personalis sumitur dupliciter: uno modo large pro suppositione qua terminus supponit pro re singulari significata per illum terminum. Et isto modo suppositio personalis non dividitur contra suppositionem simplicem et materialem sed est communis eis, quia omnis suppositio materialis vel simplex est suppositio personalis isto modo et non e contra. Alio modo sumitur suppositio personalis stricte, eo modo scilicet quo condividitur contra suppositionem materialem et simplicem, et sic est suppositio qua terminus[33] supponit pro singulari significato per ipsum non mediante suo signo sed immediate. Diceretur enim quod suppositio materialis est quando terminus supponit pro signo aliquo non in ordine ad suum significatum, sive in scripto, sive in propositione in voce, sive in mente, ut in istis 'Homo est vox', 'Conceptus est qualitas'. Suppositio simplex est qua terminus supponit pro signo in ordine ad suum significatum, sive in voce, sive in scripto sive in conceptu, ut in ista 'Homo praedicatur de pluribus'. Sed suppositio personalis isto modo est illa qua[34] terminus supponit non pro signo rei sed pro re extra significata[35] per ipsum, ut in ista 'Homo currit'.

[5] [CONTRA ISTAM OPINIONEM]

Iste modus dicendi, licet posset sustineri, habet tamen dubitationem: primo, quod non omnis suppositio sit suppositio personalis, sumendo[36] eam generalissime, quia quando unus terminus supponit pro alio termino communi ista non est suppositio personalis, ut in ista 'Homo praedicatur de pluribus'. Licet enim subiectum supponat pro uno conceptu vel voce singulari in essendo, tamen supponit pro illo conceptu vel voce quatenus est communis in significando, et per consequens non est suppositio personalis.

[5.1] Secundo est dubium, quia sumendo[37] suppositionem personalem stricte, isto[38] modo, tunc non videtur divisio suppositionis

---

33. terminus/res P
34. qua *om.* P
35. significata/signata P
36. sumendo/sustinendo F
37. sumendo/sustinendo F
38. isto/eo F

sufficiens in simplicem, materialem, et personalem, sicut patet de ista propositione 'Sortes praedicatur de uno solo'. Subiectum enim in ista non videtur supponere aliquo istorum modorum, ut supra dictum est.[39] Item, tunc hic est suppositio simplex 'Homo est vox significativa'; et hic similiter 'Conceptus est qualitas cognitiva', quia subiectum supponit pro signo in ordine ad significatum.

[5.2] Tertio est dubium in isto modo dicendi, quia termini multi supponunt simpliciter et tamen supponunt pro re extra. Patet in exemplis:

[5.3] Primum exemplum est de subiecto istius propositionis 'Homo est substantia secunda', sicut habetur in *Praedicamentis*.[40] Si dicatur quod subiectum istius supponit pro conceptu quia sensus propositionis est quod de conceptu hominis sumpto significative praedicatur hoc praedicatum "substania secunda"; contra:[41] aeque dicam tibi quod in ista propositione 'Homo currit' subiectum supponit pro conceptu, quia denotatur quod de conceptu hominis sumpto significative praedicatur hoc praedicatum "currere."

[5.4] Item, tunc habetur propositum, quia si hoc praedicatum "secunda substantia" sit verificabile de conceptu hominis significative sumpto et non verificatur de conceptu hominis sumpto significative secundum suppositionem personalem, igitur secundum suppositionem simplicem.

[5.5] Item, subiectum huius propositionis 'Homo est secunda substantia' non minus supponit significative quam subiectum huius propositionis 'Homo non est in subiecto' iuxta dictum Aristotelis ibidem in Praedicamentis[42] ubi ponit proprietatem communem omni substantiae tam primae quam secundae: quod non sit in subiecto. Sed subiectum istius propositionis 'Homo non est in subiecto' stat significative pro re extra ita bene sicut subiectum in ista 'Sortes non est in subiecto', quia sicut dictum est 'non est in subiecto' est proprietas uniformiter conveniens substantiae primae et secundae, igitur etc.

---

39. See above no. 3.7

40. Aristotle *Categories* 5 (2a10–17). Compare William Ockham *Expositio in librum Praedicamentorum Aristotelis* 4, ed. Gedeon Gàl, *Opera philosophica* 2 (St. Bonaventure: Franciscan Institute, 1978), pp. 162–171.

41. contra/est add. P

42. Aristotle *Categories* 5 (2a10–17). Compare William Ockham *Expositio in librum Praedicamentorum Aristotelis* 4 (Gàl 149–154).

[5.6] Secundum exemplum est de subiecto istius propositionis 'Homo est magis substantia quam animal'. Dicit enim Aristoteles ibidem in Praedicamentis[43] quod inter substantias secundas species est magis substantia quam genus. Si dicatur quod subiectum huius supponit pro conceptu quia sensus propositionis est quod ad quaestionem factam per quid de isto homine convenientius respondetur quod est homo quam quod est animal. Contra: per istam rationem dicetur quod animal rationale sit magis substantia quam homo, quia convenientius respondetur quod est animal rationale quam quod est homo.

[5.7] Item, per istam propositionem 'Homo est magis substantia quam animal' aut intelligitur quod haec sit magis vera 'Homo est substantia' quam haec 'Animal est substantia'; tunc habetur propositum, quia hic "homo" stat significative, igitur ibi. Aut intelligitur quod hoc totale praedicatum "esse magis substantia quam animal" verificetur de subiecto isto; adhuc tunc habetur propositum, quia non verificatur de isto subiecto pro quocumque signo rei, quia nullum signum est magis substantia quam animal, igitur verificatur de subiecto illo significative sumpto pro re extra. Unde breviter illa propositio est vera et non pro aliquo conceptu vel voce vel scripto; igitur pro re extra significata[44] per subiectum illud.

[5.8] Tertium exemplum est de subiecto istius propositionis 'Homo est substantia, quae dicitur de subiecto et non est in subiecto'. Ibidem enim in Praedicamentis[45] habetur quod substantia secunda non sit in subiecto sed dicitur de subiecto. Si dicatur quod subiectum istius stat pro conceptu, quia sensus propositionis est quod de homine significative sumpto praedicatur hoc praedicatum "substantia," quae dicitur de subiecto et non est in subiecto;—isto modo respondet Ockham ad istud exemplum et ad praecedentia in prima parte Tractatus sui de logica, capp. 32 et 34.[46] Contra: tunc habetur propositum quod haec propositio sit vera prout subiectum supponit significative pro re extra, quia non supponit personaliter, quia Aristoteles non consideraret

---

43. Aristotle *Categories* 5 (2b8–9). Compare William Ockham *Expositio in librum Praedicamentorum Aristotelis* 8, ed. Gedeon Gàl and Brown, *Opera philosophica* 2 (St. Bonaventure: Franciscan Institute, 1970), pp. 176–177.

44. significata/signata P

45. Aristotle *Categories* 2 (1a20–21). Compare William Ockham *Expositio in librum Praedicamentorum Aristotelis* 4 (Gàl 149–154).

46. Rather chapters 42–43 (Boehner 118–132).

istam 'Sortes est substantia quae est dicibilis de subiecto et non est in subiecto' eo quod negat hoc a substantiis primis; igitur stat simpliciter. Si dicatur[47] quod dici de subiecto est praedicari, sed praedicari non convenit rei extra; ad istud dicetur infra.[48]

[5.9] Quartum exemplum est de subiecto istius propositionis 'Equinitas nec est de se una nec plures', et similiter de subiecto istius propositionis 'Humanitas non est de se Sortes nec Plato', et sic de singulis.

[5.10] Et similiter de subiecto huius propositionis 'Humanitas non requirit per se quod ipsa sit Sortes vel Plato', et sic de singulis.

[5.11] Ad primum istorum dicit Ockham, in *Primo*, distinctionis secundae quaestione quinta versus finem,[49] quod per illam propositionem intelligitur quod nec unum nec plura cadit in definitione equinitatis. Contra: eadem ratione haec est vera 'Humanitas nec est de se una nec plures', et similiter ista propositio 'Animal rationale vel animalitas rationalitas nec est de se una nec plures', et tamen istam ultimam propositionem non contingit sic glossare, quia animalitas rationalitas non habet definitionem, quia sic definitionis esset definitio in infinitum.

[5.12] Ad secundum dicitur eadem quaestione:[50] cum dicitur quod 'Natura humana non est de se Sortes' aut sumitur ibi subiectum personaliter; sic est propositio vera pro Platone, et similiter sua subcontraria vera pro Sorte: 'Natura humana est de se Sortes'. Aut sumitur simpliciter pro[51] conceptu; sic vera est, quia universalis conceptus ille non est de se Sortes. Contra: licet haec propositio sit vera 'Natura humana non est de se Sortes'[52] prout subiectum supponit personaliter pro Platone, tamen ista propositio non est vera si subiectum supponat personaliter 'Natura humana nec est de se Sortes nec Plato nec Cicero', et sic de singulis. Haec enim est falsa 'Plato non est de se Sortes nec Plato',[53] et sic de singulis. Nec stat ibi subiectum pro conceptu, quia haec copulativa est vera 'Natura humana est de se

---

47. Compare William Ockham *Summa logicae* 1.32 (Boehner et al. 94–95).
48. See below, no. 8.2.
49. William Ockham *Scriptum in I Sent.* 2.6 (Brown & Gàl 219).
50. William Ockham *Scriptum in I Sent.* 2.6 (Brown & Gàl 198–200).
51. Sorte . . . pro *om.*(*hom.*) P
52. Contra . . . Sortes *om.*(*hom.*) P
53. nec Cicero . . . Plato *om.* P

realis humanitas extra et tamen natura humana nec est de se Sortes nec Plato' et sic de aliis. Et sicut subiectum primae partis istius copulativae supponit pro re extra, ita et subiectum secundae partis istius copulativae supponit pro re extra.

[5.13] Quintum exemplum est de subiecto istius propositionis 'Homo est primo animal rationale', 'Homo est primo risibilis', et sic de consimilibus. Hic dicit Ockham, in prima parte *Tractatus de logica*, cap. 65[54] quod Philosophus intelligit quod "risibile" praedicatur convertibiliter de homine et "animal rationale" praedicatur convertibiliter de ista intentione "homo," et ad istum intellectum subiectum supponit pro ipsa intentione animae; et idem dicit in *Primo*, distinctionis secundae quaestione quarta.[55] Contra: non sufficit quod praedicatum et subiectum convertantur ad hoc quod praedicatum primo praedicetur de subiecto, nam si nullum animal esset nisi homo, adhuc haec non esset vera 'Homo est primo compositus ex corpore et anima sensitiva'; sed haec esset vera 'Animal est primo compositum ex anima sensitiva et corpore', [56] et tamen "homo" et "compositum ex corpore et anima sensitiva" converterentur. Item, ad hoc quod haec sit vera 'Homo est primo risibilis' non sufficit quod "homo" et "risibile" convertantur sed requiritur quod "risibile" conveniat rei significatae per subiectum in quantum est homo et quod non conveniat alicui nisi in quantum ipsum est homo, et per consequens ad hoc quod haec sit vera 'Homo est primo risibilis' requiritur quod iste terminus "homo" supponat pro re extra cui conveniat risibilitas ex hoc quod ista res est homo et non nisi quia ipsa est homo.

[6.0] [OPINIO AUCTORIS]

Quantum igitur ad istud videtur aliter dicendum quod suppositio personalis est[57] quando terminus supponit sic pro individuo singulari quod de eius conceptu proprio natum est praedicatum illius propositionis verificari, ut cum dicitur quod 'Homo currit' hic

---

54. William Ockham *Summa logicae* 1.66 (Boehner et al. 202–203).
55. William Ockham *Scriptum in I Sent.* 2.4 (Brown & Gàl 99–152).
56. sed ... corpore *om.* P
57. suppositio ... est *om.* F

subiectum supponit pro Sorte pro quo est haec vera 'Sortes currit'. Suppositio materialis est ista qua subiectum supponit pro signo rei extra, ut 'Homo est nomen', 'Conceptus est qualitas'. Sed suppositio simplex pro re extra est illa qua subiectum sic supponit pro re extra quod praedicatum non est natum verificari de proprio conceptu illius rei extra, sicut posita sunt exempla praecedentia, et multa alia possent poni. Potest enim dici uno modo sic: quod iste homo et est Sortes et est homo et est animal, et sic de aliis. Tunc cum dicitur quod humanitas nec est de se Sortes, nec de se Plato, et sic de aliis, sicut nec de se unum vel plura, dici potest quod subiectum istius propositionis supponit pro illa re in quantum est homo et sibi repugnat respectu illius praedicati supponere pro illa re in quantum est Sortes, ideo haec non est vera 'Sortes non est de se Sortes nec Plato', et sic de aliis, et eodem modo de ista propositione 'Animal est substantia secunda', et sic de consimilibus. Alio modo potest dici quod licet natura humana pro qua subiectum illius propositionis supponit sit realiter Sortes, quia tamen supponit pro ea tali suppositione cui non repugnat formaliter quod natura pro qua supponit esset communis, ideo illud praedicatum non est natum verificari de proprio conceptu Sortis. Assumptum patet, quia haec consequentia non est formalis 'Subiectum illius propositionis supponit pro natura humana, igitur supponit pro Sorte vel[58] Platone et sic de aliis', et per consequens oppositum consequentis non repugnat formaliter antecedenti, scilicet quod subiectum illius propositionis supponeret pro natura humana, et tamen nec supponeret pro Sorte nec Platone, et sic de aliis.[59] Vel tertio modo potest dici quod verum est dicere quod subiectum illius propositionis supponit per se pro natura humana et non[60] est verum dicere quod supponit per se pro Sorte; immo magis esset verum dicere quod sibi repugnat supponere per se pro Sorte, ideo etc.

[6.1] Patet igitur quod suppositio simplex est illa pro re extra qua subiectum propositionis sic supponit pro re quae est realiter singularis quod praedicatum illius propositionis non est natum verificari proprio conceptu singularis propter causas dictas. Nec istud debet esse extraneum tenentibus oppositum, quia ipsimet, ut videtur, habent

58. vel/pro *add.* F
59. et . . . aliis *om.* F
60. non *om.* F

hoc concedere sicut tactum est. Ipsi[61] concedunt istam propositionem 'De conceptu communi substantiae sumpto significative praedicatur secunda substantia'. Quaero igitur utrum conceptus communis substantiae, quando sumitur significative, sumitur pro substantia reali communi extra animam, et hoc negant; aut sumitur significative pro re singulari, et tamen de eius conceptu proprio sumpto significative non praedicatur secunda substantia secundum eos; igitur habent concedere quod de conceptu communi rei singularis sumpto [significative] pro illo singulari praedicatur aliquod praedicatum, et tamen illud praedicatum non potest vere praedicari de conceptu proprio eiusdem singularis.

[7.0] [INSTANTIAE GUILLELMI DE OCKHAM]

Contra:[62] subiectum istius propositionis 'Conceptus hominis praedicatur de pluribus differentibus numero' non supponit personaliter nec materialiter, igitur simpliciter, et per consequens quando terminus supponit simpliciter tunc supponit pro conceptu et non pro re extra.

[7.1] Item, probo quod subiectum istius propositionis 'Homo est species' non supponat pro re extra, quia "esse speciem" est intentio secunda sicut "praedicari de pluribus," sed intentio secunda non convenit rei significatae.[63]

[8.0] [RESPONSIONES AD INSTANTIAS]

Ad primum istorum potest dici sicut solet dici a multis[64] quod duplex est suppositio simplex: una qua terminus supponit simpliciter pro re extra sicut in exemplis suprapositis, et alia qua

---

61. Namely William Ockham *Summa logicae* 1.72 (Boehner et al. 222).
62. William Ockham *Summa logicae* 1.65 (Boehner et al. 198).
63. non . . . significatae *om.* P
64. For example, Walter Burleigh, for whom see Brown, "Walter Burleigh's Treatise *De suppositionibus* and its Influence on William Ockham," *Franciscan Studies* 32 (1972): 35–36.

terminus supponit pro voce communi vel conceptu vel scripto in ordine ad significatum suum respectu praedicati quod est intentio secunda. Secundum istud concederetur quod ibi supponat suppositione una simplici, tamen praeter illam est alia suppositio simplex pro re extra, ut dictum est.

[8.1] Aliter potest dici quod triplex est suppositio materialis: una qua subiectum propositionis supponit pro voce vel conceptu vel scripto non in ordine ad aliquod significatum, ut cum dicitur 'Iste conceptus "homo" est qualitas', 'Haec vox "homo" est sonus'; alia qua subiectum propositionis supponit pro voce vel conceptu vel scripto, licet in ordine ad significatum, et isto modo potest dici in proposito quod est suppositio materialis. Nec istud videtur magnum inconveniens, nam respectu passionis grammaticalis subiectum supponit materialiter et tamen pro voce vel conceptu vel scripto in ordine ad significatum, ut cum dicimus quod ' "Homo" est nomen substantivum', ' "Homo" est nomen significativum'.[65] Tales enim praedicationes verificantur pro signis in ordine ad significata sua et tamen ibi est suppositio simplex. Ita, ut videtur, potest dici in proposito de passionibus logicalibus, ut cum dicimus quod 'Conceptus hominis praedicatur de pluribus', quod hic subiectum supponit materialiter et tamen supponit pro uno signo, scilicet conceptu, aliquo modo[66] in ordine ad significatum suum. Tertio modo diceret qui vellet, ut tactum est supra, quod subiectum illius propositionis supponit personaliter, quia subiectum illius propositionis est actus reflexus et supponit significative pro actu recto qui est res extra[67] singularis in essendo, licet sit communis in significando; et praedicatum illius propositionis est natum vere praedicari de proprio conceptu illius actus recti, igitur est aliquo modo suppositio personalis. Quiscumque istorum trium modorum ponendi detur non est magna cura quantum ad propositum, quia in proposito sufficit quod aliqua sit ponenda suppositio simplex respectu rei extra animam.

[8.2] Ad secundam obiectionem potest dici quod aliquid dicitur praedicabile de pluribus uno modo quia ipsum realiter per entitatem propriam natum est esse pars propositionis sequens copulam, et isto modo res extra non dicitur praedicari sicut nec subici; et sic

65. significativum/signatum P
66. modo *om.* F
67. extra/vera P

sumitur "praedicari" in obiectione immediate praecedente cum dicitur quod 'Conceptus hominis praedicatur de pluribus'. Alio modo sumitur "praedicari" pro "significari[68] per se et primo per praedicatum quod praedicatur de pluribus." Et isto modo convenit rei extra, nam verum est dicere quod natura humana per se et primo significatur[69] per conceptum hominis seu per istam definitionem "animal rationale," quae definitio nata est praedicari de pluribus. Unde sicut res extra dicitur cognoscibilis quia nata est significari per cognitionem, ita res extra dicitur praedicabilis quia per se et primo nata est significari[70] per praedicatum.

[8.3] Consimiliter est dicendum de specie cum dicitur 'Homo est species'. Aut enim sumitur ibi "species" pro illo quod praedicatur de pluribus eo modo quo pars propositionis praedicatur, et tunc patet quod subiectum istius propositionis supponit pro voce vel conceptu vel scripto; aut prout est idem quod per se et primo significari per praedicatum quod est pars propositionis communis multis, et isto modo res extra est species sicut humanitas; aut propositio illa valet istam 'Homo est natura quaedam specifica' et sic adhuc convenit rei extra. Ex isto patet illud quod tactum est supra, primo exemplo, quod eadem res extra ex hoc quod est Sortes est substantia prima et ex hoc quod est homo est substantia secunda, et similiter ex hoc quod est animal, et sic de consimilibus. Et eodem modo de tertio exemplo: ex hoc quod est homo[71] convenit sibi per se et primo quod sit dicibile de substantia prima ista et illa ad intellectum praedictum, sed ex hoc quod est Sortes non convenit sibi hoc.

[8.4] Aliter adhuc posset dici si homo vellet quod aliter distinguit suppositiones artifex realis et aliter artifex sermocinalis, nam artifex realis considerans de rebus extra intelligit per suppositionem simplicem illam qua terminus supponit pro re singulari extra, et tamen praedicatum illius propositionis non est natum verificari de proprio conceptu illius singularis; et intelligit per suppositionem personalem illam, scilicet, qua terminus supponit sic pro re extra singulari quod praedicatum est natum verificari de proprio conceptu illius singularis; et intelligit per suppositionem materialem illam qua terminus supponit pro signo rei extra sicut pro conceptu, voce vel scripto sive supponat

   68. significari/signari P
   69. significatur/signatur P
   70. significari/signari P
   71. est substantia [lin. 11] . . . homo *rep.* P

pro illo in ordine ad significatum sive non. Logicus autem qui est artifex sermocinalis intelligit per suppositionem personalem sicut prius, sed per suppositionem simplicem intelligit illam qua terminus supponit pro signo in ordine ad significatum et hoc respectu praedicati quod est passio logicalis, cuiusmodi est intentio secunda, sive illud signum pro quo subiectum supponit sit vox sive conceptus sive scriptum, ut 'Homo est[72] species'. Per suppositionem materialem intelligit illam qua subiectum supponit pro signo rei tam respectu praedicati grammaticalis, ut 'Homo est nomen' quam etiam respectu praedicati quod non convenit sibi in ordine ad significatum,[73] ut 'Homo est vox', ita quod artifex realis omnem suppositionem, vocet suppositionem[74] materialem qua terminus supponit pro signo rei sive illud signum sit vox sive conceptus sive scriptus et hoc tam respectu praedicati logicalis quam respectu praedicati grammaticalis quam etiam repectu praedicati quod non[75] convenit signo in ordine ad significatum, et ideo apud eum omnis suppositio simplex est pro re extra; non sic logicus, ut dictum est.

[9.0] [ARTICULUS SECUNDUS]

Secundus igitur articulus huius quaestionis est solvere quaestionem.[76]

[9.1] [OPINIO GUILLELMI DE OCKHAM]

Ad quam dicit Ockham, ubi prius, distinctionis quartae quaestione prima,[77] quod iste terminus "Deus" ex modo suo significandi solum supponit pro supposito, tamen ratione praedicati adiuncti supponit pro natura ex usu loquentium introducto ad vitandum errores et ad exprimendum identitatem summam quae est ibi. Et ideo quando praedicatum solum convenit supposito tunc solum supponit

72. est *om.* P
73. significatum/signatum P
74. vocet suppositionem *om.(hom.)* F
75. non *om.* F
76. quaestionem *om.* P
77. William Ockham *Scriptum in I Sent.* 4.1 (Brown & Gàl 12–13).

pro supposito, et quando convenit naturae, solum supponit pro natura. Tunc ad quaestionem: haec propositio est vera 'Deus generat Deum', quia praedicatum solum convenit supposito, ideo subiectum ibi solum supponit pro supposito.

[9.2] [CONTRA OPINIONEM GUILLELMI DE OCKHAM]

Contra: dubium est utrum respectu cuiuslibet praedicati convenientis naturae possit iste terminus[78] "Deus" supponere pro natura, quia dicimus quod natura Patris est communicata Filio a Patre et tamen isti non concederent istam 'Deus Patris est communicatus Filio a Patre'.

[9.3] Similiter, per Magistrum, distinctione 34, cap. "Hic considerandum"[79] haec est vera 'Una est essentia trium personarum', non tamen ista 'Deus est trium personarum'.

[9.4] Secundo, aliud est diminute dictum: quod subiectum solum supponat pro supposito[80] quando praedicatum solum convenit supposito, quia tunc ita esset propositio universalis vera sic dicendo 'Omnis Deus generat Deum' sicut haec indefinita, quia non declarant[81] quare illud praedicatum arctet magis subiectum ad solum standum pro uno quam arctet signum universale ad solum distribuendum pro uno. Similiter, forte non concederent istam 'Deus non est trinus et unus', licet concederent praedicatum solum convenire supposito. Hoc forte non concederent ne daretur aliis occasio errandi.

[10.0] [OPINIO AUCTORIS]

Aliter igitur potest dici ad quaestionem dupliciter: uno modo per praedicta quod propositio est absolute vera, nam ubi

---

78. terminus/tres P
79. Peter Lombard *Sententiae* 1.34.2, ed. Ignatius Brady (Grottaferrata: CSB, 1971), p. 251.
80. supposito/significato F
81. declarant/declaratur P

terminus supponit personaliter ibi propositio[82] est vera si praedicatum natum est verificari de proprio conceptu illius pro quo subiectum supponit. Sed ita est hic, quia subiectum istius propositionis 'Deus generat Deum' supponit pro prima persona, de cuius proprio conceptu verificari potest hoc praedicatum "generans Deum" sic dicendo: 'Ista persona non producta generat Deum', igitur etc.

[10.1] Unde iuxta praedicta contingit de divinis triplicem suppositionem praedictam assignare, ut videtur. Aliquando enim terminus supponit simpliciter de divinis, ut cum dicitur 'Deus est tres personae et quaelibet earum'. Ideo in talibus paralogismis est fallacia ex[83] varia suppositione: 'Deus est tres personae et quaelibet earum; Deus est Pater; igitur etc', quia in prima propositione subiectum supponit simpliciter et in secuna supponit personaliter pro Patre. Aliquando etiam supponit personaliter, ideo variatur suppositio in talibus paralogismis: 'Hic Deus est Pater; hic Deus est Filius; igitur Pater est Filius', quia subiectum primae propositionis supponit personaliter pro Patre et in secunda supponit personaliter pro Filio. Aliquando etiam supponit pro signo, ut cum dicimus quod 'Conceptus[84] Dei est qualitas', et sic etiam fiunt paralogismi sic arguendo: 'Haec sapientia divina est per se primo modo dicendi per se sapientia; sed haec sapientia divina est haec iustitia divina; igitur haec sapientia divina est per se primo modo dicendi per se haec iustitia divina'. Subiectum enim minoris supponit pro re extra, quia denotatur quod sapientia divina et iustitia divina sint una res extra. Sed subiectum maioris supponit pro una propositione, quia iste est sensus: haec propositio 'Sapientia divina est sapientia' est praedicatio per se primo modo dicendi per se. Hic enim subicitur iste terminus[85] "haec propositio" et supponit pro hac propositione 'Sapientia divina est sapientia'. Et similiter, sic arguendo 'Deus est Pater ingenitus; Deus est terminus communis; igitur Pater ingenitus est terminus communis', subiectum primae propositionis supponit pro re extra, sed subiectum secundae propositionis supponit pro conceptu vel alio signo rei. Patet igitur quod ista propositio potest concedi 'Deus generat Deum', quia subiectum supponit personaliter pro re de cuius proprio conceptu verificatur "generans Deum."[86]

82. propositio/propositione P
83. ex *om.* P
84. pro Filio [lin. 12]...Conceptus *om.* P
85. terminus/tres P
86. Patet [lin. 27]...Deum *om.* F

[11.0] [INSTANTIAE]

Contra: primo, quod[87] conceptus Dei supponit ibi pro hoc Deo qui est simul tres personae, igitur propositio est falsa. Assumptum patet, quia conceptus Dei primo significat hunc Deum, sed primo supponit pro suo primo significato, igitur etc.

[11.1] Secundo, conceptus Dei non supponit pro Patre nisi quia Pater est ipsa deitas, et per consequens deitas est primum significatum illius conceptus. Aut igitur supponit ibi pro deitate, igitur deitas generat Deum; aut non; tunc non supponit pro Patre, quia si non supponit pro suo primo significato non supponit pro secundario significato.

[11.2] Tertio, quia idem significant 'Deus generat Deum' et 'Deitas generat deitatem', quia concretum et abstractum idem significant; sed una istarum est falsa, igitur alia.

[11.3] Quarto, indefinita est vera pro aliquo individuo. Si igitur haec sit vera 'Deus generat Deum' non sufficit dicere quod sit vera pro persona sed requiritur quod sit vera pro aliquo individuo. Sed hic non potest dare individuum nisi "hic Deus" qui est trinitas et pro illo non est propositio vera, igitur etc.

[11.4] Quinto, melius salvantur veritates theologicae et melius vitantur difficultates in oppositum exponendo propositiones in quibus praedicantur notionalia de essentialibus per propositiones alias in quibus praedicantur essentialia de notionalibus, ut in proposito dicendo quod haec praedicatio 'Deus generat Deum' valeat istam 'Generans est Deus' et 'Genitum est Deus'.[88]

[12.0] [RESPONSIO AD INSTANTIAS]

Dicendum quod istae obiectiones licet valeant contra illos qui ponunt quod propositio ista est primo vera pro hoc Deo, non tamen valent contra me.

[12.1] Dixerunt enim aliqui[89] non solum quod "deitas" aliquo modo in re distingueretur a qualibet personarum sed etiam quod iste

---

87. quod/quia P
88. et . . . Deus *om.* P
89. John Duns Scotus *Ordinatio* 1.4.2.1.11–13, ed. Commissio Scotistica, *Opera Omnia* 4 (Vatican City: Typis Polyglottis, 1966), pp. 5–7; *Lectura in I Sent.* 4.1.4–7,

terminus "hic Deus" primo significat illam rem ut sic distinctam a personis et quod pro hoc Deo sic sumpto est haec primo vera 'Deus generat Deum'. Contra istam opinionem valent illae obiectiones, quia tunc ista propositio esset falsa 'Deus generat Deum' eo quod haec est falsa 'Deitas generat deitatem'; et similiter haec est vera 'Primo generans distinguitur a primo genito', quia nihil primo generat se. Si igitur "hic Deus" esset primo generans tunc "hic Deus" distingueretur a se.

[12.2] Obiectiones autem illae non sunt contra me. Ad primam illarum dicendum quod subiectum istius propositionis 'Deus generat Deum' supponit pro prima persona. Et ad probationem dicendum quod Pater est primum significatum illius subiecti pro quo scilicet illa propositio est vera, et hoc sufficit ad propositum. Sicut enim est verum dicere quod conceptus specificus hominis primo significat hominem et non significat[90] per se et primo Sortem, et tamen significatum illius conceptus pro quo ista propositio est vera 'Homo currit' est Sortes, ita licet sit verum dicere quod conceptus specificus Dei per se et primo significet Deum et quod non significat[91] per se et primo Patrem, tamen Pater est primum significatum pro quo ista propositio est vera 'Deus generat Deum'.

[12.3] Ad secundum dicendum quod Patri convenit ex hoc quod est Deus quod ille conceptus potest pro eo supponere, et concedo quod non est verum dicere quod[92] supponat hic pro divinitate. Sed ex hoc non sequitur quod non supponit pro Patre. Et cum dicitur de primo significato,[93] dicendum quod Pater est primum significatum pro quo ista propositio est vera, et hoc sufficit. Unde respectu huius praedicati non habet aliud significatum[94] cui vere conveniat.

[12.4] Ad tertium patebit distinctione quinta.

[12.5] Ad quartum: ubi idem individuum est plures personae distinctae ad veritatem propositionis indefinitae sufficit quod verificetur pro una illarum personarum seu pro individuo illo in quantum est

---

ed. Commissio Scotistica, *Opera Omnia* 16 (Vatican City: Typis Polyglottis, 1960), pp. 408–409.

90. significat/signat P
91. significat/signat P
92. non . . . quod *om.* P
93. significato/signato P
94. significatum/signatum P

una illarum personarum, licet non verificetur pro illo individuo in quantum est omnes simul; ita est in proposito.

[12.6] Ad quintum: illa opinio reprobatur a Magistro *Sententiarum*, distinctione ista, de qua etiam dicetur quaestione proxima.

[13.0] [ALIA RESPONSIO AUCTORIS]

Alio modo potest responderi ad quaestionem distinguendo: cum quaeritur utrum haec sit concedenda 'Deus generat Deum', quaero: quid vis significare? Aut enim intendis quaerere utrum persona quae est Deus generet personam quae est Deus alia deitate; sic falsum est. Aut intendis quaerere utrum persona quae est Deus generet aliam personam quae est Deus eadem deitate; sic est verum.

[14.0] [INSTANTIAE]

Ut tamen istud magis appareat obicio in oppositum primo, quia eadem ratione diceretur quod Deus distingueretur a Deo.

[14.1] Secundo, quia tunc Deus generat alium habentem deitatem, igitur generat alium ab habente deitatem, et per consequens generat alium ab omni habente deitatem, quia negatio importata per ly alium negat illud quod sequitur confuse et distributive.

[14.2] Tertio, quia aut generat Deum qui est Pater aut Deum qui non est Pater. Si Deus generat Deum qui est Pater, igitur per conversionem Deus qui est Pater est genitus. Si genuit Deum qui non est Pater, igitur est aliquis Deus qui[95] non est Pater et sic plures dii.

[14.3] Quarto, quia si sic: aut generat se Deum aut alium Deum eo quod generat eundem Deum vel diversum; non se Deum, quia nihil generat se, igitur alium Deum et sic plures dii.[96]

[14.4] Quinto, Deus genuit alium: aut igitur alium Deum, tunc sunt plures dii; aut alium non Deum, igitur genitus est non-Deus.

[14.5] Sexto, eadem ratione haec esset vera pro Filio: 'Deus non generat Deum'.

---

95. est Pater est [lin. 3] . . . qui *om.*(*hom.*) P
96. Quarto [lin. 1] . . . dii *om.*(*hom.*) P

[15.0] [RESPONSIONES AD INSTANTIAS]

Ad primum istorum: non est simile, quia haec est absolute falsa 'Deus distinguitur a Deo', quia negatio importata in vocabulo distinctionis negat terminum sequentem distributive et universaliter, et ideo valet istam quae est simpliciter falsa 'Deus non est idem alicui Deo'.

[15.1] Ad secundum: quid intelligis? Aut quod Deus generet alium in persona qui[97] tamen habet eandem deitatem; sic potest concedi. Et similiter quod generet aliam personam habentem deitatem. Sed ex isto non sequitur quod genuit alium ab habente deitatem, quia sensus est quod genuit alium a quolibet habente deitatem; sicut nec sequitur 'Deus genuit non eundem habentem deitatem, igitur genuit non eundem alicui habenti deitatem'; patet quod non sequitur.

[15.2] Ad tertium quaeri potest: quid intelligitur? Aut sic: utrum Deus generet Deum qui est idem Deus cum Patre; sic concederetur, ex quo solum sequitur quod Deus genitus est idem Deus cum Patre. Aut intelligitur utrum Deus generet Deum qui est eadem persona cum Patre; sic est falsum, ex quo solum sequitur quod est aliquis Deus qui non est eadem persona cum Patre, et ex hoc non sequitur quod sint plures dii.

[15.3] Ad quartum potest similiter quaeri: quid intelligitur? Aut enim intendunt quaerere utrum genuerit se Deum ad istum intellectum, utrum scilicet genuit personam quae est idem Deus cum se ipso; et sic concederetur, nec ex hoc sequitur quod genuit se, quia sunt personae distinctae licet sint idem Deus. Aut quaeritur utrum genuit personam quae est idem personaliter secum; sic falsum est. Cum etiam quaeritur utrum genuit alium Deum: aut quaeritur utrum genuit alium qui est Deus;[98] et patet quod sic. Aut quaeritur utrum genuit alium alietate deitatis; dicendum quod non.

[15.4] Ad quintum: aut quaeritur utrum genuit alium qui est Deus; potest dici quod sic, quia aliam personam quae est Deus. Aut quaeritur utrum genuit alium alietate deitatis; sic falsum est. Cum etiam quaeritur utrum genuit alium Deum: aut quaeritur utrum genuit alium

---

97. qui/quae F
98. Deus/Pater P

qui non est Deus; sic falsum est. Aut quaeritur utrum genuit alium qui tamen non est alius alietate deitatis; sic est verum.[99]

[16.0] [RESPONSIONES AD ARGUMENTA PRINCIPALIA]

Ad primum principale: dicendum quod haec praedicatio non est per se primo modo dicendi per se, ut alias[100] dictum est. Nec est praedicatio per se secundo modo dicendi per se ad illum intellectum quo passio praedicatur de primo subiecto cum quo primo convertitur. Licet enim iste conceptus "generare Deum" sit conceptus primo convertibilis cum propria descriptione quidditativa absoluta primae personae, et ideo de illa praedicetur per se secundo modo dicendi per se secundum opinionem illam quae tacta est in tertia quaestione Prologi, articulo primo, in propositione[101] tamen non est conceptus convertibilis cum conceptu isto communi omnibus personis cum dicitur "Deus," quia sic omnis qui est Deus generaret. Sed habet se ad illum sicut passio convertibilis cum conceptu inferiore se habet ad conceptum quidditativum superiorem, ut patet de ista propositione 'Animal est risibile' vel de ista 'homo generavit Platonem.' Genuisse enim Platonem est passio convertibilis cum proprio conceptu Sortis et praedicatur particulariter de conceptu communi hominis; ita in proposito secundum opinionem praedictam. Et cum arguitur quod tunc est per accidens: si intelligatur quod praedicatum conveniat subiecto per aliquod accidens seu etiam per aliquam rem distinctam in re a deitate, sic est falsum; nec consequentia valet. Si autem intelligatur sic quod "generare Deum" non convenit sibi in quantum est deitas sed magis per rationem extraneam, scilicet in quantum est talis persona, iste intellectus concederetur secundum opinionem illam, et ideo illi rei in quantum est deitas non repugnaret non generare Deum, sicut patet de Filio et Spiritu Sancto. Aliunde tamen

---

99. No reply to the sixth argument is found in the manuscripts.
100. Walter Chatton *Lectura in I Sent.* prol. 3.1, in *Commento alle Sentenze, Prologo–question terza*, ed. L. Cova (Rome, 1973), lin. 745–748; Wey 168.695–697.
101. Walter Chatton *Lectura in I Sent.* prol. 3.1 (Cova 751–767; Wey 169.700–716).

repugnat, scilicet in quantum est talis persona, ideo non potest esse sine Filio Deo.

[16.0] Ad aliud principale: conceditur quod necesse esse generat necesse esse ad illum intellectum quo conceditur quod Deus generat Deum. Et cum arguitur quod tunc necesse esse exigeret aliud a se: aut intelligitur quod necesse esse[102] per unam necessiatem essendi exigeret necesse esse per aliam necessitatem essendi; sic falsum est, quia sicut sit una deitas ita sit una necessitas essendi.[103] Aut intelligitur quod unum suppositum quod est necesse esse exigit aliud suppositum quod est necesse esse per eandem necessitatem essendi. Iste sensus, si poneretur,[104] esset concedendus. Et cum dicitur quod tunc alio circumscripto ipsum non esset[105] aut intelligitur quod, alio alietate necessitatis essendi circumscripto, ipsum non esset; sic falsum est, et non valet consequentia. Aut intelligitur[106] quod alio alietate personali circumscripto, quod tamen est necesse esse per eandem necessitatem essendi, tunc ipsum non esset; sic est verum, quia illo circimscripto circumscriberetur propria necessitas essendi et propria deitas, igitur ipsummet circumscriberetur, et ex hoc non sequitur quin ipsum sit necesse esse sicut non sequitur ipsum non esset circumscripta propria necessitate essendi, igitur non est necesse esse modo de facto. Aliter posset responderi distinguendo de necesse esse formaliter vel privative, sed transeo.

---

102. esse/est P
103. sic falsum [lin. 5] . . . essendi om.(hom.) P
104. poneretur/proponeretur F
105. concedendus [lin. 9] . . . esset om.(hom.) P
106. intelligitur om. P. I want to thank Joseph C. Wey, C.S.B., for correcting this edition.

Nominalism Meets Indivisibilism
JACK ZUPKO

Nominalists, it is said, are defined by their opposition to the needless multiplication of entities. For most fourteenth-century nominalists, parsimony was in the first instance a logico-semantic matter, raising the question of how one should explain the truth conditions of sentences without assuming any kind of strictly isomorphic relation between individual sentences and what makes them true.[1] In their analyses of the structure of continuous spatial magnitudes, this question was presented in an especially clear and unambiguous

---

1. Thus Calvin Normore argues that it is misleading to see medieval nominalism solely as a campaign against real universals. It would be more accurate to say that medieval nominalists sought to economize on entities, of which real universals were but one type. See his "The Tradition of Mediaeval Nominalism," in *Studies in Medieval Philosophy*, ed. John F. Wippel (Washington, D.C.: Catholic University of America Press, 1987), pp. 201–217. For a detailed discussion of the nominalist ontological program as found in the writings of William of Ockham, see Marilyn McCord Adams, *William Ockham* (Notre Dame, Ind.: University of Notre Dame Press, 1987), pp. 3–313. For a useful historical study of late medieval nominalism (whose author, it should be pointed out, "purposely disregards" what he calls "the traditional cliché of 'nominalism'," p. 152), see Damasus Trapp, "Augustinian Theology of the 14th Century: Notes on Editions, Marginalia, Opinions, and Book-Lore," *Augustiniana* 6 (1956): 146–274, esp. pp. 182–190. Though I am in general agreement with Normore's view, I won't take up here the controversial question of how medieval nominalism should be defined. Nor will any of the particular arguments given below depend on it.

form: "Is it necessary to posit indivisible entities to explain the truth conditions of sentences containing terms such as 'point', 'line', and 'surface'?" Affirmative answers offered one route to indivisibilism, the thesis that continua are divisible into finitely or infinitely many indivisible parts, or mathematical atoms.[2] But negative answers, besides leading to the opposing view that continua are infinitely divisible, also invited some account of how terms such as 'point', 'line', and 'surface' are to be understood, if not as standing for real mathematical points, lines, and surfaces (surfaces being indivisible in one dimension, lines in two dimensions, and points in three). The way in which such parismonious ontologies were achieved in practice, however, shows us that nominalist methodology was anything but static in the later Middle Ages, as more and more sophisticated techniques were introduced and perfected to explain the relation between terms and what they signify. This essay is addressed to one small, though representative, part of that story.

I shall focus on an example, an argument, and the reply to that argument given by a series of fourteenth-century nominalist thinkers roughly contemporary with each other: William of Ockham (*ca.* 1285–1347), Adam Wodeham (*ca.* 1298–1358), and John Buridan (*ca.* 1295–1358).[3] The example concerns an ideal sphere gradually descending onto a perfectly plane surface until they come into contact, or sometimes a sphere in contact with a plane surface and rolling across it. Its function was to raise a question: Would the sphere (first) touch the plane surface at a point? This example was a commonplace in medieval literature on continua, where it most typically arose as

---

2. These are mathematical atoms, not physical atoms. As John Murdoch has observed, "late medieval atomism was not intended, as was that of Democritus or Epicurus, as any kind of general system which might cover or explain the natural world.... It was intended rather as a single facet of natural philosophy, designed simply to explain the structure of magnitudes, and specifically of space, time, and motion as magnitudes." See his "The Development and Criticism of Atomism in the Later Middle Ages," in *A Source Book in Medieval Science*, ed. Edward Grant (Cambridge, Mass.: Harvard University Press, 1974), p. 313. Nicholas of Autrecourt is an exception insofar as he defended physical atomism, though his views are not fully understood.

3. For the date of Ockham's death as 1347 and not (as traditionally cited) 1349, see Gedeon Gàl, "William of Ockham Died Impenitent in April, 1347," *Franciscan Studies* 42 (1982): 90–95.

an argument for indivisibilism.[4] Though he did not originate it,[5] the sphere and plane example emerged as a standard topic in the medieval debate after it was discussed by the indivisibilist Henry of Harclay (1270–1317), who presents it in the following argument:

> a sphere moved on a plane touches the plane at a point. Proof: because [between] a straight [line] and a circle, or a spherical body and a circular [body], there is nothing in common but a point, and contact [*tactus*] is always at something common. But the sphere is continuously moved on the plane. Therefore, it touches continuously, point after point, and through its motion describes a line. Therefore, point after point will be continuously in that line, and consequently, such a line is composed of points.[6]

We find a variation on Harclay's touch-at-a-point argument given somewhat later by the Franciscan indivisibilist, Walter Chatton (1285–1344):

> God can make one thing truly plane in parts and another truly spherical in parts. Indeed, according to the Philosopher [*De caelo* 2.27.287a11–22],

---

4. Adam Wodeham, who is usually careful about naming his sources, refers to it only as "the common argument [*communis ratio*] concerning the touch of a plane by a spherical body." Adam de Wodeham *Tractatus de indivisibilis* 2.3.3, ed. Rega Wood (Boston: Kluwer, 1988), p. 138, lines 26–27.

5. Rega Wood has indicated to me in correspondence that the probable first appearance of this common argument in the West is in Book 6 of an anonymous *Physics*-commentary preserved in Erfurt, Amplonian Q.312, at fols. 9va and 10rb. She believes that the commentary can be attributed to Richard Rufus of Cornwall. Richard, who knew Averroës's writings well, most likely found the argument in Averroës's commentary on *De caelo*. As Vassili Zoubov notes, in "Jean Buridan et les concepts du point au quatorzième siècle," *Medieval and Renaissance Studies* 5 (1961): 61–62, the example is cited not only by Averroës (*De caelo* 1.32 [Venice, 1560] f. 27^r with reference to 1.4 [271a]), but also by Sextus Empiricus (*Adversus mathematicos* 3.27–28) and Plutarch (*De communibus notitiis* 40.7).

6. Henry of Harclay, as paraphrased in William of Alnwick's *Determinationes* 2, fol. 7^v (Latin text quoted in Wodeham *De indiv.* [Wood p. 290, n. 6]). For Alnwick as a reliable expositor of Harclay's views, see John Murdoch and Edward Synan, "Two Questions on the Continuum: Walter Chatton (?), O.F.M. and Adam Wodeham, O.F.M.," *Franciscan Studies* 25 (1966): 212, n. 2. Harclay's argument is also paraphrased by Adam Wodeham in his *Tractatus de indivisibilibus* 1.2 (Wood p. 94), as well as in his *Quaestio de continuo*, ed. Murdoch and Synan in "Two Questions on the Continuum," pp. 276–277, sect. 25. The latter may be an early draft of the former. Except for passages from Wodeham's *De indiv.* (which I quote from Rega Wood's edition and translation), all translations in this paper are my own.

the heavens are spherical, or there would be a vacuum in the recess of the indented or protruding parts. Since it happens that those two are together, the sphere touches the plane. I ask whether [they touch] at a number of parts, or only at one. [1] If at many, then it is not a sphere, because it will be molded to the plane in its parts; this I demonstrate [as follows]: those parts make a plane, or [else] some [of them] will penetrate the plane and there will be some parts protruding into the plane and others indented. [2] If only at one, I have what [the argument] proposed [to show]; for it follows formally: only one part, therefore not many, therefore indivisible by necessity.[7]

The gist of the argument seems clear: a sphere and plane must touch each other at *something*, but not at a divisible part, since any such part is divisible into further parts, and contact between more than one part of the sphere and plane would involve the compression and/or penetration of the one by the other; therefore, the sphere and plane must touch each other at a single, indivisible part, i.e., at a point.

The trouble with this argument, however, is that it offends against certain divisibilist principles also established by the Philosopher. At the beginning of *Physics* 6, Aristotle argues that continuous magnitudes cannot be composed of indivisible points because indivisibles have no *extremities* (i.e., first and last parts) by means of which they could be continuous (meaning that their extremities are one) or even in contact (meaning that their extremities are together).[8] Furthermore, continua must be infinitely divisible, because if they were divisible into indivisibles, we would *per impossibile* have indivisibles in contact with each other, since the extremities of what is continuous must be in contact with each other.[9]

---

7. Wodeham *Quaestio de continuo* (Murdoch and Synan p. 249, sect. 68). Compare Chatton *Reportatio* 2.2.3.1,4 as in Paris, BN lat. 15887, fol. 93rb–94va. I have abandoned the editors' suggested emendation of *tenet* for *contingit* in the third sentence of this passage. There is a refinement which should be mentioned, but which need not detain us. Although both were indivisibilists, Chatton, unlike Harclay, argued that continua were composed of a finite number of indivisibles in consecutive contact. For the details, see John Murdoch, "Infinity and Continuity," in CHLMP pp. 571–578, and Rega Wood, "Introduction" to *De indiv.*, pp. 4–8.

8. See *Physics* 6.1 (231a21–b5).

9. *Physics* 6.1 (231b15–18). Although both Harclay and Chatton reject the first Aristotelian contact argument, only Chatton rejects the second. He does so by modifying Aristotle's definition of 'touch'. See second section, below, and Chatton *Reportatio* 2.2.3 (fol. 94vb).

The indivisibilists who rejected Aristotle's contact argument did so for a variety of reasons: Harclay, to avoid the mathematical absurdity that would result if continua of unequal magnitude were composed of equally infinite parts; Chatton, as part of his defense of the theological doctrine of angelic motion;[10] still others, because of difficulties they saw in Aristotle's own refutation of indivisibilism.[11] My aim here, however, is not to determine which theory, divisibilism or indivisibilism, is better suited to deal with various mathematical and theological constraints.[12] Rather, I am interested in ontological constraints, and specifically in the way in which one group of divisibilists tried to reply to the indivisibilist touch-at-a-point argument without multiplying entities, viz. mathematical atoms.

A point of clarification: although the ontological question raised by the fourteenth-century divisibilist-indivisibilist debate over the structure of continua seems clear enough, this is not to suggest that rejection of indivisible entities is what nicely separates the nominalist position from all others. Parsimony can be achieved in a number of ways, of course, so that it would not have been inconsistent for a participant in the debate to express traditional nominalist scruples about the existence of universals,[13] while still embracing mathematical atoms on the grounds that we cannot do without them if we want to explain the structure of continuous magnitudes. Moreover, although indivisibilism

---

10. Aristotle goes on to argue in *Physics* 6.10 (241a6–14) that it is impossible for anything indivisible to be in motion, an argument with obvious applications to angels, which are indivisible beings. Duns Scotus, for example, offers a mathematical argument against indivisibilism in the context of a discussion of angelic motion in *Opus Oxoniense* 2.2.9.

11. For discussion of the various contexts in which medieval indivisibilism was defended, see Murdoch and Synan, "Two Questions on the Continuum," pp. 212–225; Murdoch, "Infinity and Continuity," pp. 575–577; and Wolfgang Breidert, *Das aristotelische Kontinuum in der Scholastik* (Munster: Aschendorff, 1970).

12. That task has already been embarked upon by others, and the story it reveals is in any case extremely complex. I direct the reader to John Murdoch's authoritative writings on this subject over the past quarter-century.

13. These scruples were often expressed in connection with Porphyry's first question about the nature of genera and species, "whether they subsist or are placed in bare [acts of] the understanding alone." See Boethius *In Isagogen Porphyrii* editio altera 1.10–11. Both Abelard and Ockham, for example, agree here that genera and species (1) exist in the understanding alone and (2) have no extramental significance except as conventional names. For discussion, see McCord Adams, *William Ockham*, pp. 3–12.

was certainly the minority view, there were indivisibilists, such as Harclay, who held that universal terms do not signify anything real outside the mind, and divisibilists, such as Walter Burley (*ca.* 1275–1345), who defended a moderate realist position on the nature of universals.[14] What this means is that there is no reason why the divisibilist-indivisibilist debate could not have taken place as an in-house disagreement between one group of nominalists who thought it necessary to add indivisible entities to one's ontology for mathematical and/or theological reasons, and another group who rejected this. But at least by second quarter of the fourteenth century, it hardly ever did. Since most nominalists found it natural to identify with divisibilism,[15] the ontological aspect of the debate was not usually separated from it in practice. Indeed, the popularity of the problem of the *existence* of indivisibles is distinctively medieval,[16] and, as John Murdoch has suggested, may have been "to some extent a result of the kinds of questions about entities a particularist ontology urged one to ask."[17]

The three nominalist thinkers I shall be discussing—Ockham, Wodeham, and Buridan—all subscribed to a trio of doctrines characteristic, though (except for the first) by no means definitive, of fourteenth-century divisibilism:[18]

---

14. Although Harclay maintained that universal and particular terms are distinct only in reason, his view does represent, as McCord Adams has suggested, an "attempt to combine a nominalist ontology of singulars and concepts with a realist vocabulary" ("Universals in the Early Fourteenth Century," in CHLMP, p. 439). Accordingly, Harclay is best thought of as occupying a middle ground between moderate realists, such as Duns Scotus and Burley, and more radical nominalists, such as Ockham, who is unwilling to concede even that much. For discussion and references to the relevant texts, see McCord Adams, *William Ockham*.

15. The naturalness of the identification can be partly explained, no doubt, by the influence of Ockham's views on indivisibles. For discussion, see Murdoch, "Infinity and Continuity," pp. 574–575.

16. There is, for example, no direct treatment of the existence problem in Aristotle's *Physics*.

17. John Murdoch, "*Scientia mediantibus vocibus*: Metalinguistic Analysis in Late Medieval Natural Philosophy," in *Sprache und Erkenntnis im Mittelalter*, ed. Wolfgang Kluxen et al. (Berlin: Walter de Gruyter, 1981), p. 89, n. 43. Compare Murdoch, "William of Ockham and the Logic of Infinity and Continuity," in *Infinity and Continuity in Ancient and Medieval Thought*, ed. Norman Kretzmann (Ithaca: Cornell University Press, 1982), pp. 165–168 and 175–183.

18. For the variations on medieval divisibilism, see Murdoch, "Infinity and Continuity," pp. 571–584; Wood, *Adam de Wodeham*, pp. 10–15 (to whom the useful

(1) *Divisibilism*: A continuum is not composed of atoms, but of parts divisible without end.
(2) *Non-entitism*: Indivisibles do not exist in the physical world.
(3) *Infinitism*: the composite parts of a continuum are infinitely divisible, or constitute a potentially infinite set.

The ontological question raised by the indivisibilist touch-at-a-point argument is especially worrisome for divisibilists who are non-entitists, of course, since it is not open to them to conceive of the point of contact between the sphere and plane as some kind of real limit. Despite their shared theoretical commitments, Ockham, Wodeham, and Buridan defuse the argument in surprisingly different ways. These differences cannot be explained, I think, solely by the various contexts in which the touch-at-a-point argument arose. Rather, as I hope to show, they demonstrate both the evolution and the increasing sophistication of explanatory methods used by fourteenth-century nominalist thinkers.

WILLIAM OF OCKHAM

William of Ockham discusses the indivisibilist sphere and plane example twice: once in the *Expositio Physicorum*, and once in the *Quodlibeta septem*.[19] The first and more physicalistic context is in Book VI of the *Expositio*, a work directed in large part against

---

classificatory term 'non-entitism' is due). Duns Scotus, for example, rejected non-entitism, but is still classified as a divisibilist because he maintained that continua are not *composed* of indivisible entities. Scotus's arguments against non-entitism are cited verbatim and then attacked by Ockham in *Tractatus de quantitate* 1, in *Opera Theologica* 10, ed. C. A. Grassi (St. Bonaventure, N.Y.: Franciscan Institute 1986), pp. 26–45. The non-entitist form of divisibilism defended by Ockham, Wodeham, and Buridan was actually less common than the orthodox Aristotelian variety (whose defenders included Aquinas, Duns Scotus, and Giles of Rome), according to which indivisibles are to be understood as real limits, though not as constituent parts, of continua. In fact, the only non-entitist prior to Ockham seems to have been Peter John Olivi, for whom see Wood, *Adam de Wodeham*, p. 25, n. 44. The definition of divisibilism given here is that of Thomas Bradwardine (*ca.* 1295–1349), *Tractatus de continuo* (quoted in Murdoch, "Infinity and Continuity," n. 36): "continuum non componi ex athomis, sed ex partibus divisibilibus sine fine."

19. The argument is not mentioned in Ockham's other discussions of the structure of continua, namely in the *Summa logicae* and *Tractatus de quantitate*. The latter is his most comprehensive theological treatment of the continuum problem.

Giles of Rome, a divisibilist who conceived of indivisibles as *real limits* based on the assumption that quantity is a *res absoluta* distinct from substance and quality.[20] In Chapter 14, Ockham replies to Giles's view that, contrary to Aristotle, it is possible for indivisibles to be moved.[21] Ockham notes that some have tried to refute this argument by proving that continua are composed of indivisibles, in connection with which he cites the following disjunctive argument for indivisibilism:

> it is supposed that a completely spherical body touches an absolutely plane body. To which, I ask whether it touches at something divisible, or at something indivisible. The first cannot be given, because at whichever divisible you choose, there will be a curve, and consequently the whole [divisible] will not fit the plane, but there will be an intermediate body [*corpus medium*] between some part of the curve and that plane. If the second is given, we have what the argument proposes to show.[22]

In other words, if we imagine a perfect sphere descending onto a perfectly plane surface beneath it, they must first touch at an indivisible point, because (ruling out compression or penetration) divisible

---

20. Giles was thus a divisibilist who rejected non-entitism. For discussion of the influence of Giles's views on Ockham in the *Expositio Physicorum*, see Ernest Moody, "Ockham and Aegidius of Rome," *Franciscan Studies* 9 (1949): 417–442. In contrast, Ockham denies that quantity is an absolute thing, distinct from substance or quality, and likewise rejects the notion that Aristotle meant to posit limits of continua really distinct from continua themselves. See Ockham *Expos. Phys.* 5.5.7, in *Opera Philosophica* 5, ed. Wood et al. (Bonaventure, N.Y.: Franciscan Institute, 1985), p. 382, lines 33–34. For discussion of Ockham's views here, see McCord Adams, *William Ockham*, pp. 201–213; Murdoch, "Infinity and Continuity," pp. 573–575; Murdoch, "Logic of Infinity"; and Eleonore Stump, "Theology and Physics in *De sacramento altaris*: Ockham's Theory of Indivisibles," in *Infinity and Continuity*, pp. 207–230, which takes issue with the interpretation offered in Murdoch, "Logic of Infinity."

21. Giles of Rome *Commentaria in octo libros Physicorum Aristotelis* 6.18 (Venice, 1502; rptd. Frankfurt a. M.: Minerva, 1968), fol. 160rb. Aristotle had argued in *Physics* 6.10 (241a6–14) that there can be no motion of a point or any other indivisible because before anything moving can traverse a space greater than itself, it must first traverse a space less than or equal to itself; but since there can be no space less than an unextended indivisible, the notion of a *moving* indivisible is incoherent. It is perhaps worth noting that Ockham, Wodeham, and Buridan were not about to deny the existence of *immaterial* indivisibles (e.g., angels or human intellectual souls) or, for that matter, the possibility of their motion. The touch-at-a-point argument, of course, concerns the necessity of positing indivisibles to explain the structure of continuous *spatial* magnitudes.

22. Ockham *Expos. Phys.* 6.14.4 (Wood et al. 583.63–68).

curved parts do not "fit" divisible plane parts. Except for their single point of contact, there will always be space between them, and more space as one moves along the plane surface in any direction away from that point.

Ockham's reply to this argument is quick and direct. He denies that any two absolutely spherical and absolutely plane bodies can be said to touch, if by that we mean that there is no intermediate body between them. This is for two reasons. First, the sphere and plane cannot touch each other as a whole, since both are divisible entities composed of parts *more* immediate to their place of contact. Second, they cannot touch each other at some part, because any first touching parts of the sphere and plane you choose will be further divisible into smaller parts that touch each other even more immediately. Thus, if we call the first touching parts of the sphere and plane A and B, respectively, Ockham says that it is "manifestly false" to suppose that there is nothing intermediate between any part of A and B. He argues for this as follows:

> each would be divided into three equal parts, viz. A into C, D, and E, and B into F, G, and H. It is obvious that between C and F there is an intermediate body; for otherwise, they would be both curves or both planes. Therefore, A and B do not first touch each other. And so it can be proved of any parts that they do not first touch each other....[23]

Furthermore, to the counter-argument which supposes that a hard spherical body must immediately touch a soft plane bodily yielding easily to it (imagine a ball bearing dropped into a bowl of jello), Ockham replies that they would still not touch immediately, since there must always be an intermediate body between any sphere and plane parts you choose at the place of penetration.[24]

Ockham's reply here is interesting, to say the least. But one might argue that he arrives too quickly at what is, to be sure, a counterintuitive conclusion, namely, that "one must say, following Aristotle, that a purely spherical body cannot touch a purely plane body."[25] For it seems a kind of philosophical overkill to reply to the indivisibilist touch-at-a-point argument by saying that the sphere and plane do not

---

23. Ockham *Expos. Phys.* 6.14.4 (Wood et al. 583.83–584.87).
24. Ockham *Expos. Phys.* 6.14.4 (Wood et al. 584.101–115).
25. Ockham *Expos. Phys.* 6.14.4 (Wood et al. 584.98–100).

touch each other at a point because they do not touch each other *at all*. Ockham is, of course, willing to say that the sphere and plane touch each other, if by that we mean that they touch "mediately," or in such a way that there are always other extended bodies between them. He apparently does not think it necessary to take some of the counterintuitive edge off the divisibilist solution by further exploring in his reply the notion of mediate contact.[26] This is doubly unfortunate in view of Ockham's non-entitism, since a more precise definition of contact would surely help to explain the truth conditions of sentences such as 'The spherical and plane bodies are touching'. Unless predicates of contact can be assigned an interpretation that is both plausible and consistent with the assumption that indivisibles do not exist in the physical world, the indivisibilist query remains unanswered. If it is still true to say that continuous, divisible bodies touch at something, why not posit something, namely, indivisible points, at which they touch?

Ockham takes a more decided step towards addressing this issue in his reply to the touch-at-a-point argument in the *Quodlibeta septem*, a work composed after the *Expositio Physicorum*. Here his opponent

---

26. He does provide at least the beginnings of an account elsewhere in the *Expositio physicorum*, when he modifies Aristotle's definition of contact ("Things are said to be in contact when their limits are together," *Phys*. 5.3 [226b23]) to make it more amenable to his non-entitist brand of divisibilism. The reason seems clear. If by 'together' [rendered into Latin as *simul*] Aristotle means that their limits are in the same place, then the two things must be continuous. No two distinct things could touch each other in that sense without ceasing to be distinct. If two distinct things are to be in contact, then, their limits cannot literally be immediate, but only mediate. See Ockham *Expos. Phys*. 5.5.2 (Wood et al. 377.98–100 and 378.43–45). The conditional reflects Ockham's view that although Aristotle sometimes speaks as if points are things distinct from bodies, he does not mean this literally, as implying the existence of indivisible entities. See Ockham *Expos. Phys*. 5.5.2 (Wood et al. 377.38–378.42). Such remarks are rather to be treated as *conditional propositions*. This is also the intrepretation that Ockham suggests for mathematical propositions that mention indivisible points. Such points, he says, exist only in the imagination of the mathematicians. See Ockham *Expos. Phys*. 5.5.7, 5.7.1, 6.1.2 (Wood et al. 382.25–383.61, 402.28–31, 461.304–462.323). For discussion, see Murdoch, "Logic of Infinity," pp. 175–179. As we shall see below, Wodeham and Buridan also make use of the notions of mediate contact and entities indivisible only *secundum imaginationem*, respectively, but (unlike Ockham) they do so specifically in the course of their own non-entitist replies to the touch-at-a-point argument.

is definitely Chatton, and his target is Chatton's version of the argument, which as we saw above concerns the hypothetical case of God placing completely spherical and completely plane bodies in contact with each other. To this argument, Ockham objects:

> it is impossible and includes a contradiction [to say] that the sphere touches the plane, because if it does, since [it does] not [touch] at something indivisible, it must touch at a divisible part. And for any part of the spherical thing you choose, because it is part of something spherical, by necessity one part of it is ascending and another descending. And so by necessity there is some intermediate body [between them], say, the air, if it touches in the air.[27]

Again, the curved surface of the spherical body will prevent it from being in contact with a plane at any of its *divisible* parts.

Yet Ockham also recognizes something in the *Quodlibeta septem* discussion that is present, but not made explicit, in his earlier treatment of the sphere and plane example: his conclusion that the sphere and plane would not touch is based on the *indivisibilist* assumption that contact must be immediate. "Otherwise," he says, "it can be said (and perhaps better) that a spherical body touches a plane at some divisible part of it."[28] That the latter is Ockham's preferred definition of contact is evident in the next paragraph, where there is a reply to the objection that the divisible part of the sphere actually touching the plane would not itself count as a spherical body, presumably because it would lack a curved surface. Ockham says that this follows only if we assume that

> ...some first part is touching as a whole, such that each part of that part touches the plane, since then the argument would conclude by necessity that it would not be completely spherical.[29]

It would follow, in other words, that no spherical part would touch any plane part if by 'touch' we mean contact between each and every divisible part of those parts. A glance at the curved surface

---

27. William of Ockham *Quodlibeta septem* 1.9 in *Opera Theologica* 9, ed. Joseph C. Wey (St. Bonaventure: Franciscan Institute, 1980), pp. 58–59, lines 200–205.
28. Ockham *Quodl.* 1.9 (Wey 59.205–207). For immediacy of contact as a characteristic thesis of indivisibilism, see Wood, *Adam de Wodeham*, pp. 3–10.
29. Ockham *Quodl.* 1.9 (Wey 59.210–212).

of the sphere and the flat surface of the plane should be sufficient to confirm that.

Unable to talk about immediate contact between divisible parts, Ockham tries another strategy:

> I now posit that [the sphere] does *not* touch by means of any first part of which each part touches the plane. Therefore, it does not touch by means of any first [part] that is prior to all other touching [parts]; but for any touching part you choose, still one half does not touch immediately, nor half of that half, and so on to infinity.[30]

Ockham's view is that we can say that the sphere touches the plane as long as we do not mean that it touches immediately, or at any first part. His reasoning here reprises the argument from the *Expositio Physicorum*: any two parts of the sphere and plane taken to be immediate would be infinitely divisible into parts even more immediate, e.g., into halves, quarters, eighths, and so on.

Although Ockham considered these replies sufficient to refute the touch-at-a-point arguments offered by Giles and Chatton,[31] his divisibilist and non-entitist successors do not seem to have regarded the issue as settled. Both Wodeham and Buridan take the indivisibilist sphere and plane example quite seriously, and, rather than merely repeating Ockham's arguments from the *Expositio Physicorum* and *Quodlibeta septem*, fashion their own *positive* accounts of how the sphere and plane may be said to touch. These seem intended to supplement Ockham's much briefer account in two ways: first, by precisely defining the divisibilist concept of mediate contact in the context of the touch-at-a-point argument; second, by turning the notion of the infinite divisibility of touching parts from a rough illustration into a quasi-mathematical procedure, thereby adding formal rigor to the non-entitist reply.

ADAM WODEHAM

Adam Wodeham focuses much more attention than Ockham on the indivisibilist sphere and plane example, quoting

---

30. Ockham *Quodl.* 1.9 (Wey 59.212–217), emphasis added.
31. See notes 22 and 7 above, respectively.

directly from both the Harclay and Chatton versions of the touch-at-a-point argument in his main discussion of the indivisibilist controversy, the *Tractatus de indivisibilibus*.[32] Still, he prefers to call it a "common argument [*communis ratio*]" for the view that a point is an absolutely indivisible entity, a fact suggesting that, by the time Wodeham was writing, it had ceased to be associated with any particular indivisibilist thinker.[33] Indeed, Wodeham observes that the question of whether the sphere would touch the plane or not "is a great point of dispute between [adherents of different] schools [of thought], and they make the difficulty emerge nicely for each side."[34]

Wodeham argues, following Ockham, that either (1) it is not possible that the sphere touch the plane, or (2) if it does touch the plane, it touches it "at something infinitely divisible."[35] The second alternative, of course, involves the divisibilist concept of mediate contact. But before considering that, Wodeham offers an argument in defense of the first alternative, namely, that there can be no contact at an indivisible point.

Unlike anything in Ockham, this argument seems designed to confront Chatton's touch-at-a-point argument head on, even down to the way it sets up the sphere and plane example as a thought experiment about divinely produced ideal bodies. Wodeham asks us to imagine God placing a sphere at some distance above a plane in a medium of air, then causing the sphere to descend until it is prevented from descending further by the surface of the plane, but

---

32. See Harclay's version in Wodeham *De indiv.* 1.2.4 (Wood); and Chatton's in Wodeham *De indiv.* 1.2.16 (Wood 94.18–24, 100.14–17). The Chatton version quoted by Wodeham is not exactly the same as the version cited in note 7 above. It involves, like the Harclay version, a sphere being moved across a plane surface. For the source of the latter, see Chatton, *Reportatio* 2.2.3 (fol. 94va); of the former, note 6 above. Both versions of the indivisibilist argument are likewise reproduced by Wodeham in his *Quaestio de continuo* (Murdoch and Synan, "Two Questions on the Continuum," pp. 276, sect. 24; 280, sect. 34). Wodeham also considers the question of indivisibles and the composition of continua in his *Lectura secunda* 24.1–2, ed. Rega Wood and Gedeon Gàl (St. Bonaventure: Franciscan Institute, 1990) 3:321–411, although the sphere and plane example is not discussed there.

33. Wodeham *De indiv.* 2.2.3 (Wood 138.26). Wood argues that it was composed between 1323 and 1331, probably closer to the earlier date (pp. 15–16).

34. Wodeham *De indiv.* 2.3.4 (Wood 146.7–8).

35. Wodeham *De indiv.* 2.3.3 (Wood 146.5).

without either body suffering compression or penetration. "This once accomplished," Wodeham argues, "the air interposed would still be continuous, although not everywhere uniformly or equally thick, but always thinner or more and more tenuous, as we approach the place of contact."[36] To demonstrate this conclusion, Wodeham embellishes his thought experiment as follows:

> suppose that God annihilates that spherical body and the plane joined to it in the manner described above, without effecting any change of place in regard to the air, one part of which previously surrounded the spherical body and the other part of which touched the plane surface—[namely], the solid plane body previously withdrawn [below] the spherical body. Once this is done, I ask: will we find that that air is continuous or not? [1] [If it is continuous, then] this is what we proposed to show. [2] [If it is not continuous], then there will be a hole, either a divisible or indivisible hole. [2.1] [If it is divisible], then either [2.1a] there was a vacuum there before, which appears incongruous; or [2.1b] the plane was immediately touched by the sphere divisibly in a straight line, which is contrary to the nature of sphericity and of a straight line. [2.2] If [the hole is] indivisible, then it could be filled by an indivisible; or at least there would be an indivisible vacuous space, where before there had stood an indivisible belonging to the spherical body joined to the plane. And the opposite of this was proven above.[37]

The problem with the indivisibilist option [2.2] is that since indivisibles cannot together make something continuous,[38] indivisible points cannot be part of any continuum, such as the sphere; hence, their annihilation would make no difference to the way in which the sphere touches the plane.[39]

But even if the continuity of the air, in this example, shows that the sphere and plane cannot touch in the way Harclay and Chatton want them to touch, Wodeham still hopes to make sense of our intuition that they must touch *somehow*. Here he has a twofold

---

36. Wodeham *De indiv.* 2.3.6 (Wood 146.24–27).
37. Wodeham *De indiv.* 2.3.7 (Wood 146.32–35 and 148.1–10).
38. Wodeham *De indiv.* 2.1.7–8 (Wood 124.10–27). Wodeham refers to a preceding argument at *De indiv.* 1.3.1 (Wood 102.1–13), as well as quoting from Ockham's argument that an indivisible point cannot be posited as part of something existing *per se*. For the latter, see Ockham *Expos. Phys.* 6.1.2 (Wood et al. 454.57–65).
39. Wodeham *De indiv.* 2.3.3 (Wood pp. 144–146).

strategy. First, tempered by (of all things) Chatton's indivisibilism, he takes Ockham's notion of mediate touching as contact at some divisible part, but not at any first such part, and he refines it into a new account of touching which further modifies the Aristotelian notion of contact so that he can talk about divisibles being immediate to each other. Second, he introduces the quasi-mathematical procedure he calls "proportional division *ad infinitum*" to illustrate how the sphere and plane could be said to touch by *means* of a divisible, but in the *manner* of an indivisible. Wodeham begins by noting that in his argument against indivisibilism, it also follows that the sphere and plane do not touch at anything *divisible*. For the reason, he refers the reader first to Ockham's *Expositio Physicorum* argument that between any two "first" touching parts of divisible bodies, there will always be a *corpus medium*, or intermediate body.[40] For Wodeham, however, the real source of the problem is what he takes to be Aristotle's definition of contiguous contact. The sphere and plane do not touch each other, he says, if

> we understand by 'touch each other' that their limits are together and in the same primary place according to the description of contiguous things laid down by Aristotle in *Physics* 5 and repeated in book 6. [41]

According to Aristotle, however, things are contiguous if they are (1) in succession (nothing of their own kind is intermediate between them), and (2) in contact, or touching (their extremities are together),[42] suggesting that Wodeham has run together Aristotle's definition of contact (things are touching if their extremities are together) with his definition of continuity (things are continuous if their extremities are one).[43] No divisibles can be contiguous on this understanding of Aristotle because divisibles have spatially distinct parts, and it is not possible for two things having spatially distinct

---

40. See notes 23–24 above.
41. Wodeham *De indiv.* 2.3.11 (Wood 150.6–9).
42. Aristotle. *Phys.* 5.3 (227a9).
43. See Aristotle. *Phys.* 5.3 (226b21–227a9); 6.1 (231a21–29). Compare Wodeham *De indiv.* 2.3.11 (Wood 151.13–14): "no such [sphere and plane] limits are together in that fashion." The source of Wodeham's (perhaps deliberate) confusion here might well have been Ockham, who likewise found it necessary to reinterpret the Aristotelian notion of contact so that it would apply to non-continuous divisible bodies.

parts to occupy "the same primary place." Nevertheless, Wodeham uses the occasion to offer his own, alternative definition of 'touch each other'. This definition is interesting because it looks very much to have been inspired by his indivisibilist arch-rival, Chatton, who had tried to refute Aristotle's contact argument with the novel assumption that continua can be composed of indivisibles not in the sense that they are in the same place (which is, after all, why Aristotle found indivisibilism to be absurd), but in the sense that they are next to each other such that whole touches whole without there being anything else in between.[44] With Chatton, Wodeham proposes that "things 'touching each other' or 'contiguous' are those whose limits are together, or [whose limits] are immediate [to each other]" by what he terms a "simultaneity or positive immediacy [*simultate seu immediatione positiva*]."[45] The sphere and plane would touch each other in this sense, he says, since each extends to the other without stopping short of, or extending beyond, the other.[46] But what, exactly, is the significance of them touching with "simultaneity or positive immediacy"?

Wodeham attempts to answer this question in a further step, illustrating the notion of contact between positively immediate limits by means of a procedure he calls "proportional division *ad infinitum*." Although neither the sphere nor any part of it touches the plane "primarily and exactly [*primo et adaequate*]," he says, it does touch by itself and in its parts, viz. "by any part of it extending to and reaching the plane."[47] Thus, the sphere and plane can be said to touch each other immediately if the sphere and each part of it is treated as a kind of *macro-indivisible*, extended towards the plane until

---

44. Chatton *Reportatio* 2.2.3 (fol. 94ᵛᵇ): ". . . placet mihi quod totum tangat totum, id est quod nihil est medium inter ea." Wodeham, who was intimately familiar with Chatton's writings, quotes directly from this passage at *De indiv.* 1.1.24 (Wood 48.5–8). The source of Chatton's alternative definition of contact (though not, of course, its application to indivisibles) could well have been Ockham. See Ockham *Expos. Phys.* 5.5.2 (Wood et al. 377.98–100, 378.43–45).

45. Wodeham *De indiv.* 2.3.12 (Wood 150.17–18). Chatton, of course, characterizes such contact negatively, namely as involving "nothing else in between" things that are touching, rather than positively, as is suggested by the notion of positive immediacy.

46. Wodeham *De indiv.* 2.3.12 (Wood 150.18–20).

47. Wodeham *De indiv.* 2.3.14 (Wood 150.34 to 152.1).

it can go no further without compression or penetration.⁴⁸ And there are infinitely many such positively immediate limits:

> For example, [a sphere would touch a plane] by means of its [lower] half, constructed transversely; and by means of a half of that same [half] constructed in parallel—[that is], the lower half similarly reaching the plane, and so on *ad infinitum*, as can be proven by argument and also using the examples introduced above here.⁴⁹

We might illustrate Wodeham's procedure as follows: a perfect sphere and the plane on which it rests would, ruling out compression or penetration, touch each other immediately, since the sphere would be extended towards its place of contact with the plane. But if we were to divide the sphere by slicing it horizontally through its middle, thus removing its top half, no change would be effected in the way the remaining half-sphere touches the plane, and so it, too, would touch the plane immediately. But then we can use the same procedure to produce a quarter-sphere having the same manner of contact, and then an eighth-sphere, and so on *ad infinitum*. And furthermore, adds Wodeham, we can say the same thing "analogously regarding the parts of the plane touched by the sphere."⁵⁰ Wodeham's non-entitist reply to the indivisibilist touch-at-a-point argument is that although we must say, following Ockham,⁵¹ that the sphere always touches the plane either as a divisible whole or at some divisible part (and there are infinitely many such divisible parts in contact with the plane, as

---

48. I owe the term 'macro-indivisible' to Norman Kretzmann, "Adam Wodeham's Anti-Aristotelian Anti-Atomism," *History of Philosophy Quarterly* 1 (1984): 388.

49. Wodeham *De indiv.* 2.3.14 (Wood 152.1–5).

50. Wodeham *De indiv.* 2.3.15 (Wood 152.12–13). Wodeham contends that proportional division *ad infinitum* can likewise be applied to the diameter of the sphere perpendicular to the plane. See the passage at *De indiv.* 2.3.16 (Wood 152.14–22). Wodeham's solution here appears to involve the mathematical notion of asymptotic division to a limit. His assumption (via his definition of mediate contact) would be that angles of tangency have a finite minimum limit, whereas one would expect an indivisibilist to argue that such angles are of infinitesimal magnitude. For a discussion of curvilinear angles and their relation to the continuum problem, see Murdoch, "Infinity and Continuity," pp. 580–582.

51. Wodeham mentions Ockham by name in this context at *De indiv.* 2.3.18 (Wood 154.6–7). He appears to have in mind Ockham's handling of the indivisibilist touch-at-a-point argument in *Expositio Physicorum* 6.

the method of proportional division demonstrates) it does so *in the manner of an indivisible*.[52]

What Wodeham has done here, I believe, is to combine, rather ingeniously, Ockham's thoroughly divisibilist and non-entitist account of continua with a definition of contact inspired by Chatton's explanation of how continua can be composed of indivisibles (*pace* Aristotle), in order to suggest a way in which *divisibles* can be said to touch each other positively and immediately.[53] It is as if Wodeham were saying, "I know that no two absolutely spherical and absolutely plane bodies can be said to touch each other if by that we mean that there is no intermediate body between them. After all, each is divisible into infinitely many parts that touch each other with greater and greater immediacy. But if we think of them just as wholes, as Chatton conceives of indivisible points existing next to each other in a continuum, then they can touch each other immediately in the positive sense that each is extended towards the other as far as it can go, without compression or penetration." What Wodeham borrows from Chatton is a way of thinking about the composition of continua which he then applies to divisibles. Though *de facto* divisible, continua (or their parts produced by proportional division) are to be thought of as indivisible wholes, a move which enables the non-entitist to talk about immediate contact between continuous bodies while shielding his claims from being reduced to absurdity by Ockham's argument.

But non-entitist and indivisibilist alike may object that it is wrong to speak of the sphere and plane touching each other immediately, especially in view of Wodeham's earlier concession that there will always be a continuous body of air between them. Chatton in particular might want to stress that, on his definition of contact, there is nothing between the immediately touching indivisible points of which continua are composed. But Wodeham could handle such objections

---

52. Wodeham *De indiv.* 2.3.18 (Wood 152.32–34).

53. Again, Wodeham not only knew Chatton's definition of contact, but quotes from it directly near the beginning of the *De indiv.* See note 44 above. In a note on Wodeham's second definition of contact, Wood assumes (correctly, in my view) that "'positive immediacy' means that the immediate things are together, as opposed to there being nothing between them." She does not, however, make the further suggestion (which I am making here) that Wodeham got the idea from Chatton.

with a neat *distinguo*. First, he would say, if you are talking about the sphere and plane as divisible entities, then of course they will touch each other only mediately because any sphere and plane parts you choose will have more immediate parts, to say nothing of the air, between them. But if, on the other hand, you are talking about the sphere and plane (or of any of their parts produced by proportional division) as wholes, then the divisibilist *reductio* argument no longer applies, and we must instead define immediacy in terms of their being so close to each other that, if they were any closer, their sphericity and/or planeness would be compromised by compression and/or penetration. That this latter, immediate sense of contact is compatible with the former, mediate sense is something Wodeham concedes in the final section of his discussion of the sphere and plane when he remarks, "and nevertheless, as was made clear [i.e., in the refutation of the indivisibilist touch-at-a-point argument], something mediates, or could mediate, between any part touching the plane in this fashion and the plane, when there is such contact."[54] That is, the sphere and plane can still touch each other immediately as wholes, even though there is air between them.

The influence of this novel strategy for defusing the sphere and plane example is evident in the writings of Wodeham's somewhat younger Parisian contemporary, John Buridan. Buridan's writings suggest that he adopted not only Wodeham's indivisibilist-inspired definition of immediate contact, but also the method of proportional division *ad infinitum* as an illustration of how the parts of divisible bodies can be said to touch each other. Yet Buridan did not embrace Wodeham's reply to the indivisibilist argument without first augmenting and refining it. It is to that final part of our story that I now turn.

JOHN BURIDAN

Buridan is more interested than either Ockham or Wodeham in exploring the logico-semantic underpinnings of the debate over the structure of continuous magnitudes. He sees the indivisibilist touch-at-a-point argument primarily as presenting the problem

---

54. Wodeham *De indiv.* 2.3.19 (Wood 154.16–18).

NOMINALISM MEETS INDIVISIBILISM   177

of how a non-entitist should understand the terms occurring in it, i.e., 'point' and 'touch', rather than as raising questions about the mode of contact between ideal spheres and planes. The logical and mathematical aspects of the problem are related, or course, but the difference we see in Buridan is one of emphasis. "If only we could be clear about the signification of our terms," he seems to be saying, "such mathematical questions about modes of contact will answer themselves."

Buridan's approach is best exemplified in Book 6 of his *Questions on Aristotle's Physics*, where the sphere and plane example is mentioned in an argument on the affirmative side of Question 4, which asks whether points are indivisible things [*res indivisibiles*] in a line.[55] After presenting and defending his own divisibilist, non-entitist, and infinitist views on the question, Buridan proceeds to reply to the arguments on the opposing side. To the touch-at-a-point argument, he replies as follows:

> As for the sphere placed on the plane, we say that the whole sphere touches the whole plane, taking 'whole' categorematically. But it is not the case that the whole sphere, or some whole part of the sphere, touches the plane, taking 'whole' syncategorematically. Indeed, no part of the sphere taken syncategorematically touches the plane, except the last [part] next to that plane. And we wish to signify these concepts [*intentiones*] when we say that it touches at a point.[56]

So would a sphere placed on a plane surface touch it at a point? Buridan is willing to say, following Wodeham, that they touch each other as wholes, but only if the term 'whole' is understood in its categorematic sense, which he elsewhere says should be expounded as 'having parts'.[57] In this way, the proposition 'The whole sphere

---

55. The argument Buridan presents here looks like a minimalist version of the Harclay/Chatton touch-at-a-point argument. See Buridan *Quaestiones super octo physicorum libros Aristotelis* 6.4, in *Kommentar zur Aristotelischen Physik* (Frankfurt a. M.: Minerva, 1964), fol. 96rb. Buridan's clipped rendering of the argument both here and in his other writings suggests that it had perhaps acquired in mid-fourteenth-century Paris the same status Wodeham had earlier ascribed to it in England, namely that of a "common argument" (*communis ratio*) for indivisibilism.

56. Buridan *Q. in Phys.* 6.4 (fol. 97vb).

57. Buridan *Quaestiones in De anima* 2.7, ed. Peter Gordon Sobol, in "John Buridan on the Soul and Sensation: An Edition of Book II of His Commentary on Aristotle's

touches the whole plane' is true if sphere and plane are both seen as wholes *having parts*, namely, as *divisible* wholes. But if 'whole' is understood in its primary syncategorematic sense,[58] where it is expounded as 'each part', it will distribute the predicate 'touches the whole plane' over each and every integral part of its subject. The proposition will thus be false, because only the last part of the sphere immediately next to the whole plane would touch it in that sense. Furthermore, since Buridan maintains that continua are infinitely divisible, nothing answers to the description, 'last part of the sphere', if by that we mean 'whole last part' in the latter, syncategorematic sense. Buridan explains this consequence in an argument reminiscent of Ockham's proof that infinitely divisible spheres and planes cannot have any first touching parts:

> no whole part of any continuum is its limit [*terminus*], and I am [here] taking the name 'whole' syncategorematically. This thesis is obvious because no whole part is the first or last. For which reason, assume the opposite, viz. that some whole part of any continuum is its first or last part. It follows that each part of that part will be the first or last, and that it will be the limit of that continuum. And this is false, because if the part which is posited first were divided into A and B, it is certain that A will be before B, and so B will not be the first part.[59]

Buridan therefore sees the problem of the sphere touching the plane in terms of the logical distinction between categorematic and syncatgorematic words. We can talk about whole continuous entities in contact with each other as long as 'whole' is taken in its categorematic, divisibilist sense of 'having parts'. But we cannot do so if we assume, following the indivisibilists, that there is some whole indivisible part

---

Book of the Soul, with an Introduction and a Translation of Question 18 on Sensible Species," doctoral dissertation, Indiana University, 1984, pp. 103–104; *Tractatus de suppositionibus* 3.7, ed. Maria Elena Reina in *Rivista critica di storia della filosofia* 12 (1957): 326, lines 482–483.

58. In its primary syncategorematic sense, 'whole' effects a distribution over the integral parts of its subject. See (for Buridan's discussion of this sense) Q. in *De anima* 2.7 (Sobol pp. 102–105); *Tractatus de suppositionibus* 3.7 (Reina 326.490–495). For general discussion, see Norman Kretzmann, "Syncategoremata, Exponibilia, Sophismata," in CHLMP, pp. 230–240.

59. Buridan Q. in Phys. 6.4 (fol. 97ra). This is the seventh thesis (*conclusio*) defended by Buridan in the main part of the question.

of the sphere in the syncategorematic sense that each part of it is in contact with the plane. This is because indivisibles by definition have no parts.

What is the point of such precision? In a comment just prior to his discussion of the sphere and plane example, Buridan reveals that his aim is to underwrite certain figurative modes of discourse. The logico-semantic problem here is that even if the last part of a continuum is called a point in the divisibilist, categorematic sense that some whole part of it, i.e., some part of it having parts, is its last part, "a point is commonly said by everyone to be indivisible."[60] To this Buridan replies that a point is called an indivisible "not because it is so, or because it is literally true [*quia sit ita, vel quia sit verum de virtute sermonis*]" that a point is indivisible,[61] but because it is treated as such in conventional usage. He gives several examples here, the first and foremost of which has to do with the practice of mathematics. Although points are not strictly speaking indivisible,

> in one way, this is said in keeping with the imagination of mathematicians [*secundum imaginationem mathematicorum*], as if there were an indivisible point, not because they must believe that there really is, but because they revert to those assumptions in measuring, just as if it were so. For if an indivisible point is limiting a line, it is agreed that that whole line would be exclusively beneath it, and likewise, the whole [line] itself is exclusively beneath its last part.[62]

Likewise, says Buridan, we observe that in commerce, a cloth merchant measures lengths of cloth from an imaginary first point.[63] In more philosophical contexts, we see that a point is sometimes called

---

60. Buridan Q. in Phys. 6.4 (fol. 97rb).
61. Buridan Q. in Phys. 6.4 (fol. 97rb).
62. Buridan Q. in Phys. 6.4 (fol. 97$^{rb\text{-}va}$). Compare Buridan *Quaestiones super libros quatuor De caelo et mundo* 1.22, ed. Ernest A. Moody (Cambridge, Mass.: Medieval Academy of America, 1942), pp. 105, 112–15; and Ockham *Expos. Phys.* 5.5.7 and 6.1.2 (Wood et al. 383.48–49, 462.320–323), discussed in note 26 above.
63. Cloth merchants aren't worried about the structure of continua, of course, but (and this is Buridan's point) the practice of measuring an ell of cloth clearly assumes the existence of indivisible first and last points. If such points are treated as infinitely divisible, how could they give rise to determinate and non-arbitrary measurements? For analogous remarks regarding the utility of other concepts of measurement, e.g., length, width, and depth, none of which Buridan supposes to be really distinct from quantity, see Q. in De caelo 1.2–3 (Moody pp. 10–16, esp. 15.29–33).

the indivisible limit of a line in the sense that "it is not divisible into parts of which each part is the limit of the line." In other words, 'point' can refer to some whole last part of a line in the categorematic but not the syncategorematic sense of 'whole'.[64] Alternatively, the first or last part of a line is sometimes treated as a single thing distinct from every other part, in which case it would acquire the qualitative or formal indivisibility Aristotle ascribes in *Metaphysics* X to that which is one.[65] Like the cloth-merchants, mathematicians and philosophers sometimes ply their trade on the assumption that points are indivisible.

Buridan's sensitivity to the logico-semantic underpinnings of mathematical language enables him to appreciate an aspect of the sphere and plane example missed by both Ockham and Wodeham. This emerges in Buridan's reply to the touch-at-a-point argument in his "Quaestio de puncto," an independent treatise on the continuum problem.[66] He begins by citing Averroës's comment that although natural bodies can touch only at a divisible part, a geometrically conceived sphere and plane surface would touch at a point.[67] Accordingly, Buridan concedes that there is indeed a sense in which continua must be assumed to be in contact at a point.

---

64. Buridan Q. in Phys. 6.4 (fol. 97rb).
65. Buridan Q. in Phys. 6.4 (fol. 97va). See Aristotle Metaph. 10.3 (1054a20–29).
66. The *Quaestio de puncto* asks essentially the same question as Q. in Phys. 6.4, namely "whether a point is some indivisible thing added to a line or body." See Buridan *Quaestio de puncto*, ed. V. Zoubov in "Jean Buridan et les concepts du point au quatorzième siècle," *Mediaeval and Renaissance Studies* 5 (1961): 63, line 3. Though there are similarities between the two discussions, the actual texts differ in both their structure and argument. The editor of the *De puncto* prefers to describe them as "complementary" (Zoubov p. 46). Unlike Q. in Phys. 6.4, the *De puncto* is directed against a certain "doctor venerabilis" who is not further identified. The author of the table of contents of the volume in which one of the manuscripts of the *De puncto* is found (Paris, BN lat. 16621) calls it a treatise written "contra magistrum de Montescalerio" (Zoubov, "Jean Buridan," p. 43). Michalski has suggested that the *magister* in question is Burley. The editor of the *De puncto* regards this as a possibility, but also maintains (sensibly, in my view) that it cannot have been the entire aim of the *De puncto* to refute Burley. See Zoubov, "Jean Buridan," pp. 50–52.
67. Buridan *De puncto* 3.2 (Zoubov 91.21–25). The editor of the *Quaestio de puncto* gives the reference to Averroës as *In De coelo* 1.32 (Venice, 1560), 5:27r. The touch-at-a-point argument is presented in highly abridged form at *De puncto* 3.1 (Zoubov 85.10).

NOMINALISM MEETS INDIVISIBILISM 181

> in order to verify the thought of the mathematicians, you must know that when a body is touching another body, it touches the other as a whole—taking 'whole' unitively [unitive]—because the body that is one whole touches the other body that is also one other whole, but not as a whole dividedly [divisive], because this would signify that each part would touch each part, which cannot be without penetration.[68]

The upshot for the sphere and plane example is clear.

> if a spherical body is placed on a plane, they would not touch each other in their parts by any division. And so they are said to touch at a point.[69]

The similarity between these remarks and Wodeham's view, namely, that spheres and planes conceived as positively immediate macro-indivisibles would touch each other at a point, can hardly be accidental. Like Wodeham, Buridan stresses that continua said to touch at a point must be thought of positively as *wholes*, rather than negatively as mere aggregates of parts producible by division. But this is not simply an endorsement of Wodeham's position. Buridan adds sophistication to the non-entitist reply in two ways. First, like Wodeham, he shows that Ockham's counterintuitive denial of contact is not the only option available to the non-entitist: by exploiting the logical distinction between the categorematic and syncategorematic senses of the term 'whole', one can show how the touch-at-a-point argument is actually compatible with divisibilist and non-entitist assumptions about the structure of continua. Second, Buridan sees this compatibility as exemplified in the practice of mathematicians, who use terms such as 'point' connotatively to refer not to a new class of entities, but to already existing entities in a certain, abstract way, namely, as quantities.[70]

---

68. Buridan *De puncto* 3.2 (Zoubov 91.26–92.1).
69. Buridan *De puncto* 3.2 (Zoubov 92.14–15).
70. Buridan *In Metaphysicen Aristotelis quaestiones argutissimae magistri Joannes Buridani* 6.2 (Paris: 1588 [actually 1518]), rptd. as *Kommentar zur Aristotelischen Metaphysik* (Frankfurt a. M.: Minerva, 1964), fol. 33vb. For discussion of Buridan's philosophy of mathematics, see J. M. M. H. Thijssen, "Buridan On Mathematics," *Vivarium* 23 (1985): 55–78. Though Buridan is parsimonious about positing entities, he sees nothing wrong (unlike Ockham) with proliferating modes of entities to account for the truth conditions of sentences concerning certain kinds of physical change. See *Q. in Metaph.* 5.8, *Q. in Phys.* 2.3. For discussion, see Calvin Normore, "Buridan's Ontology," in *How Things Are: Studies in Predication and the History and Philosophy*

That Buridan eventually came to develop his account into something of a fine art is evident in one of his last works: Book 3, Question 14 of the third and final redaction of his *Questions on Aristotle's De anima*.[71] After discussing the ways in which indivisibilists and divisibilists nominally define the term 'point', he notes that "students have occasionally asked whether a sphere placed on a plane would touch it at a point." To this query, he offers a split reply, depending upon which nominal definition of 'point' is used.[72] If 'point' is defined in the indivisibilist sense as 'an indivisible having position in a magnitude', he says, then a sphere placed on a plane surface would *not* touch it at a point, since "a point is nothing," and touching obviously involves something. Recall that this is essentially Ockham's reply to the argument: if contact has to be at a point, then there can be no contact. But if 'point' is defined in the divisibilist sense as 'the first or last part of a line', Buridan replies conditionally, stating that "if it touches, it touches it at a point in such a way that it touches at [the sphere's] last part." Not only that, it touches "at infinitely many last parts," since the sphere has infinitely many last parts, which may be produced, he says, "by dividing the sphere at circles parallel to each other and to the plane itself"—in other words, by slicing the sphere horizontally so that the cuts are parallel to the plane on which it rests. This is, of course, the method of proportional division *ad infinitum*

---

of Science, ed. James Bogen and J. E. McGuire (Boston: Reidel, 1985), pp. 189–203; and Zupko, "How Are Souls Related to Bodies? A Study of John Buridan," *Review of Metaphysics* 46 (1993):575–601. For Ockham's contrasting views on this point, see McCord Adams, *William Ockham*, pp. 178–186 and 277–285. Buridan also sees mathematical or, more properly, geometrical terms such as 'sphere' and 'plane' as referring to natural entities conceived in a certain abstract and generalized manner, namely, in so far as they exhibit the inherence of a magnitude. One might say that Buridan proliferates 'hows' rather than 'whats'. See, e.g., Buridan *De puncto* 1.1 (Zoubov 65.10–15). I should perhaps add that Buridan's strategy here would be of little use to Ockham, and not merely because Ockham balks at proliferating modes. The traditional interpretation of the role of connotative terms in Ockham's ontological program (as strictly synonymous with their nominal definitions, and hence as eliminable in mental language), has been recently, and very effectively, criticized by Claude Panaccio, "Connotative Terms in Ockham's Mental Language," *Cahiers d'épistémologie* [Montreal] no. 9016 (1990): 1–21.

71. For evidence suggesting that Buridan's *Q. in De anima* was composed after May 1347, see Zupko, "John Buridan's Philosophy of Mind," doctoral dissertation, Cornell University, 1989, pp. xxii–xxiii.

72. Buridan *Q. in De anima* 3.14 (Zupko 155.98–156.110).

Wodeham uses to illustrate how the notion of contact at some whole part of the sphere is compatible with the divisibilist assumption that the sphere has infinitely many such parts. Thus, says Buridan, a sphere sliced in half would touch the plane at the point which is its bottom half; the sphere sliced in quarters would touch the plane at the point which is its bottom quarter; and so on *ad infinitum.*

All of this is, Buridan concedes, subject to the condition that the sphere does touch the plane. Should the objector be dissatisfied with this hypothetical reply, and "ask categorically whether [the sphere] touches [the plane surface at a point]," Buridan has a second twofold reply, depending this time on the nominal definition of the word 'touch'.[73] If the definition is based on Aristotle's remark in Physics 5 that two things touch if their extremities are together,[74] then we need to ask about the nominal definition of 'together'. Buridan says that 'together' can be defined in terms of 'adjacent'. The latter term, it appears, has an ambiguous signification: it could signify either (1) two bodies such that no other body is between them; or (2) the situation of two bodies such that they could not be closer "without the penetration or compression of one of them."[75]

If 'adjacent' signifies in the second way, Buridan says, "the sphere and the plane would touch each other." Contact of this sort is defined using Wodeham's notion of positive immediacy: the sphere and plane are said to touch if they extended towards each other as far as possible without compression or penetration, regardless of presence of other, intermediate bodies (e.g., the air) between them.

But if 'adjacent' signifies in the first way, Buridan argues that the sphere and plane "do not touch each other" because then they would have to touch at a point, which is nothing.

> if you place an actual sphere above an actual plane here in the air, then there will be air between them and between any and every part of them, because the air on the right would touch against the air on the left, for if

---

73. Buridan Q. in De anima 3.14 (Zupko 156.111-124). Compare Buridan De caelo 1.22 (Moody 107.31-32); Ockham Expos. Phys. 5.5.2 (Wood et al. 377.98-100); Wodeham De indiv. 2.3.11 (Wood 151.13-14).

74. See Physics 5.3 (226b23).

75. Although Buridan does not acknowledge his sources here, we can easily recognize the former as Chatton's negative definition of contact between indivisibles, and the latter as Wodeham's positive definition of contact between continuous wholes.

there were indivisible points as some imagine, those volumes of air would be separated only by a single indivisible point, which would not separate the parts joined to it. And since there would be nothing indivisible in the sphere or in the plane, and air is between any indivisible of that sphere and of that plane, it follows that there is nothing belonging to the one that is touching something belonging to the other in such a way that there is not some body between them, namely, the air.[76]

In other words, if we imagine the cross-sectional view of an actual sphere S being lowered onto an actual plane P, S and P will be separated by a continuum of air—call it 'LR'—as long as S is above P. But when S has been lowered as far as it can go, L and R would be separated, the case assumes, only by the point of contact between S and P. But since this same point is also the point of contact between L and R, S cannot really touch P, for the continuum LR still separates them. Therefore, S and P cannot touch at a single, indivisible point. To divide these volumes of air, that point would have to be extended and hence divisible—something Ockham and Wodeham also both recognized.

CONCLUSION

The replies of Ockham, Wodeham, and Buridan to the indivisibilist touch-at-a-point argument based on the sphere and plane example show, on a small scale, how medieval divisibilism evolved from a relatively unsophisticated defense of Aristotelian assumptions into a highly complex and subtle theory about the structure of continua. The portion of the story I've told appears to go something like this: in Ockham, the indivisibilist argument is addressed mostly in terms of definitions and arguments from Aristotle's *Physics*, with little concern about its initial or intuitive plausibility. In Wodeham, that plausibility is both confronted and resolved in terms of an alternative account of contact (inspired, ironically, by the indivisibilists), and by means of the quasi-mathematical technique known as "proportional division *ad infinitum*," which is used to illustrate how the sphere and plane can be said to touch by means of a divisible, but in the manner

76. Buridan Q. *in De anima* 3.14 (Zupko 156.124–157.134).

of an indivisible. Finally, in Buridan, the conclusion of the argument is treated like a sophism sentence and disarmed using logic, so that the paramount concern is to understand the signification of terms such as 'point' and 'contact'. The mathematical problem of explaining contact between ideal continuous bodies is raised only secondarily, almost as an afterthought. The divisibilist and non-entitist solution is hardly free of counterintuitiveness, of course, since it stipulates that if 'point' is to be a referring expression, it must pick out some divisible macro-object. From a dialectical standpoint, however, what really blunted the force of the indivisibilist touch-at-a-point argument was the development by Wodeham and Buridan of particular methods by which it could be interpreted without positing indivisible entities. In the fourteenth-century debate over the structure of continua, nominalism did indeed meet indivisibilism, and at least in the case of the touch-at-a-point argument, it emerged with its ontology intact.[77]

San Diego State University

---

77. For comments on previous drafts of this paper or arguments contained therein, I would like to thank Mary Gregor, Norman Kretzmann, Tom Weston, and Rega Wood. An abridged version was presented at a session on medieval metaphysics at the 1992 Annual Meeting of the Medieval Association of the Pacific at the University of California, Irvine. I am grateful to several members of the audience on that occasion, especially Marilyn Adams, Calvin Normore, and Martin Tweedale, for a number of helpful suggestions.

The Church in the Light of Learned Ignorance

THOMAS M. IZBICKI

The years between 1436 and 1442 were vital ones in the life and thought of Nicholas of Cusa, who entered that period as the leading conciliar theorist of his generation and emerged from it as a papal apologist, "the Hercules of the Eugenians," as well as one of the most original speculative thinkers of the Renaissance. Cusanus's change of ecclesiological emphasis coincided with the eclipse of Cardinal Giuliano Cesarini, with whom he was closely associated, as leader of the Council of Basel, and the rise of Cardinal Louis d'Aleman, an ardent foe of Eugenius IV, to supplant him. This change of leadership itself coincided with the factional division of the assembly over the site of a council of union with the Greeks and a change in emphasis from open debate on issues of faith, unity, and reform to the attempt to declare conciliar supremacy a dogma.[1] Cusanus's own change of allegiance cannot be divorced from his own self-interest;[2]

---

1. On the change in the council, see Giuseppe Alberigo, *Chiesa conciliare: Identità e significato del conciliarismo* (Brescia: Paideia, 1979), pp. 256–340. On Cesarini's eclipse, see Gerald Christianson, *Cesarini, the Conciliar Cardinal: The Basel Years, 1431–1438* (St. Ottilien: EOS, 1979), pp. 149–180.

2. See, most recently, Joachim W. Stieber, "The 'Hercules of the Eugenians' at the Crossroads: Nicholas of Cusa's Decision for the Pope and Against the Council in 1436/1437—Theological, Political and Social Aspects," in *Nicholas of Cusa in Search*

nor can it be separated from the fortunes of Cesarini, to whom, together with Emperor Sigismund, he had dedicated *De concordantia catholica*, and whom he had supported in the climactic struggle over the location of a council of union.[3] This transformation, however, cannot be divided from the contemporaneous changes occurring in Cusanus's internal life, which caused him to emphasize speculative rather than institutional themes in his later writings. Following a mystical experience on a ship returning from Constantinople, where he had been representing both Eugenius and the minority faction at Basel, Cusanus entered the middle phase of his literary life, during which he developed his idea of learned ignorance and his methodology of conjecture.[4]

Reviewing these changes in Cusanus's life and thought, scholars have been inclined to emphasize discontinuity, especially between his speculative concepts and his previous ecclesiological and political themes. Also little attention is given Nicholas's papalist polemics, either because his major treatises put them in the shade or because they seem like puny siblings of *De concordantia catholica*.[5] A closer examination of them reveals, however, that they both reflect Cusanus's struggle to establish a new identity apart from the Council of Basel and an effort to fit his papalism into the larger frame of his speculative thought. Both of these developments coincided in Nicholas's letter to Rodrigo Sánchez de Arévalo (1442), which determined the nature of his later ecclesiology, as expressed in his sermons and his *Reformatio generalis* (c. 1459). This ecclesiology, however, could not free Cusanus

---

of God and Wisdom: Essays in Honor of Morimichi Watanabe, ed. Gerald Christianson and Izbicki (Leiden and New York: Brill, 1991), pp. 221–255.

3. See, respectively, Nicholas of Cusa, *The Catholic Concordance*, tr. Paul Sigmund (Cambridge: Cambridge University Press, 1991); H. Lawrence Bond, Christianson, and Izbicki, "Nicholas of Cusa: On Presidential Authority in a General Council," *Church History* 59 (1990): 19–34; *Der Briefwechsel des Eneas Sylvius Piccolomini*, ed. R. Wolkan, 1/1 (Vienna: Hölder, 1909), pp. 58–76, no. 24, at p. 65.

4. J. E. Biechler, "Nicholas of Cusa and the End of the Conciliar Movement: A Humanist Crisis of Identity," *Church History* 44 (1975): 5–21.

5. See, respectively, Pauline Moffitt Watts, *Nicolaus Cusanus: A Fifteenth Century Vision of Man* (Leiden: Brill, 1982) and the brief treatments of Cusanus's later ecclesiological works in Morimichi Watanabe, *The Political Ideas of Nicholas of Cusa* (Geneva: Droz, 1963), pp. 97–114; Paul E. Sigmund, *Nicholas of Cusa and Medieval Political Thought* (Cambridge, Mass.: Harvard University Press, 1963), pp. 261–280.

from German suspicions that he had betrayed the Council of Basel and that, whatever his reforming efforts, he could not be trusted as papal legate or as bishop of Brixen.[6]

Cusanus's struggle to define himself as a papalist evolved in the context of his role as a papal representative in Germany between 1439 and 1444, where he attended several of the diets and other meetings which tried in vain to choose between the Council of Basel and its pope, Felix V, and Eugenius IV and his council at Ferrara, Florence, Siena, and, ultimately, Rome. The Germans attempted to maintain a stance variously described as "neutrality" or "eitherness" (*utralitas*), refusing to make a final decision for either party while negotiating with both. A common proposal for ending the "conciliar crisis" was a council, preferably at Constance, which would continue the Council of Basel as if it never had been divided and would choose between Eugenius and Felix.[7] These German deliberations would fail to enforce such a policy and, ultimately, would be abandoned for recognition of Eugenius on terms favorable to the princes.[8]

In 1439, however, Cusanus could not foresee these results; and he had to put on a bold face to confront conciliarists and neutralists alike. His earliest polemics, beginning with a letter to an imperial advisor, arguing in vain against the policy of neutrality adopted by Albrecht II, the brief-lived Hapsburg king of the Romans, emphasized a theme consistent with his earlier, more conciliar works, that of

---

6. Izbicki, "Auszüge aus Schriften des Nikolaus von Kues im Rahmen der Geschichte des Basler Konzils," *Mitteilungen und Forschungsbeiträge der Cusanus-Gesellschaft* 19 (1991): 117–135; Donald Sullivan, "Nicholas of Cusa as Reformer: The Papal Legation to the Germanies, 1451–1452," *Mediaeval Studies* 36 (1974): 382–428; Erich Meuthen, "Die deutsche Legationsreise des Nikolaus von Kues 1451/52," *Lebenslehren und Weltentwürfe im Übergang vom Mittelalter zur Neuzeit*, ed. Hartmut Bookmann et al. (Gottingen: Vandenhoek & Ruprecht, 1989), pp. 421–499; Watanabe, "Nicholas of Cusa and the Tyrolese Monasteries—Reform and Resistance," *History of Political Thought* 7 (1986): 53–72.

7. This proposal sometimes is described as a plan for a "third" council; see R. Bäumer, "Eugen IV und der Plan eines 'Dritten Konzils' zur Beilegung des Basler Schismas," *Reformata Reformanda: Festgabe für Hubert Jedin*, ed. Erwin Iserloh and Konrad Repgen (Munster: Aschendorff, 1965) 1:87–128.

8. Joachim Stieber, *Pope Eugenius IV, the Council of Basel and the Secular and Ecclesiastical Authorities* (Leiden: Brill, 1979).

consent. The case for Eugenius and against both Felix and neutrality drew on both law and history; but Cusanus emphasized the need for Basel to prove, to justify its actions against a reigning pope, that the princes or the Church dispersed throughout the world had consented.[9] The same argument would recur in 1441 in a polemical exchange with a Carthusian monastery concerning the nature and powers of a council. Nicholas argued that a valid council requires concords and the consent of the entire Church, including pope and cardinals. Basel, he said, was a seat of discord; but the Church was represented at Florence, where concord prevailed and the pope was present consenting to conciliar acts.[10] Also in 1441, in a letter to the archbishop of Trier, Cusanus made the first of several attempts to prove that Germany must give up neutrality and, without evasion, embrace Eugenius.[11]

How little the argument from consent mattered, even in the narrow public of ecclesiological debate, can be seen from Cusanus's dispute with Thomas Ebendorfer, the theological architect of neutrality, at the time of the Diet of Mainz (1441). Nicholas argued that papal consent was required to validate any conciliar enactment, even the decree *Frequens* of the Council of Constance, on which much of the argument against translation of the Basel assembly to Ferrara turned. The pope could be disobeyed only if his actions endangered the Church, a threat absent when Basel acted against a reigning Roman pontiff.[12] This argument and others like it weighed little

---

9. *Acta Cusana: Quellen zur Lebensgeschichte des Nikolaus von Kues* 1/2, ed. Erich Meuthen and Hermann Hallauer (Hamburg: Meiner, 1983), pp. 268–273, no. 408. On Nicholas's ability to recycle his older ideas within the broader context of medieval "political languages," see Antony Black, "Political Languages in Later Medieval Europe," in *The Church and Sovereignty c. 590–1918*, ed. Diana Wood, Studies in Church History Subsidia 9 (Oxford: Blackwell, 1991), pp. 313–328. These languages, however, should be understood as sources employed within the broader language of arguments from reason and authority; see Juan de Torquemada, *A Disputation on the Authority of Pope and Council*, tr. Izbicki (Oxford: Blackfriars, 1988), pp. xvi–xvii.

10. *Acta Cusana* 1/2:305–13, no. 468.

11. *Acta Cusana* 1/2:313–20, no. 469. See also pp. 322–325, no. 473, and pp. 432–436, no. 527.

12. *Acta Cusana* 1/2:342–52, no. 481. On Ebendorfer's role, see Alphons Lhotsky, *Thomas Ebendorfer* (Stuttgart: Hiersemann, 1957), p. 36.

with German theologians like Ebendorfer, Bartholomew of Maastrich, and Johann Wenck, the leading critic of Nicholas's speculative doctrines.[13] Cusanus himself revealed his awareness of how vulnerable his conciliar past left him by arguing, in his contemporaneous *Dialogus concludens errorem Amadeistarum*, a first essay at a literary genre which would be used often in his later writings, the imaginary conversation. The interlocutors in this dialogue were a master, obviously Cusanus himself, and his disciple. The latter's request for an explanation of his teacher's change of ecclesiastical allegiance led to a remarkably benign interpretation, for a papalist, of both the Council of Constance and of the earliest sessions at Basel. Radicalization was the fault of latecomers; and their acts were invalid, since the pope had not consented to them. This argument was coupled with a lame contention that God would not let the reigning pope damage the Church and an insistence, almost in the teeth of that argument from Providence, that the pope had to act to build up the Church.[14] This last emphasis would be taken up in the letter to Arévalo and Cusanus's other writings on the Church.

The discontent Cusanus must have felt at such lame arguments, so lacking in speculative content or originality, is apparent from his letter to Rodrigo Sánchez de Arévalo,[15] written in 1442, when he expected that Castilian canonist, who was representing his king, Juan II, in Germany, to join him at the Diet of Frankfurt in defending Eugenius IV and his council against Basel, Felix V, and neutrality. This letter must be read, however, in the light of Cusanus's great speculative treatises *De docta ignorantia* and *De coniecturis*, the major works of the middle phase of his writing career, which had been

---

13. *Acta Cusana* 1/2:359–62, no. 484; pp. 325–326, no. 474; pp. 326–328, no. 475. See also *Nicholas of Cusa's Debate with John Wenck*, ed. and tr. Jasper Hopkins, 2d ed. (Minneapolis: Banning, 1981).

14. Erich Meuthen, "Nikolaus von Kues: Dialogus concludens Amadeistarum errorem ex gestis et doctrina concilii Basiliensis," *Mitteilungen und Forschungsbeiträge der Cusanus Gesellschaft* 8 (1970): 11–114. See also *Acta Cusana* 1/2:363, no. 488.

15. Richard H. Trame, *Rodrigo Sánchez de Arévalo, 1404–1470* (Washington, D.C.: Catholic University of America Press, 1958), pp. 53–57; Juan Maria Laboa, *Rodrigo Sánchez de Arévalo, alcalde de Sant'Angelo* (Madrid: Publicaciones de la Fundación Universitaria Española, 1973), p. 45.

completed in this same period.¹⁶ Although the nominal topic of the letter was the present state of the Church, it also contains a more general theological statement, an expression of Cusanus's Christology and, in the light of this Christology, a contribution to the ongoing debate on the True Church (*vera ecclesia*). Cusanus would conclude, as shall be demonstrated below, that the True Church could not be seen by men; but its presence could be discerned through "sacred signs" where the faith of Peter in the Incarnate Lord was professed and the body of Christ was built up by Peter's successor, the "sacred prince," the pope.¹⁷ Only in this speculative context would Cusanus find a papalist idiom with which he could rest content.

The place of Christ at the heart of Cusanus's thought cannot be emphasized too strongly. The hypostatic union of Divinity and humanity in Jesus bridged the gap between "finite mind" and "Infinite Truth."¹⁸ This emphasis was not limited to any one work. One need only mention that place of the Word as interlocutor in the irenic discussion of religious differences in *De pace fidei*, the central role of the icon in *De visione Dei*, or the winning score of 34 in *De ludo globi*, which equals the age of Jesus at the time of His Passion.¹⁹ The key exposition of Cusanus's Christology, however, at least for our purposes, can be found in *De docta ignorantia* 3. The first two books were concerned with a doctrine of creation which left the Creator

---

16. For the periodization of Cusanus's works, see F. Edward Cranz, "The Late Works of Nicholas of Cusa," in *Nicholas of Cusa in Search of God and Wisdom*, pp. 141–160.

17. Quotations from Cusanus's letter to Rodrigo Sánchez de Arévalo are taken from the translation included as an appendix to this article.

18. H. Lawrence Bond, "Nicholas of Cusa and the Reconstruction of Theology," *Medieval Christian Tradition: Essays in Honor of Ray C. Petry*, ed. George H. Shriver (Durham, N.C.: Duke University Press, 1974), pp. 81–94; Rudolf Haubst, *Die Christologie des Nikolaus von Kues* (Freiburg i. B.: Herder, 1956); Haubst, "Der Leitgedanke der *repraesentatio* in der cusanischen Ekklesiologie," *Mitteilungen und Forschungsbeiträge der Cusanus-Gesellschaft* 9 (1971): 140–159.

19. Nicholas of Cusa, *On Interreligious Harmony*, ed. James E. Biechler and H. Lawrence Bond (Lewiston: Mellen, 1990); *Nicholas of Cusa's De pace fidei and Cribratio Alkorani*, tr. Jasper Hopkins (Minneapolis: Banning, 1990); *Nicholas of Cusa's Dialectical Mysticism*, tr. Jasper Hopkins, 2nd ed. (Minneapolis: Banning, 1988); Nicholas of Cusa, *The Games of Spheres*, tr. Pauline Moffitt Watts (New York: Abaris, 1986).

unknowable by the faculties of the creatures, including a defense of Negative Theology, in which Truth "shines incomprehensibly within the darkness of our ignorance."[20] In Book 3, Nicholas set out to show the coincidence of the "absolutely Maximum" and the "contracted maximum" in Jesus.[21] These opposites coincided in the hypostatic union of divine and human natures in Christ, a union transcending human knowledge, since "Absolute God" did not become confused with created matter.[22] This union produced the maximum individual, of whom there only could be one; but He elevated human nature above the angels, becoming the "universal contracted being of each creature," "the Word [of God] in whom all things were created."[23]

In this light, Cusanus explicated the Incarnation, Passion, and Resurrection of Jesus as the means of salvation and as the fulfillment of the hypostatic union.[24] The Saracens, that is, the Muslims, and the Jews were censured for affirming certain truths of the faith while denying others. Here we find a negative form of what appears as a positive argument in *De pace fidei*, the argument that other religions approach the truth without attaining it.[25]

Only in the last two chapters of *De docta ignorantia* did Cusanus address directly the ecclesiological dimensions of his subject. In chapter 11, Cusanus's emphasis fell upon faith as understanding's guide, with understanding, in turn, helping faith to increase.[26] Faith, God's gift, revealed the treasures of wisdom and knowledge to the limited human intellect.[27] Faith united the believer with Jesus, receiving from Him power over "nature and motion." The wondrous deeds of the saints were evidence of the power Jesus conferred on the

---

20. The Latin text of this work can be found in Nicholas of Cusa, *Opera omnia* 1 (Leipzig: Meiner, 1932). The English quotations are taken from *Nicholas of Cusa on Learned Ignorance*, tr. Jasper Hopkins (Minneapolis: Banning, 1981), pp. 49–124, esp. p. 85.
21. *On Learned Ignorance*, p. 125.
22. *On Learned Ignorance*, pp. 128–130.
23. *On Learned Ignorance*, pp. 130–133.
24. *On Learned Ignorance*, pp. 135–142.
25. *On Learned Ignorance*, pp. 143–144. On Cusanus and Islam, see James E. Biechler, "Nicholas of Cusa and Mohammed: A Fifteenth Century Encounter," *Downside Review* 101 (1983): 50–59.
26. *On Learned Ignorance*, p. 149.
27. *On Learned Ignorance*, pp. 149–151.

believer.[28] The Thomist tradition, represented in Cusanus's day by Juan de Torquemada, among others, distinguished between unformed faith, expressed in baptism, and formed faith, enlivened by charity, Augustine's mark of membership in the True Church.[29] Cusanus reflected this distinction, without making specific mention of baptism. As far as possible, it was necessary for "perfect faith in Christ" to be "most pure, maximum, and formed by love." Faith could not be maximum unless it passed into the realm of action. The truth of the faith required an active response. Otherwise it was dead and, in Cusanus's words, "is not faith at all." Faith made the believer more like Christ, leaving the desires of the flesh for those of the spirit, the visible for the invisible, the mundane for the divine.[30]

In chapter 12, Cusanus set forth his understanding of the Church to round out the book. It is worth noting that the institutional apparatus of the Church, so prominent in Cusanus's conciliarist writings, went without mention. Nonetheless, the fundamental idea of building up the Church was presupposed in this chapter. In *De docta ignorantia*, Cusanus spoke of humans as pilgrims, imitating Jesus, who had obtained, as no one else could, "unqualified maximum faith and unqualified maximum love."[31] Christ became the exemplar to which every Christian was expected to conform to be able to enter into the Church Triumphant. They could seek union with Christ without either attaining it perfectly, because of human limitations, or losing "their respective degrees on account of the union."[32] Resorting to Pauline terminology, Cusanus spoke of membership in one body through faith. In Johannine terms, he spoke of believers as branches of the one vine. The result, in Nicholas's words, was that, "Christ's humanity will be in all men, and Christ's one spirit will be in all

---

28. *On Learned Ignorance*, p. 151.

29. *On Learned Ignorance*, pp. 151–152. On Torquemada's doctrine of the Church, see Izbicki, *Protector of the Faith: Cardinal Johannes de Turrecremata and the Defense of the Institutional Church* (Washington, D.C.: Catholic University of America Press, 1981), pp. 31–41.

30. *On Learned Ignorance*, p. 152. Cusanus preached a similar message in his 1440 sermon on the text "Dies sanctificatus"; see his *Opera omnia* 16/4:333–57, no. 22. Compare this with his earlier, more Anselmian preaching on the Incarnation, e.g., his sermon on *In principio erat verbum* in *Opera omnia* 16/1:1–19, no. 1.

31. *On Learned Ignorance*, p. 153.

32. *On Learned Ignorance*, p. 154.

spirits."[33] Although the achievement of union was described in terms of hunger and thirst, Cusanus made it clear that he was speaking of the intellect, which could not achieve its true food and drink, the Maximum, the Divinity, in this life, even as a member of the Church Militant.[34] Only in the Church Triumphant would the human intellect share, as far as possible, in the hypostatic union by which "the true man Christ Jesus is united, in supreme union, with the Son of God."[35]

In Cusanus's eyes, Church meant "a oneness of many [members], each seeking union without the loss of its identity and achieving that union in the maximal Church, the eternal now of the Church Triumphant." This union was achieved as the "maximum union" of all natures without distinction of greater or lesser in "the maximum union of the natures of Christ," which gives unity to the Church.[36] Through Christ, the Church shared the "Absolute Union," the Holy Spirit, which unites the Father and the Son in living love. Here Cusanus affirmed not only the highest bond of ecclesial union but the Western doctrine of the Double Procession of the Holy Spirit, which had been harmonized, however briefly, with Eastern theology in the decree of union between the Greek and Latin churches promulgated at the Council of Florence less than a year before *De docta ignorantia* was completed.[37]

In Cusanus's doctrine of the Church, as set forth in *De docta ignorantia*, the metaphysics, epistemology, and psychology of mystical union leave behind, for the moment, the vexing problems of pope, council, and princely politics. The True Church lies in the hereafter in the realization of faith in love in the Church Triumphant.

This doctrine of the Church might seem too esoteric to confront those same problems, but Cusanus saw it as the clue to the right ordering of the ecclesiastical institution. It allowed him to reject the declaration of the assembly at Basel, issued in 1439, the year which saw the Greek and Latin Churches declare themselves reunited, that

33. *On Learned Ignorance*, p. 154.
34. *On Learned Ignorance*, pp. 155–156.
35. *On Learned Ignorance*, p. 156.
36. *On Learned Ignorance*, pp. 156–157.
37. *On Learned Ignorance*, p. 157. See also Joseph Gill, *The Council of Florence* (Cambridge: Cambridge University Press, 1959), pp. 227–269, 412–415.

conciliar supremacy is a dogma. On the basis of that dogma, the assembly had deposed Eugenius IV and elected Amadeus VIII of Savoy to reign as Felix V.[38] It also permitted Cusanus, at least in his private writings, to avoid the excessively institutional emphasis of Eugenius and the apologist resident at his court. Eugenius had responded to Basel's attempt to depose him by issuing the decree *Moyses*, which condemned Basel as a congerie of rebels against hierarchical authority, like Dathan, Abiram, and Korah, the opponents of Moses.[39] Eugenius also staged a debate between Cardinal Giuliano Cesarini, defending conciliarism, and the Dominican theologian Juan de Torquemada, defending papalism, as a prelude to a renewed diplomatic effort to win the princes to the papal cause.[40] In that diplomatic struggle, as has been noted above, Eugenius and Basel competed to win over the princes through argument, persuasion, and outright bribes.[41] In this context, Cusanus tried to apply the doctrine of learned ignorance to practical problems in quest of a solution which was theologically sound, spiritually oriented, papalist, and yet oriented to building up the Church.

As has been noted above, the occasion of this effort, made in the letter to Rodrigo Sánchez de Arévalo, was the Diet of Frankfurt (1442), the most recent of a series of meetings, involving the electors and other powers, lay and clerical, which sought to coordinate the Empire's response to the Conciliar Crisis. Arguments supporting conciliarism, papalism, and neutrality were heard; but, as had become typical of these gatherings, no final decisions were made. The diet was preceded by informal meetings from June 8 to July 7, which were interrupted by the coronation at Aachen of Frederick III, another Hapsburg prince, as King of the Romans. Formal proceedings occurred between July 7 and August 18. The combination of meeting and

---

38. Aeneas Sylvius Piccolominus (Pius II), *De gestis concilii Basiliensis*, ed. D. Hay and W. K. Smith (Oxford: Clarendon Press, 1967).

39. *Unity, Heresy and Reform, 1378–1460*, ed. C. M. D. Crowder (New York: St. Martin's Press, 1977), pp. 172–177.

40. Juan de Torquemada, *Oratio synodalis de primatu*, ed. Emmanuel Candal (Rome: Pontificium Institutum Orientalium Studiorum, 1954), and the translation by Izbicki, *A Disputation on the Authority of Pope and Council*.

41. Antony Black, *Monarchy and Community: Political Ideas in the Later Conciliar Controversy* (Cambridge: Cambridge University Press, 1970), pp. 86–129.

coronation caused both Eugenius and Basel to choose their delegations carefully. The Eugenian delegation was led by the Castilian canonist Juan Carvajal and by Nicholas of Cusa. Basel's delegation was led by Louis d'Aleman, president of the council, the canonist Panormitanus and the theologian John of Segovia. Panormitanus and Cusanus presented the cases of their respective parties in almost purely institutional terms, including Nicholas's papalist version of the idea of consent, while John of Segovia and Cusanus argued in writing about the proper interpretation of *Etsi non dubitemus*, Eugenius's latest official statement of his claims.[42] Instead of taking sides, Frederick took the occasion to advance his own plan for reunion, the latest plea that a council be gathered which would absorb the rival assemblies of the two parties. Neither party found this idea palatable, since it implied both the continued validity of the council sitting at Basel and the invalidity of its deposition of Eugenius IV.[43]

These were the public events, both oral and written, of the Diet of Frankfurt. In comparison, Cusanus's letter to Arévalo is a breath of theological fresh air, placing institutional concerns in a cosmic context. It may not have pleased the recipient, who neither arrived in Frankfurt nor reacted to the letter publicly. As a canonist, one adhering to a thoroughly monarchic view of the Church, he may have found Cusanus's ideas peculiar, or at least irrelevant. Despite the presence of the letter in the Paris edition of Cusanus's works, the manuscript tradition is exiguous, suggesting private distribution of the text and a minimal reading public.[44] The letter has been taken

---

42. For the written version of Panormitanus's speech *Quoniam veritas*, see *Deutsche Reichstagsakten* 16, ed. Hermann Herre and L. Quidde (Stuttgart, 1928; rptd. Gottingen: Vandenhoeck & Ruprecht, 1957), pp. 439–538, no. 212. For the written version of Cusanus's reply to that speech, see *Acta Cusana* 1/2:376–421, no. 520. On their doctrines, see Arnulf Vagedes, *Das Konzil über dem Papst?* (Paderborn: Schöningh, 1981); Heinz Hürten, "Die Konstanzer Dekrete *Haec sancta* und *Frequens* in ihrer Bedeutung fur Ekklesiologie und Kirchenpolitik des Nikolaus von Kues," in *Das Konzil von Konstanz*, ed. August Franzen and Wolfgang Müller (Freiburg i. B.: Herder, 1964), pp. 381–396. On *Etsi non dubitemus* and its role in these debates, see Remigius Bäumer, "Die Stellungnahme Eugens IV zum Konstanzer Superioritätsdekret in der Bulle Etsi non dubitemus," in *Das Konzil von Konstanz*, pp. 337–356.

43. Stieber, *Pope Eugenius IV*, pp. 94, 123.

44. *Acta Cusana* 1/2:372–73, no. 516; F. Nägel, "Die Schlettstader Handschrift 340 und ihre Bedeutung für die Uberlieferungsgeschichte des Nicolaus Cusanus am

as a defense of absolutism or, at least, as setting only vague limits on any possible abuse of papal power.[45] A closer reading finds Cusanus straining against the limits of institutional theory, even as he defends the papacy.

At the very beginning of the letter to Arévalo, Cusanus made a leap from the question of pope or council more perfectly representing the Church to more speculative matters. His topic was the Word of God "through which all things came to be." Creation participated "in an unfolded, varied way in the unity of the eternal Word." Cusanus maintained, as in *De docta ignorantia*, the imparticipable nature of the Word, despite the dependance of creation upon It. In Christ, grace is "added over and above nature," opening the way to God through the hypostatic union. As in his previous discussion of the Church Triumphant, Nicholas dwelt on Jesus as "the enfolding of all the blessed," satisfying the intellectual need that nothing created can satisfy. The saved "participate variously" in Christ, making Him head of the Church, holding its "principate."

The Church Militant, "acknowledging the truth through faith and awaiting in hope the happiness which comes through charity" seeks to pass over to the Church Triumphant. The Church Militant has no knowledge of a believer's state of soul. Thus each believer participates in Christ according to individuality of natures; each, unable to grasp knowledge of God directly participates in truth through "enigma and mirror image" in hope of attaining the Truth at last. For Cusanus, the Church is the mystical body of Christ, because in it "the grace of Jesus Christ is unfolded" to all those adhering to Him in the Spirit. Since the Spirit "remains concealed in this sensible world," this is the "concealed Church," which "cannot be known in its sensible particularity of members." Reason can grasp generally who believes and lives in love. Conjectural knowledge of Christ's Church can be gained "through sensible signs." According to the "limited

---

Oberrheim," *Mitteilungen und Forschungsbeiträge der Cusanus-Gesellschaft* 6 (1967): 155–166.

45. These differing emphases can be found in Sigmund, *Nicholas of Cusa and Medieval Political Thought*, pp. 266–272, 280; Erich Meuthen, *Nikolaus von Kues, 1401–1464: Skizze einer Biographie* (Munster: Aschendorff, 1964), pp. 77–78; Trame, *Rodrigo Sánchez de Arévalo*, p. 57, citing Hubert Jedin; Watanabe, *Political Ideas of Nicholas of Cusa*, pp. 106–108.

understanding of this world," what can be perceived from these signs is the True Church, though the discernible Church "contains both those adhering to Christ in the Spirit and [those who do] not," though they acknowledge Christ. This "Church has sacred signs," "so that we may know through them those who are Christ's in the way in which conjectural knowledge can be obtained from signs."

This opinion on the concealed Church was not entirely new in Cusanus's writings. The opening chapters of *De concordantia catholica* had noted human inability to discern who were the true members of the Church, those united to Christ, the Word Incarnate; but that theological point was obscured by the great mass of the work, which focused on the institutional aspects of Christendom, both the reform of the ecclesiastical apparatus and the amelioration of conditions in the Empire.[46] More in his speculative vein, Cusanus, just before writing the letter to Arévalo, had offered Cardinal Cesarini, in *De coniecturis*, his speculations on human diversity, pointing to the existence of one ultimate religion perceived by the human mind, itself the image of God, in a variety of manners.[47] Although this speculation can be read as presaging the more irenic statements in *De pace fidei*, they also indicate the wellsprings of the unusual form of papalism found in the letter to Arévalo. Because the human mind was like unto God, man was most perfect when most like the divine exemplar. Thus the text of the letter emphasized Christ as the exemplar to which all members of the true, invisible Church must conform, however imperfectly. Even the pope, as we will see below, was obliged to conform to an exemplar, Peter, whose regime had been sanctioned by Christ for the work of building up the Church. Cusanus offered here, through his own version of the distinction between the Church Militant, known here and now through signs, and the Church

---

46. Nicholas of Cusa, *Opera omnia* 14, 2nd ed. (Hamburg: Meiner, 1963), pp. 33–36, 42–52. This passage was noted, but only to compare Cusanus's ideas with those of Gerard Groote, by Albert Hyma, *The Christian Renaissance: A History of the Devotio Moderna*, 2d ed. (New York: Century, 1925; rptd. Hamden, Conn.: Archon Books, 1965), pp. 262–263. For the limits of the Church's knowledge see Clyde L. Miller, "Perception, Conjecture and Dialectic in Nicholas of Cusa," *American Catholic Philosophical Quarterly* 64 (1990): 35–54.

47. In Nicholas of Cusa, *Opera omnia* 3 (Hamburg: Meiner, 1972), pp. 138–152. See also Watts, *Nicolaus Cusanus*, pp. 87–116. The *De coniecturis* is assigned to late 1441 or early 1442 in *Acta Cusana* 1/2:370, no. 507.

Triumphant, to be known hereafter, a larger vision than the present crisis demanded, one which addressed the ultimate concern of his age about the nature of the True Church.

Medieval ecclesiastics regarded the Church as possessing four marks, signs which distinguished it from the gatherings of heretics. These were unity, holiness, catholicity, and apostolicity. Of them, holiness, once it became ascribed to the visible Church, was the most controversial. Both good and bad persons obviously were present among the baptized.[48] Cusanus, who was well aware of Basel's negotiations with the Hussites,[49] addressed this issue. He argued that the Church was holy by inference from its sacred signs, despite the presence of "evil and hypocritical men." Those who did not manifest these signs inwardly were excluded, since Christ "admits only the good to union." Since the mind could not know God directly, only through the inward divine image, the True Church of those united to the divine could not be known directly either, only located through signs.

Having set forth these larger premises, Cusanus went on in the letter to Arévalo to discuss the visible order of the "sensible Church," including the papacy. This order was given by Christ according to the "best manner in which it can be." This contention differed little from the papalist contention, advanced by Torquemada in his tracts, that monarchy was Aristotle's most perfect polity and so had been Christ's chosen design for His Church's governance.[50] This portion of the letter to Arévalo is the best known. The Church, Cusanus said, was "unfolded" in Peter, the first to acknowledge Jesus as the Christ. On that profession, and on the one who professed it, the Church was founded. What was enfolded in Peter was unfolded in the Church, producing "one Church participating in the same confession in a varied diversity of believers." The Church needed to be both diverse and one, sharing "one entire confession in all and each part of it." As Adam was unfolded in humanity, Peter, the head of the visible Church, was unfolded in its members, in

---

48. Izbicki, *Protector of the Faith*, p. 37; Scott H. Hendrix, "In Quest of the *vera ecclesia*: The Crises of Late Medieval Ecclesiology," *Viator* 7 (1976): 347–378, at pp. 348–353, 356, 371–374.

49. E. F. Jacob, "The Bohemians at the Council of Basel," in *Prague Essays*, ed. R. W. Seton-Watson (Oxford: Clarendon Press, 1949), pp. 81–123.

50. Izbicki, *Protector of the Faith*, p. 83.

a "variety of powers, orders and prelacies in the unity of faith in the Church." That entire unfolding of Peter (*explicatio Petri*) depended on God; but, within that limit, the supreme power "contains in its plenitude every power of all others." In the language of papalism, as represented by Torquemada, Peter had the plenitude of power; the lesser prelates, a share in the responsibility for ecclesiastical œgovernment.[51]

The "most absolute divine power" conferred this power on Peter; the papal principate, in a more limited sense, was absolute, "set above the people over which it rules." In the language of Roman law, the pope was the prince "not bound by the laws" and "cannot be judged by his subjects."[52] Basel, unnamed in this passage, had committed the crime of rebellion by breaking away from "obedience and unity" when it tried to judge a "sacred prince." In terms derived from Boniface VIII's decree *Unam sanctam*,[53] Cusanus argued that all spiritual and temporal powers were obliged to obey the pope. In case of doubt, the sacred prince must be presumed to be right, that his power was used correctly; and his command must be obeyed. Lesser prelates shared in Peter's powers, but less perfectly. Without saying so, Cusanus here answered the question about pope or council representing the Church more perfectly, since the lesser prelates had nothing which Peter did not possess more perfectly. As Christ was the exemplar of the invisible Church, the *vera ecclesia*, Peter was the exemplar of the visible Church, to whom all its members, including pope and prelates, had to conform. The pope especially was bound to imitate Peter, being most like him when engaged in building up the Church. The more closely the pope conformed himself to Peter, who had been empowered by Christ to be the enfolding

---

51. Gerd Heinz-Mohr, *Unitas christiana: Studien zur Gesellschaftsidee des Nikolaus von Kues* (Trier: Paulinus, 1958), pp. 95-105. This discussion of Peter's role may be understood as a reference to the Primitive Church: see Giuseppe Alberigo, "*Forma ecclesiae* nell'umanesimo cristiano, sopratutto secondo Nicolò da Cusa," *Chiesa per il mondo: Miscellanea teologico-pastorale* (Bologna, 1974) 1:351-375, at pp. 356-357. On Torquemada, see Izbicki, *Protector of the Faith*, pp. 59-60.

52. *Digest* 1.3.31.

53. *Corpus Iuris Canonici* Extrav. commun. 1.8.1, ed. E. Friedberg (Leipzig: Tauchnitz, 1879; rptd. Graz: Akademische Druck-Universität Verlagsamstalt, 1959) 2:1245-46. Cusanus made particular use of *Unam sanctam* in the memoranda against neutrality cited in note 11 above.

of all prelacy, the more heinous any unjustified dissent from his rule became.[54]

All of these ideas argued for obedience to Peter, to his successors, to his present successor, Eugenius IV. Cusanus warned, however, that "a prelate may not abuse the power granted for the building up of the Church for the destruction of a subject church." Likewise, Cusanus wrote, "Peter's universal successor has no power over any particular successor of Peter through which the particular power of building up [the Church in dealing with] those subject to him suffers any change or is impeded." No pope had any power except from Peter. Having been raised in Peter's faith, he was obliged to the common good, building up that faith. The pope had no "free power of casting off, even once, the power enfolded through Peter healthily ordained for the rule of the Church, as long as it requires help in the building up [of the Church]." If the pope "receded from the unity of the Church," by pertinaciously exceeding his office and powers, the Church might recede from him. He had shown "himself unworthy of the sacred principate which he diminishes through abuse." Here it is worth noting that Cusanus emphasized the right order of the Church, the *status ecclesiae*, rather than heresy, in setting limits on the "absolute power" of the sacred prince.[55] It also is worth noting that the pope is not described as reflecting automatically the perfection of his exemplar, Peter. Rather, his conduct was expected to be directed

---

54. This conformity, which was to bring the Church Militant home to the Church Triumphant, is emphasized by Alberigo, "*Forma ecclesiae*," pp. 358, 369–371. According to Alberigo, Peter becomes parallel to Christ, especially as an exemplar for the pope, in Cusanus's preaching; see p. 372, esp. note 84. An excerpt from a sermon on Peter appears in the *Libri excitationum in Nicolai Cusae cardinalis opera* (Paris, 1514; rptd. Frankfurt a.M.: Minerva, 1962), vol. 2, fol. 72^r. A text of Sermon 284, *Beatus es Simon bar Iona*, which emphasizes Peter's faith, his power enfolding all the faithful, and the need to follow him, was kindly provided to the author by Heinrich Paulli.

55. Heinz-Mohr, *Unitas christiana*, pp. 79–84. The term "status ecclesiae" had several possible meanings; see Yves Congar, "*Status ecclesiae*," *Studia Gratiana* 15 (1972): 1–31; Gaines Post, *Studies in Medieval Legal Thought: Public Law and the State, 1100–1322* (Princeton: Princeton University Press, 1964), esp. pp. 241–414. The rendering here, "right order of the Church," fits the use of the term by the papalists, who regarded this concept as a limit on papal power only in the most dire emergencies. See Torquemada, *A Disputation on the Authority of Pope and Council*, pp. xv, 50, 56–57.

toward conforming more fully to the image of Peter, especially through actions which built up the Church. Only if the pope departed from his exemplar, obscuring the Petrine image, could his power be resisted. Such instances were expected to be uncommon, not frequent excuses to turn on the reigning pope. Nonetheless, here we see that Cusanus brought to the problems of a divided Church his awareness that even his own party, the Eugenians, ultimately fell short of realizing the *vera ecclesia* here on Earth, just as no human could realize fully the image of the incarnate Word.[56]

Despite these limits, Cusanus returned to his emphasis on the pope's building up the Church through obedient prelates. Nicholas pointed to the efforts made at the Council of Ferrara-Florence to build up the Church. For that purpose the Council of Basel had been translated to Italy. The remnant of that assembly had attempted to "impose on the sacred prince a horrid abomination," deposition. Its members had succeeded only in "cutting off themselves most pertinaciously from him and from the universal catholic Church throughout the world." Cusanus concluded by speaking of affairs in Germany, urging Arévalo to use his visit to Frankfurt to uphold Frederick III's intentions, wrongly understood by the author at that time to be an effort to bring the Empire into the Eugenian camp.

The letter to Arévalo, as was noted above, can be understood as absolutist or as qualifying papal sovereignty with a teleological imperative to build up the Church. The latter view ties in quite naturally with Cusanus's churchmanship. Even his reply to Panormitanus at the 1442 Diet of Frankfurt, a papalist polemic, still emphasized the pope's role in building up the Church.[57] Later the same emphasis

---

56. Augustine's idea of Peter having received the power of the keys as the Church's representative was known to Cusanus from Gratian's Decretum; see *Corpus Iuris Canonici* 24.1.6 (Friedberg 1:968), which is excerpted from Augustine's fiftieth tract on John. See also Giuseppe Alberigo, *La chiesa nella storia* (Brescia: Paideia, 1988), pp. 119–128, which emphasizes *De concordantia catholica*. On the conciliarist use of this passage, as well as of the more specifically Neoplatonic idea of Peter having received the keys *in figura ecclesiae*, often cited by the Decretists, see Brian Tierney, *Foundations of the Conciliar Theory* (Cambridge: Cambridge University Press, 1955), pp. 34–36. For a papalist refutation of the holistic interpretation of this text used by the conciliarists, see Izbicki, *Protector of the Faith*, pp. 31–51.

57. Acta Cusana 1/2:376–421, no. 520, at pp. 406–407 and 416. This work also made sporadic use of terms derived from the letter to Arévalo, describing all power as "contracted" in Peter and his successors (399) and all power "explicated" in the

would appear in Cusanus's bitter public dispute with Pius II over the promotion of Jean Joffroy to the cardinalate, in which the German expressed his feeling of isolation in the curia, and in his *Reformatio generalis*, which stressed consultation in the exercise of ecclesiastical government and did so in the light of the mission of the hierarchy, in imitation of Christ, to build up the Church.[58] Cusanus even made efforts to bring this vision into practice, especially when, as papal legate to the Empire in 1451–1452, he tried to curb practices he thought led the faithful away from the true center of Christianity, devotion to Christ, toward superstition.[59] This effort was impeded by political and social realities beyond Nicholas's control; but the reforming impetus remained, even when Cusanus's efforts in the diocese of Brixen were undermined by their author's legalism and rigidity.[60]

The Christocentric vision of the Church in the letter to Arévalo remained dear to Cusanus's heart through all of these adversities, a connecting thread in a career too often seen as discontinuous. This becomes apparent when the entire letter is read, looking back from its passages on *explicatio Petri* to the opening passages on the Incarnation and the conjectural Church. Those passages, in turn, must be read in the light of *De docta ignorantia*, particularly of its closing chapters. Without them, the idea of an inferential or conjectural Church seems a pallid sequel to Cusanus's conciliarist writings.[61] Taking those

---

Church as being in Peter and his successors complicatorie at the beginning (402–403). Cusanus also argued that the supporters of Basel thought of the Church geometrically, as located in one city, rather than mathematically and abstractly reduced to one, Peter, and thus unstained by human failings (406, 412).

58. Pius II, *Memoirs of a Renaissance Pope*, tr. Florence A. Gragg, ed. Leona C. Gabel (New York: Putnam, 1959), pp. 227–230; Stephan Ehses, "Der Reformentwurf des Kardinals Nikolaus Cusanus," *Historisches Jahrbuch* 32 (1911): 281–297; Rudolf Haubst, *Studien zur Nikolaus von Kues* (Munster: Aschendorff, 1959), pp. 10–11. The same theme of *imitatio Christi* appears in Cusanus's sermons from this time, especially those from his visitation of Rome's major basilicas on the pope's behalf. See John W. O'Malley, *Praise and Blame in Renaissance Rome* (Durham, N.C.: Duke University Press, 1979), pp. 96–101.

59. See note 6 above.

60. See note 6 above and Pardon Tillinghast, "Nicholas of Cusa vs. Sigmund of Hapsburg: An Attempt at Post-Conciliar Church Reform," *Church History* 36 (1967): 371–390.

61. James E. Biechler, *The Religious Language of Nicholas of Cusa* (Missoula: Scholars Press, 1975), p. 169. According to Alberigo, *Chiesa conciliare*, pp. 291–354, papalism ossified after rejecting Cusanus's fusion of hierarchy and consent. See

chapters into account, Cusanus's understanding of the Church in the light of learned ignorance fits into its proper place.

In the light of learned ignorance there could be no certain knowledge of the True Church by the human intellect, in ultimate terms. The True Church contained those whose inward tie with Christ through faith and charity led them to God through the hypostatic union. The *locus* of the True Church could be discerned through sacred signs, but its true nature only could be known in the Church Triumphant. The visible institution, despite its admixture of good and bad members, remained, under the absolute power of God, the qualifiedly absolute power of the pope and the less perfect Petrine powers of other prelates, the best guide to the locus of the True Church.

Cusanus's idea of the Church fits uneasily into the late medieval concern about the True Church (*vera ecclesia*); but it is grounded in the patristic source materials he, like his contemporaries, used in their debates on institutional structure. Cusanus returned to the Augustinian emphasis on the invisible Church of those united to Christ by charity, an emphasis that did not preclude affirmation of the visible institution with its rites and structures. Like his contemporaries, however, he retained the medieval version of Augustine's ecclesiology, which emphasized faith formed through charity.[62] The emphasis upon faith, in this context, was one on the visible profession of defined truths. It was on this externalized understanding of faith that medieval writers, especially the canonists, had based their arguments about hierarchic exercise of the powers of orders and jurisdiction and their concept of Christendom, a society founded on the profession of Christian truth.[63] Even the Pauline idea of the Church as the mystical body of Christ, once that term had been divorced from the eucharist, described as the true body, also took on

---

also Alberigo, "L'unità della chiesa nel servizio del papato," in *Nostalgie di unità: Saggi di storia dell'ecumenismo* (Genoa: Marietti, 1989), 53–71, at pp. 57–61.

62. Scott H. Hendrix, *Ecclesia in via* (Leiden: Brill, 1974). For the impact of Augustine's emphasis on charity upon later writers, especially in the idea of avoidance of scandal, see Heinz-Mohr, *Unitas christiana*.

63. Gerhard Ladner, "Concepts of *ecclesia* and *Christianitas* and their Relation to the Idea of Papal *plenitudo potestatis* from Gregory VII to Boniface VIII," *Miscellanea Historiae Pontificiae* 18 (1954): 49–77.

THE CHURCH AND LEARNED IGNORANCE   205

an institutional meaning.⁶⁴ Academic argument had been able to hypothesize a visible Church at variance with the truth, but theologians were as ill prepared to deal with the division of the Church Militant by the Great Western Schism as canonists were to face the possibility of really deposing a pope. The Schism and the subsequent conciliar crisis forced them to struggle on two fronts, attempting to reunite and reform the institution while defending its validity against new and threatening heresies. Thus the theories now called conciliarism attempted, through use of corporation theory, texts from Scripture, and ideas of the mystical body, to find a ground on which the Church could act, through a council representing it, to renew the institution, while papalists reasserted a role for the ecclesial body dependent on the pope and attacked the holist theories of their opponents.⁶⁵ Both parties, however, united in rejecting the theologies of Wyclif, Hus, and their followers, who, on the basis of a different reading of inherited texts, emphasized the invisible Church of those predestined to be saved to the extent of questioning the validity of the visible institution and rejecting the sacraments administered by priests not known to be among the elect.⁶⁶

Cusanus's ideas about the Church permitted him to find a theological justification for papalism within his doctrine of learned ignorance; but it permitted him to do so while affirming the primacy of the invisible Church in a manner close to Augustine's theology, which left room for the visible institution with its rites and structures, including a papacy obliged to act to build up the Church. The closest congruence of this ecclesiological construct, to which Cusanus adhered for the rest of his life, is not to his former conciliarism or to the papalism of Torquemada and other contemporaries, it is to Luther's doctrine of a Church hidden from men but whose location is known by certain signs. Luther's signs, though they include ministry, differ drastically, however, emphasizing the proclamation of the pure Gospel. There was no room for the papacy, since truth was not to be found in "the

---

64. Henri de Lubac, *Corpus mysticum*, 2d ed. (Paris: Aubier, 1949), pp. 13–19, 116–135.
65. For conciliarist holism, often grounded in Neoplatonic ideas, see Antony Black, *Council and Commune* (London: Burns & Oates, 1979). For the papalist attack on it, see Izbicki, *Protector of the Faith*.
66. Hendrix, "In Quest of the *vera ecclesia*," pp. 371–374.

synagogue of the papists and the Thomists."[67] This congruence may be explained by a common use of common sources or a common effort to merge the mystical elements of the late medieval heritage with nominalism.[68] It also represents a common desire to reach beyond the limits of the Church in the present day to eternal verities. Cusanus's desire to find the concealed Church, even while serving the papacy, may be an intellectual measure of his frustration with his situation, at odds with his fellow Germans and yet not fully at home in the curia, just as his speculative thought represents a discontent with the limits of human reason in grasping eternal truth.

The Johns Hopkins University

APPENDIX: NICHOLAS OF CUSA'S LETTER TO RODRIGO SÁNCHEZ DE ARÉVALO

This translation is based on a partial one kindly provided by H. Lawrence Bond, Appalachian State University. The Latin text can be found in De auctoritate presidendi, ed. G. Kallen, Cusanus-Texte 2: Traktate 1 *(Heidelberg, Carl Winter, 1935), pp. 106–112, which reprints the version found in vol. 2 of the Paris, 1514 edition as Epistle 1.*

Most learned man, much venerated by me, lord Rodrigo [Sánchez] de Arévalo, archdeacon of Treviño, [I am writing to you] in order that, in these disturbances in the Church, in which you see the thoughts of many learned men being tossed from side to side by the opinion of the vulgar, you may be able to hunt down a final and truer conjecture according to the rules of learned ignorance. Observe that (although the subject of inquiry is about the pope and a council representing the Church), since all things are in the Word of God, through which

---

67. Paul D. L. Avis, *The Church in the Theology of the Reformers* (Atlanta: John Knox Press, 1981), pp. 13–24, esp. p. 19.

68. F. Edward Cranz, "Cusanus, Luther and the Mystical Tradition," in *The Pursuit of Holiness in Late Medieval and Renaissance Religion*, ed. Charles Trinkaus and Heiko Oberman (Leiden: Brill, 1974), pp. 93–102.

all things came to be, that Word then enfolds all things and through It all things are unfolded in a diversity of difference participating in the Word Itself. All created things participate in an unfolded, varied way in the unity of the eternal[1] Word, which enfolds all things, so that the Word Itself, although it is imparticipable, is participated in by the variety of a multitude of participants in that best way possible. All things, therefore, only exist in so far as they participate in the existence of the Word. The existence of every creature, therefore, flows from that absolute existence in the most immediate manner, since it is present equally in all things; but the diversity of creatures arises from the diversity of all things participating.

Proceeding to the next step, by affirming the grace which is added over and above nature, they are related thus to Christ, for, in rational human nature, every rational creature hypostatically united to divinity by grace in Christ Jesus can attain the grace of elevation to union with God, which is the ultimate happiness. Consequently, the blessed Jesus is the enfolding of all those made blessed. All rational creatures, therefore, can achieve the ultimate happiness in no other way than through participation in the grace of Jesus. In all those participating in that grace, therefore, the grace of Jesus is unfolded in a variety of participants. In this way the grace of Jesus is everything which is in all who are pleasing to God; and all those pleasing to God are, in Jesus, everything that is pleasing to God. The grace of Jesus, therefore, is one thing in which all the saved participate variously. Thus Peter, the greatest of all theologians, wishing to teach us, (as Luke says in Acts)[2] referring to the ancient fathers, said [that] we believe he was made well in some manner through the grace of our lord Jesus Christ. This is the gospel's clear meaning and Saint Paul's doctrine, since Christ is the one holding the principate in all things and the head of the whole Church.

There are rational men, however, wayfarers in hope of salvation, to whom the truth of this grace was revealed through the incarnation of Christ; and [there are] some, acknowledging the truth through faith and awaiting in hope the happiness which comes through charity, who make up the Church Militant, which has through the grace

---

1. The text reprinted by Kallen wrongly has "alterni" at p. 106.
2. Compare Acts 4:10.

of Jesus Christ all things which are necessary for this, that, after the struggle, it may pass over to the Church Triumphant and attain to blessedness in Jesus Christ. This is the Church in which the grace of Jesus is unfolded according to the participatory nature of this world, because, although corruptible man, on account of the condition of his nature, cannot understand the truth without enigma and mirror image, at least he touches it through enigma and mirror image, or faith.

This requires the unique grace of Jesus Christ, by means of which the faithful, those laying hold [of truth] through faith, are wayfarers in hope of participating in unifying love in their own way and in a varied diversity. Wherefore, we call this Church mystically the body of Christ, because nothing but the grace of Jesus Christ is unfolded. Since, however, this is that one dove, the spotless bride,[3] who has as high priest Jesus, who entered the heavens,[4] whom she acknowledges, adhering to Christ in the Spirit, which remains concealed in this sensible world, then this concealed Church of Christendom cannot be known in its sensible particularity of members, who hold this confession and remain worthy of love, but only is grasped in a certain generality of reason through the power of reason. Just as the Church Triumphant, above reason, is accessible only in simplicity of understanding, so [the Church] Militant [is accessible only] in generality of reason. It is necessary, therefore, in the sensible world to try conjecturing about Christ's Church through sensible signs, since otherwise the truth of reason could not be grasped. For this reason that conjectural Church in this sensible world, according to the limited understanding of this world, is the True Church, although within this conjecture, received from signs, it contains both those adhering to Christ in the Spirit and [those who do] not. This Church of this sensible world is constituted of those who show by sensible signs that they participate in Christ, since they are those who acknowledge Christ, the son of God. For this reason this Church has sacred signs constituted so that we may know through them those who are Christ's in the way in which conjectural knowledge can be obtained from signs.

---

3. Compare Song of Songs 6:9 and Ephesians 5:27.
4. Compare Hebrews 9:11–14.

I say, therefore, that this Church of Christ is regarded as holy, judged in this sort of conjectural way, even if evil and hypocritical men mingle themselves under these sacred signs, which signs are sacred as far as conjecture reaches. This Church, therefore, does not contain all who adhere to Christ. Those who have manifested no sensible sign inwardly remain excluded from this judgment; nor do all those in this Church adhere to Christ, who admits only the good to union. Since, however, the condition of this life is such that the Church has to be this way, we do not hesitate [to say] that it was ordered by Christ in the best manner in which it can be. Thus, just as the Church is perfect in its own way, in so far as it has a head; it is fitting for the sensible Church to have a sensible head; and, for this reason, the sensible head of this Church is the pontiff, who is chosen from among men. In him this Church exists in an enfolded manner as in the first confessor of Christ. We know that Peter was the first confessor of Christ among men; and for this reason, from his confession of the Rock who is Christ, Peter, receiving a name [from It], unfolded the Church enfolded in himself first of all through the word of doctrine.[5] There is not, therefore, any other Church than the union of the faithful in the confession of Peter, which has its inception from Peter through supernal revelation. The unfolding of Peter, therefore, who is named after the Rock, and enfolding the Church, is one Church participating in the same confession in a varied diversity of believers. Since, however, the multitude can participate in unity only in a varied diversity, the Church cannot subsist, consequently, except in a varied participation in unity. For this reason it is necessary for there to be various members of the one body of the Church, in whom there is that one entire confession in all and in each part of it. The unity of the Church, therefore, exists in a varied diversity. Just as the strength of unity cannot be attained except in a diversity, so the strength of the enfolding origin can be grasped only in the unfolded things originated. The strength of the nature of Adam, the enfolding father, is not grasped otherwise than in the men unfolded from him; nor [the strength] of the Creator, except in those creatures. In the manner mentioned above, the enfolded strength of Peter, the head of the Church, cannot be grasped except in the Church unfolded from

---

5. Compare Matthew 16:18-19.

him. Thus, when we behold the variety of powers, orders, and prelacies in the unity of faith in the Church, seeing in it the entire well-ordered, decorous variety originally enfolded in Peter, we are moved to conjectures concerning the admirable power and strength of Peter; and we grasp the plenitude of all things possible in the Church for its preservation and the unique power of Peter for [its] direction. There is no unfoldable unity in the multitude unless the strength of unity exists in an unfolded way. We know this universal principate, originally enfolding every particular principate, [to be] inexhaustible through multiplication of particular [principates]. If, therefore, the powers of patriarchs, archbishops, metropolitans, bishops, and priests are in the Church, they have to be enfolded. The enfolding, however, does not originate with itself; rather it depends on the absolute. Wherefore, the power of the first and supreme one contains in its plenitude every power of all others. Thus there is no power except one, that of the first, which is shared variously in a diversity of prelates, by none, however, maximally. As such it is imparticipable.

You see now, most prudent father, how incorrect it is to say that the power of particular prelates can equal or surpass that of the universal prince. You see the divine dictum of Pope Leo[6] how every power first receives its being from that most absolute divine power; but in the Church [this is received] through Peter, the head and prince of the Church. Note, therefore, how there is no absolute power of the prince, except that of the most high God. But every principate participates variously in the diversity of the contracted [power]. The principate in the Church, therefore, is absolute in its own way, since in it the Church is enfolded. Thus any principate participates in its own way in this absoluteness, when it is set above the people over which it rules. Wherefore, it is unreasonable to say that a prince in his kingdom, where he is prince, shares power equally or is subordinate. The principle of non-contradiction does not permit such a sharing [of power]. Some wise men, who said the prince is not bound by the laws and cannot be judged by his subjects, understood this.[7] Therefore, it should be sufficiently clear to you what an execrable crime it is to break away from obedience and unity and how presumptuous [is] a

---

6. *Corpus Iuris Canonici* 19.7 (Friedberg 1:62).
7. *Digest* 1.3.31.

judgment of subjects against the sacred prince, under whatever guise this might be attempted. You even see every sacred principate in the Church placed under the first, in so far as it is enfolded within it and not otherwise; for the sacred universal principate exists to build up the Church. Wherefore, every principate, spiritual or temporal, in so far as it serves this end, can be in the Church; and in so far as it resists this end, the principate is not in the Church, since it does not participate in the sole universal ecclesiastical power, which, in every power which is in the Church, is whatever that [power] is in a contracted way.

You see different powers, spiritual and temporal, unfolded clearly within the Church by coming together in the unity of the universal power. It is not difficult now for you to understand how every faithful person, whether king, or ruler or any other [power] must be subject to the sacred prince of the Church, insofar as they wish to be part of the Church which that universal power encompasses. And this [is true] when the prince of the Church, according to the strength of this principate, decides on commands. Where, however, the prince commands that things be done which they do not believe pertain to the end of building up the Church entrusted to him, the command does not proceed from the principate; wherefore, it is not necessary to obey it. If, however, there is a doubt and the prince's intention is not clear, it must be assumed of the sacred prince that [he has] used correctly the power entrusted [to him]; and [he] must be obeyed.

Although we understand, therefore, that in the Church, where there are good and bad people, the sacred prince can be good or evil, and we see that his power cannot oppose the Church. Since, in those things which are not enfolded in that power, no one is subject to him, there is no peril in obeying in doubtful matters; but great peril in not obeying. Augustine[8] says here that no reason can be given why it is necessary to start a schism; wherefore, schism is a diabolical, inexcusable crime.

Note, father, how, since the primitive Church was unfolded variously from the universal, contracted, enfolded power of Peter according to various particular prelacies, any prelate participating in his particularity, in the contracted power of Peter, [has] the same power

---

8. Compare *Corpus Iuris Canonici* 23.4.19 (Friedberg 1:906).

which Peter had, except for its contraction. Wherefore, because in this all who have care of the Lord's flock are Peter's successors, it is apparent to the wise that the universal power of the sacred prince of the Church cannot be above any particular [power] except according to the condition [of holding] the sacred principate, that is for the building up [of the Church]. Thus, in so far as he is Peter's universal successor, he could have no power over any particular successor of Peter through which the particular power of building up those subject to him suffers any change or is impeded. Otherwise, however, when the sacred universal prince acts to oversee, a prelate may not abuse the power granted for the building up of the Church for the destruction of a subject church.

From this I see murmurs arising, which easily could remove the universal sacred prince, alleging Peter's successor [to have originated] after the Church unfolded by Peter, not as if he were another Peter, called after the Rock on which the Church with its order had to be built, since to undermine order and state of the universal Church is not to follow Peter. Every Roman and chief pontiff, however, in the unfolded scheme and right order of the Church has no power except from Peter, since this unfolding was founded through the power of Peter for the building up of the Church, which already was formed through him, when a son born in the Church is raised up to the principate of Peter. Because those things which are found unfolded now in the Church by Peter's successors in the aforesaid way are those which originate from the power of the universal prince, it is not convenient for that same power, now existing unfoldedly in the elected pontiff to be infringed in some way. There are rules, an order of estates, and other universal things of this sort, except in the case in which the pontiff himself discerns either equity or useful change for the building up of the Church; in this case it has to be noted that, when he does not attempt to promote the common good, he offends and scandalizes [his] brothers.

In the same manner, those more wise always have understood that, although the hand of the sacred prince extended to build up the Church can be inhibited or impeded by no observance or rule of the fathers, even in councils, there is not in him, nevertheless, a free power of casting off, even once, the power enfolded through Peter healthily ordained for the rule of the Church, as long as it requires help in the building up [of the Church]. But it befits no see more to execute what was established inviolably by the holy fathers than [it befits] the true successor of Peter in those things which proceed in an unfolded manner from the same power of Peter.

You see now [that], when the sacred prince of the Church presumes [to do] anything against the statutes of the holy fathers, where he does not seem to be moved by reason of utility or necessity but rather from some particular, unworthy cause in such a manner [that] he then offends in it against the previous mandates of Peter himself, he exceeds the nature of his power. For which reason it would not be inconvenient, if he should persist in this pertinaciously, [that] the Church could recede from him; when he has receded from the unity of the Church, without which the Church cannot exist, this does not introduce schism. In this way the pontiff must be understood to be subject to the canons of the holy fathers, as if there were in him no power of abusing according to his desire things well ordered; and, if he should persist in this pertinaciously, then he would show himself unworthy of the sacred principate which he diminishes through abuse.

In some manner Peter lives in his universal successor; just so in the canons of the fathers those fathers [live], and the Church, in the fathers. Thus Peter is said to live in the Church in those rules of the holy fathers, as long as that [power] gives aid for that purpose of building up the Church. And thus it is, according to the intellectual rule of learned ignorance, [that] the Church is in the pontiff in an enfolded manner. And [the sacred prince] equally is in the Church, that is when it keeps watch over its holy ordinances in a fitting manner; these things, if they are extended to certainty, open the intellect, so that the most incorrect writings of some are spurned easily.

It should be seen how easily our holy lord cannot be prohibited by any ordinance of any synod, when the council for leading back of the eastern Church [is] in session, in that place which was more convenient for doing such things; and he ordained that he would dissolve all other assemblies for that purpose; and he dismissed the fathers from Basel, so that they could concur freely in that holy union. For, just as there is not power of the pontiff for the destruction of things done well by the fathers, so there is no power under heaven which can diminish his authority; rather he should bring back the erring to the fold. Those purblind men are seen to have been out of all sense in a spirit of fury when they claimed for themselves some sort of judicial power over the sacred prince; and the savages tried to impose on the sacred prince a horrid abomination, cutting off themselves most perniciously from him and from the universal catholic Church throughout the world. That is enough now, since what they did is well known to you.

Clearly you have the illuminated eye of intelligence so that you can see very well that their sophistic excuses are supported by no authority or reason. Their vain ambition and apostate rebellion are apparent to the whole world, into which those desperate men strive with great diligence and care to infuse a worse poison; and particularly, to the king of Castile and Leon,[9] most serene and most worthy of highest praise, who shows through you the solicitude, so dear to God, of conserving unity in these far distant regions of the Germanies with such zeal, so that nothing at the diet may happen unfortunately to the king, [who is] most preoccupied with the daily pressures of the Saracens,[10] lest such bitter foes of Christendom should be tolerated under some perilous subterfuge by those who seek, by a rash deed, to strike down with anathema the vicar of Christ.[11] That most clement prince will carry back imperishable glory for his inward devotion. That man of most holy desires cannot be left unconsoled by God and the Church. For these his most holy vows cannot be turned away from heaven unaccepted because of your most circumspect actions in this illustrious diet of the unconquered king of the Romans[12] and the most glorious electors of the sacred Roman Empire, since, rejoicing in the Lord over all things done well, you will return to narrate [them]. I wish most cordially that you will bring that about, the more so since you know I have labored for the same thing most fervently for many years.

Farewell.

---

9. Juan II.
10. Literally "Agarenorum."
11. Eugenius IV.
12. Frederick III.

B
56
.M4
v.3

66121